Key Words
A Journal of Cultural Materialism

Configurations of the Real

12
(2014)

edited by
Elizabeth Allen
Catherine Clay
Tony Crowley
Sarah Davison
Simon Dentith
Kristin Ewins
Ben Harker
Angela Kershaw
Stan Smith

Key Words: A Journal of Cultural Materialism

Editors: Elizabeth Allen (Regent's College, London), Catherine Clay (Nottingham Trent University), Tony Crowley (University of Leeds), Sarah Davison (University of Nottingham), Simon Dentith (University of Reading), Kristin Ewins (Örebro University), Ben Harker (University of Manchester), Angela Kershaw (University of Birmingham), Stan Smith (Nottingham Trent University).

Editorial Advisory Board: John Brannigan (University College Dublin), Peter Brooker (University of Nottingham), John Connor (Colgate University, NY), Terry Eagleton (National University of Ireland Galway and Lancaster University), John Higgins (University of Cape Town), Andreas Huyssen (Columbia University, New York), Peter Marks (University of Sydney), Sean Matthews (University of Nottingham), Jim McGuigan (Loughborough University), Andrew Milner (Monash University), Meaghan Morris (Lingnan University), Morag Shiach (Queen Mary, University of London), Dai Smith (Swansea University), Nick Stevenson (University of Nottingham), John Storey (University of Sunderland), Will Straw (McGill University), Jenny Bourne Taylor (University of Sussex), John Tomlinson (Nottingham Trent University), Jeff Wallace (Cardiff Metropolitan University), Imelda Whelehan (University of Tasmania), Vicki Whittaker (Publishing Advisor).

Contributions for prospective inclusion in *Key Words* should comply with the style notes printed on pp. 158–60 of this issue, and should be sent in electronic form to Catherine Clay, School of Arts and Humanities, Nottingham Trent University, Clifton Campus, Nottingham NG11 8NS, UK (catherine.clay@ntu.ac.uk).

Books and other items for review should be sent to Angela Kershaw, Department of French Studies, College of Arts and Law, University of Birmingham, Birmingham B15 2TT, UK. The Reviews Editor, Stan Smith, can be contacted at stanwsmith1@gmail.com.

Key Words is a publication of The Raymond Williams Society (website: **www.raymondwilliams.co.uk**).

Contributions copyright © The Raymond Williams Society 2014.

All rights reserved.

Cover design by Andrew Dawson.

Printed by Russell Press, Nottingham.
Distributed by Central Books Ltd, London.

ISSN 1369-9725
ISBN 978-0-9929916-0-9

Contents

Editors' Preface: Configurations of the Real	5
Raymond Williams and Ecocriticism Michael Malay	8
'A Specific Contemporary Sadness': Raymond Williams and the Speculative Socialist Tradition Rosalind Brunt	30
The Long Recuperation: Late-Nineteenth/Early-Twentieth-Century British Socialist Periodical Fiction Deborah Mutch	46
'The Rich Harmonics of Past Time': Memory and Montage in John Sommerfield's *May Day* Elinor Taylor	60
Future Imperfect: Mass and Mobility in Williams, Orwell and the BBC's *Nineteen Eighty-Four* Sean McQueen	74
Sovereign Is He, Who Knocks: The Neoliberal State of Exception in American Television Liane Tanguay	93
Cultural Immaterialism: Wallace Stevens in Virtual Paris Tony Sharpe	108
'A Smell of French Bread in Charlotte Street': Louis MacNeice Revisited Stan Smith	125
Keywords Tony Crowley	135
Stuart Hall (1932–2014): A Personal Tribute Peter Brooker	137

Contents

Reviews	140
Notes on Contributors	154
Raymond Williams Foundation (RWF)	156
Style Notes for Contributors	158

In memoriam

Stuart Hall, FBA, 3 February 1932–10 February 2014

Richard Hoggart, FRSL, 24 September 1918–10 April 2014

Editors' Preface: Configurations of the Real

Raymond Williams wrote in *Marxism and Literature* that 'the thrust of Marx's whole argument' in *Capital* was that '[c]onsciousness is seen from the beginning as part of the human material social process, and its products in "ideas" are then as much part of this process as material products themselves'. Whether as Marx's 'necessary element of "imagination" in the labour process', or as 'the necessary conditions of associated labour, in language and in practical ideas of relationship', or as 'the real processes – all of them physical and material' which 'are masked and idealized as "consciousness and its products,"' all these are, in Williams's gloss, 'necessarily social material activities' (1977, 59–62).

Marxism and Literature contains, under the heading 'Structures of Feeling' (128–35), Williams's fullest exposition of what is probably his most familiar interpretative device, what he calls here the 'cultural hypothesis' (132) that would permit a non-reductive reading of the complex relations between the 'real' and its configurations in consciousness. The concept of 'structures of feeling' provides an implicit context for the otherwise very disparate articles in the current issue, and the discussion in *Marxism and Literature* is referenced explicitly in several of them. Michael Malay's wide-ranging survey of the politics of ecology, for example, cites Williams's acknowledgement there that, in speaking of 'structures of feeling', '"feeling" is chosen to emphasize a distinction from more formal concepts of "world-view" or "ideology"', going 'beyond formally held and systematic beliefs' to examine 'meanings and values as they are actively lived and felt, and the relations between these and formal or systematic beliefs' (132).

Malay elucidates the demystification of pastoral in *The Country and the City* (1973) by referring to another instance of the trope in *Politics and Letters*, where Williams proposes that 'a dominant set of forms or conventions – and in that sense structures of feeling – can represent a profound blockage for subordinated groups in society, above all an oppressed class' (1979, 164). Such a formulation speaks directly to the issues raised by Rosalind Brunt's reading of Williams's own novels in relation to the working-class fiction of Robert Tressell and Edward Bellamy. Brunt develops Williams's angry reflections, in his 1982 Robert Tressell Lecture, on the power of the hegemonic structure of feeling to imprison working people in 'an ignorance that gets built in, inside people themselves – an ignorance that becomes their common sense', so that '[b]eing a prisoner can come to seem common sense, or can be made to seem what is human'. Deborah Mutch, examining the serial fiction of two popular socialist authors of the later nineteenth and early twentieth centuries, Charles Allen Clarke and A. Neil Lyons, extends these considerations, invoking the argument in *The Long Revolution* that the 'connexion between the popular structure of feeling and that used in the literature of the time is of major importance in the analysis of culture', for it is here that 'the real relations within the whole culture are made clear: relations that can easily be neglected when only the best writing survives' (1965, 85).

Mutch contends that working-class literature can only be properly recuperated from marginalisation when its literary hybridity is recognised, dismantling what *Marxism and Literature* calls 'the crippling categorizations and dichotomies of "fact" and "fiction", or of "discursive" and "imaginative" or "referential" and "emotive"' (146). Elinor Taylor's subtle reading of *May Day* (1936), described by Jack Lindsay as 'the best collective novel that we yet have produced in England', likewise deconstructs the hierarchies of traditional bourgeois fiction and criticism by situating Sommerfield's novel, in the context of contemporary debates about the nature of 'socialist realism', at the interface of modernist experimentation and the cultural formation and problematic politics of the Popular Front. For Sean McQueen, examining the structure of feeling embodied in successive cinematic and televisual adaptations of Orwell's *Nineteen Eighty-Four*, imagining the future is always already a way of imagining the present, a reconfiguration of the real in the subjunctive future perfect which is 'the logically informing tense of dystopia'. In a penetrating critique which draws effectively on the analysis provided by *Marxism and Literature*, Liane Tanguay links Williams to such recent theorists as Giorgio Agamben to define the dominant structures of feeling articulated by the legitimating narratives and enabling fantasies of the US culture industry. These, she argues, normalise the practices of the security state, offering 'cultural mediations of a more fundamental state of exception' which relocate sovereignty in the market rather than the state, subordinating political and social spheres and disarticulating lived experience from the 'dominant abstract' of contemporary capitalism. Invoking the same passage in *Marxism and Literature* cited by Malay, she argues that we must look instead beyond neoliberalism's 'formally held and systematic beliefs' to those 'meanings and values as they are actively lived and felt, and the relations between these and formal or systematic belief' (132), if we are ever to recover 'not only a consciousness of history but a consciousness of alternatives', that 'consciousness of aspirations and possibilities' of which Williams wrote in *Problems in Materialism and Culture* (1980, 223).

Tanguay extracts from *Breaking Bad*, the TV series at the centre of her critique, a technical term from chemistry, 'chirality', which she sees as a 'deliberate metaphor' for the series' narrative strategies. This is, she says, 'a property of certain chemical compounds that form non-superimposable mirror images of one another and that, while identical, can have very different effects'. It's a highly suggestive image that could open up the varying configurations

Preface

of the real explored in this issue. Wallace Stevens's (equally imagined) 'virtual' and 'real' Parises, for example, as described by Tony Sharpe, summed up in the assertion of the poem 'Adagia' that 'Reality is a cliché / From which we escape by metaphor', can be seen as one instance of the Modernist structure of feeling with which politically committed writers such as Sommerfield were in strenuous contention. Even the most rarefied aesthetic discourses, as Williams affirms, are in the end 'themselves necessarily social material activities', and as such are suffused with historical affect. Thus Louis MacNeice, that least 'political' of the Thirties poets, nevertheless found himself assuming an implicitly political stance in his ostensibly 'anti-political' prioritisation of the lived, immediate moment. In a variation on our regular 'Recoveries' feature, Stan Smith here reconsiders, half a century after the poet's death, his changing reputation, and his emergence as a writer with a profound commitment to the politics of everyday life.

The present issue of *Key Words* is dedicated to the memory of two men who, together with Raymond Williams, were the undisputed intellectual progenitors of the cultural materialist tradition, each of them in his way dedicated to making sense of the full richness and complexity of 'the human material social process, and its products in "ideas" […] as much part of this process as material products themselves'. Co-founders of the Centre for Contemporary Cultural Studies instituted at Birmingham University in 1964, Stuart Hall and Richard Hoggart died within months of each other earlier this year. We publish here a personal memoir of Stuart Hall by Peter Brooker, former editor of this journal and chair of the Raymond Williams Society, who was one of the first postgraduates to attend the Birmingham programme. News of Richard Hoggart's death came too late for the journal to do more than note his passing. We hope to carry an extended tribute to his work by Sean Matthews in the 2015 issue.

Raymond Williams and Ecocriticism
Michael Malay

Abstract: This article argues for the importance of Raymond Williams as an ecological thinker. In particular, it examines how Williams's writing offers a critical methodology whereby a complex series of practices and activities – from pastoral poetry to industrialisation, from English manor houses to African junkyards – are understood as dialectical manifestations of related processes. It begins by considering 'apocalyptic writing' as a genre which exercises an unduly strong hold on our conception of environmental problems, before turning to Williams's detailed accounts of our relations with the natural world as a methodological counter-example. Its central argument is that Williams, especially in *The Country and the City*, foreshadowed certain developments in 'ecocriticism', particularly 'second-wave ecocriticism', which stresses the importance of environmental and social justice issues in our reading of literary texts. It concludes by suggesting future points of contact between Williams and ecocriticism.

*

I

There is a sense in which apocalyptic literature – writing geared towards the end, the cataclysmic finale – is unhelpful for ecological thought. This is because teleology is at odds with the processes of nature. In the environment, the 'end' never comes. Nature continues (severely damaged, perhaps, by human intervention) but with little deference to our conceptions of time. Yet apocalyptic thinking is a common feature of writing about the environment. The urge to imagine the end-point has been obsessive and perennial, as with Richard Jefferies's *After London* (1885), Rachel Carson's *Silent Spring* (1962) or Cormac McCarthy's *The Road* (2006). This impulse is often connected to a troubled sense that the *status quo* cannot continue – that our relations with the world (and our relations between ourselves) will soon reach a crisis point. For some writers, such as the cultural critic and philosopher Slavoj Žižek, the future tense should be discarded: the apocalypse is already immanent – in our current forms of governance, our weakening market economies and our unsustainable exploitation of the environment. As Žižek announces at the outset of *Living in the End Times* (2010), the 'global capitalist system is approaching an apocalyptic zero-point'.[1]

Given their sensitivity to the ills of civilisation, it is not surprising that apocalyptic thinkers can sometimes be misanthropic. D.H. Lawrence's Birkin from *Women in Love* (1920) is a good example of this phenomenon:

'So you'd like everybody in the world destroyed?' said Ursula.
 'I should indeed.'
 'And the world empty of people?'
 'Yes, truly. You yourself, don't you find it a beautiful clean thought, a world empty of people, just uninterrupted grass, and a hare sitting up?'
 The pleasant sincerity of his voice made Ursula pause to consider her own proposition. And really it *was* attractive: a clean, lovely, humanless world. It was the *really* desirable. Her heart hesitated, and exulted.[2]

Of course, there *is* something attractive about this idea: it's hygienic. The various problems of modernity implicit in this passage – industrialism, pollution, the 'crowd' – are sublimated into a pastoral vision. We return to the cleanliness of the world before man: 'uninterrupted grass', a 'hare sitting up'.[3]

To varying degrees, all apocalyptic writing participates in Birkin's sublimating impulse (though not necessarily in his misanthropy). Central to apocalyptic thinking – especially apocalyptic thinking about the environment – is an anxiety over the scale of the problem, a bewildering feeling that the issues are beyond comprehension.[4] This seems a natural response, especially when one considers the variety of the problems at hand as well as the detailed complexity of each *particular* problem (from the hole in the ozone layer above Australia to farming practices in North America). The multiplicity of issues resists our capacity to be experts.

This essay is concerned to show the theoretical problems of maintaining apocalyptic thinking in the light of current environmental issues. To this end, it takes Williams's *The Country and the City* (1973) as an example of a method of criticism which blends the critical and the ecological, the textual and the social, and which is insistently anti-apocalyptic in its approach, in that it tries to make sense of, rather than sublimate, the multiplicity of issues involved in our dealings with the natural world. Section II briefly sketches the background of apocalyptic thought and its environmental implications; section III looks more closely at the 'ecological' critique Williams developed in *The Country and the City*; and section IV details the particular ways ecocriticism might appropriate and adapt the blend of sociology and environmentalism to be found in Williams's work.

II

One consequence of apocalyptic thought is that the concrete problems of environmental degradation are strangely emptied of content. There is an issue, in other words, with the *form* of cataclysmic writing, in the sense that its dominant tone (prophetic, admonitory) and its narrative structure (the fulfilment of a predetermined crisis), actively militate against a detailed consideration of specific environmental concerns. The less literary, but arguably more important daily issues of water contamination, despoliation of the soil, the decline of bee populations, just to name some instances, are merged into a totalising apocalyptic narrative. At the critical point, where the burden of careful thinking becomes most important, attention to particularities is replaced by an abstract notion of ecological catastrophe. Tracing the complex patterns of cause and effect, the connections between acid rain, say, and our patterns of consumption, proves to be too much.

Of course, apocalyptic visions may sting readers into developing a larger environmental consciousness. Carson's *Silent Spring*, for instance, or McCarthy's *The Road*, are now canonical environmental texts, both of which continue to propel discussion about our present – and unsustainable – uses and abuses of the natural world. Yet one possibility is that attention to the end may replace a sensitivity to the present, in that apocalyptic writing transfigures the variegated and the confusing into the sublime. This transformation is part of its strategy, its coping mechanism. In Birkin's case, for example, the pressure of the sublime leads to pastoral romance of a very odd kind: there is simply no one there to enjoy it. In other strains of apocalyptic thought, as in McCarthy's *The Road*, the future ends in violent catastrophe. But the two visions, the catastrophic and the utopian-pastoral, are linked. There is something cathartic in imagining civilisation's complete disappearance or its frenzied descent into violence, a purgative release in having 'apocalypse now'. One implication, however, is that we may become so used to catastrophic scenarios that we do not pay attention to the particular, more worrying problems of our material activities within the environment. The apocalyptic, after all, asks us to think in terms of grand scenarios. Environmental problems, on the other hand, are always localised issues, connected to specific processes and practices. Degradation is not a trope, but an active relationship, and we potentially lose this sense of materiality by accepting the generalisations of catastrophic thought.[5]

But if apocalyptic writing is inadequate as a mode of intellectual engagement, it is nevertheless marked by deep human feeling and urgency. As Damian Thompson remarks, apocalypticism is a genre 'born out of crisis, designed to stiffen the resolve of an embattled community by dangling it in front of the vision of a sudden and permanent release from its captivity. It is underground literature, the consolation of the persecuted'.[6] In Thompson's conception, apocalyptic writing is connected to danger and the threat of disappearance. This is why it can be movingly melancholic and desperate, as well as violent and purgative. As a tactical response, however, it is severely limited. By accepting 'underground literature' as a category, apocalyptic thinkers may normalise a narrative of loss and catastrophe, promoting the 'consolation of the persecuted' over the activism of the persecuted. This is because apocalyptic writing does not always 'stiffen the resolve' of a community. By reducing its writers to commentary, indeed, apocalyptic thought can have the opposite effect. This weakening of resolve is especially pronounced in nihilistic visions of the future, where teleology replaces agency, and eschatology, rather than analysis, becomes the main mode of engagement. One becomes witness to an event that has passed, is passing or is to come.

On the other hand, if underground literature wants to overcome inertia, it must become more articulate about its particular disenchantments, more forceful in its suggestions for improvement, and an expert in the problems it tries to diagnose rather than perennially identifying with the 'persecuted'. Otherwise, apocalyptic thinking may deepen a groove in our thinking that itself is part of a larger problem – a sense that it is already 'too late', that the problems are 'too many' and that 'nothing can be done'. The fatalism of this position can be attractive, as it releases one from the onus of careful action, but it ends up evoking what might be called a 'bad sublime', in which thought, confronted by a variety of problems – each with its own internal intricacies – seeks repose outside of those problems. Instead of 'staying with the trouble' (Donna Haraway's phrase), the issues are displaced by an act of apocalyptic force.[7]

Raymond Williams's various discussions of nature – 'perhaps the most complex word in the language'[8] – may help us evaluate our current attitudes towards the environment, as well as call attention to the various problems we may be unaware of (and therefore unwillingly perpetuate) in our relations with the natural world. Of particular interest is Williams's emphasis on the impact of our activities upon the environment, and the network of ideas, customs and ideologies that provide the framework for those activities. The relationships, of course, are often combined in ways that elude our powers of description: as Williams recognises, 'nature' contains an 'extraordinary amount of human history'.[9] But this reckoning asks for a more complex methodology, as well as an acknowledgement that the most complex methodology will not be enough. To express the relationships between culture, politics and the environment, Williams notes in 'Ideas of Nature', we 'need not only a more sophisticated but a more radically honest accounting than any we now have'.[10]

III

Although Williams died before 'ecocriticism' became a popular critical term, many of his ideas are germane to ecocritical aims and principles. In its simplest form, Cherryl Glotfelty defines ecocriticism as the

> study of the relationship between literature and the physical environment. Just as feminist criticism examines language and literature from a gender-conscious perspective, and Marxist criticism brings an awareness of modes of production and economic class to its reading of texts, ecocriticism takes an earth-centred approach to literary studies.[11]

Glotfelty's definition – perhaps the most cited in ecocritical literature – is deliberately broad, and while it has the merit of inclusiveness, its conceptual malleability makes it potentially nebulous. For there is a sense in which every text evinces *some* form of relationship between 'literature' and the 'physical environment', even if that relationship is understood as the piece of paper on which a text is printed. This may be a trivial sense of 'relationship', as well as a simplification of Glotfelty's ideas on ecocriticism, but it nevertheless points to the problem of what ecocriticism might mean, in practice and theory, if it is too generally defined.

A tighter focus has been provided by others. For Richard Kerridge, for instance, ecocriticism is charged with a practical dimension:

> The ecocritic wants to track environmental ideas and representations wherever they appear, to see more clearly a debate which seems to be taking place, often part-concealed, in a great many cultural spaces. Most of all, ecocriticsm seeks to evaluate texts and ideas in terms of their coherence and usefulness as responses to environmental crisis.[12]

But this definition suffers the opposite fate of Glotfelty's: it is too specific. For should all texts be measured according to their 'coherence and usefulness as responses to environmental crisis'? I may, for instance, enjoy a Ted Hughes poem about a fox, and it may tell me a great deal about my relation to other animals – as well as the symbolic force they exert over my imagination – but I may find it completely unpractical when it comes to dealing with particular problems in my local environment. But I would not for that reason want to dismiss Hughes's poem as uninteresting for ecocriticism.

Certain definitions, then, can be extremely broad while others seem prescriptively limited, such that, decades after the term was first used by William Rueckert (who called ecocriticism 'the application of ecology and ecological concepts to the study of literature'), there is still no common agreement on what the term might mean.[13] As Nirmal Selvamony pointed out as recently as 2007: 'ecocritics are not agreed on what constitutes the basic principle in ecocriticism, whether it is *bios*, or nature or environment or place or earth or land. Since there is no consensus, there is no common definition.'[14]

In one sense, this plurality of approaches to ecocriticism is healthy. Just as biodiversity can be a good indicator of environmental strength, the increasing complexity of ecocriticism (and its subvariants of ecofeminism, eco-Marxism, ecotheology) points towards organic intellectual growth. On the other hand, as Steven Lovatt points out, the increasing 'biodiversity' of ecocriticism is potentially a negative development, since it might indicate the 'co-option or unhelpful assimilation of a fresh approach into (overly) familiar channels of interpretation'.[15] Ecocriticism may thus become a trend or a fashion, interchangeable with other modes of reading – an 'aesthetic' position among many. As such, part of ecocriticism's initial urgency, as a response to concrete environmental problems, risks being diluted through its uncritical absorption into other 'isms'. Environmental degradation may become a purely formal problem, a series of textual motifs, rather than something happening on the ground.

This fear, for instance, is partly the subject of S.K. Robisch's 'The Woodshed', an essay suspicious of any integration between ecocriticism and theory, especially poststructuralist theory.[16] This is because 'theory' for Robisch (his quotation marks) has been co-opted by English departments increasingly characterised by ideological battles and 'political jockeying' (700), an arena which threatens to turn ecocriticism away from its primary subject, which for Robisch is simply 'to write about literature under the influence of ecology' (701). Ecocriticism is in no danger of insufficient 'theorizing', Robisch writes, responding to claims that it needs a stronger theoretical foundation. If anything, he continues:

> 'Theory' regularly indicts itself as a participant in the destruction of biospheric health by promoting a thought process that renders the biosphere an immaterial idea subject to the laboratory of abstraction – a characteristic shared with economic 'theories' that have contributed to monoculture and the erasure of ecosystems. (702)

It is clear that Robisch's urgency is deeply felt: he believes theory is 'obfuscating' our relations with the natural world and therefore stymieing any real action we might take in it. As Kate Soper reminds her readers in *What is Nature?* (1995), 'it is not language that has a hole in its ozone layer […] the "real" thing continues to be polluted and degraded even as we refine our deconstructive insights at the level of the signifier'.[17] But Robisch's position is a precarious one, as his wholesale rejection of theory presupposes a way of relating to 'nature' – a word, Williams reminds us, with an extremely tangled pedigree – free of ideology and politics. As Dominic Head shows in 'Beyond 2000: Raymond Williams and the Ecocritic's Task' (2002), Williams was acutely aware, during his academic career, of the same co-option Robisch is wary of now.[18] Unlike Robisch, however, Williams's response was to radicalise theory within academic institutions rather than abandon it. As Head writes:

> If Williams was prepared to see new intellectual trends as potentially beneficent he was also aware of the danger of being incorporated or confined through their specialisation with existing dominant institutions. For academic work this is a particularly pressing problem but the kind of problem, so Williams suggests, which is at the very heart of the broader political challenge. So nevertheless, despite the dangers of incorporation, 'it is essential', writes Williams, 'that the carriers of the new and positive interests should move in on institutions, but in their own still autonomous way'. (27)

Ecocriticism's passage into academic institutions is not a settled question. It may become institutionalised, as Robisch fears, and sapped by its engagement with theory – or it may revitalise the institutions it intrudes upon, by opening up different methods of interpretation that frustrate and challenge orthodox readings of the natural world. The results will probably be mixed, with much depending on whether ecocritics can work within institutions in 'their own still autonomous way'.

What, then, is Williams's particular relevance for ecological thinking? Dominic Head and Martin Ryle have suggested some convincing points of contact. In 'Raymond Williams and Ecocriticism' (2000), Head calls *The Country and the City* a 'masterpiece of ecocriticism *avant la lettre*' in which Williams 'systematically exposes the various constructions of pastoral since the sixteenth century, and insists on the economic and social interdependence of the urban and the rural'.[19] Head also observes that Williams's 'creative work might finally become as significant as his criticism', because he discerns in Williams's fiction an intense concern with the political and social forces that shape rural and urban environments, as well as a sensitivity to how those forces are experienced and lived through by individuals and communities.[20] Ryle also emphasises the significance of *The Country and the City* and fastens on the text's 'persistent vigilance vis-à-vis any literary representation in which images of the rural and natural are offered as emblematic of the good life, especially when the perspective is backward-looking'.[21] Unlike Head, however, Ryle is cautious about identifying it as a work of ecocriticism, noting that 'contemporary ecocritics may well find unsympathetic both Williams's a priori skepticism about country writing, and his lack of interest in the non-human' (50). But Ryle also suggests that *The Country and the City*, through its 'reflection on the forces and processes that threaten nature and humanity alike', provides a helpful corrective for 'the celebration of wild nature and the other-than-human, which gives the keynote of much writing favoured by ecocritics' (50). Indeed, Ryle makes a general case for Williams's relevance for ecological thought:

> Williams's distinctive contribution to ecocritical thinking is not a matter of a discrete paradigm, elaborated in theoretical mode. Rather, we can learn from his practice of politically engaged criticism, attentive to environment and ecology and committed to reading cultural works in social and historical contexts. (44)

My effort in the following is to supplement some of Head's and Ryle's ideas and suggest further affinities between Williams and ecocriticism. In particular, I suggest that the investigative scope of Williams's work – his analytical method of keeping one eye on the 'text' and the other on the 'forces' that produced it – serves as a useful corrective for ecocritical studies that cleave off the text from history, or environment from politics, as though the various elements could be separated.[22] This is not to suggest that studies conducted from an explicitly literary angle are not incisive or important ways of practising ecocriticism. 'Literary theory cannot be separated from cultural theory', Williams writes, 'though it may be distinguished within it'.[23] A study of Gerard Manley Hopkins's poetic forms, for example, is not weakened by ignoring the details of Victorian industrialism.[24] As long as these boundaries are defined clearly and knowingly (which includes a sense of their being arbitrary), then literary approaches to texts are entirely legitimate. Indeed, there are times when a materialist or economic analysis can say very little about literary writing. What might a Marxist critic say, for instance, about the imaginative nature of poetic metaphors?[25] It is to suggest, however, that there is never a *pure* association between literary texts and the physical environment, since this relationship involves many other kinds, not least cultural, political and religious ones. As Williams writes in *Keywords*: 'Any full history of the uses of nature would be a history of a large part of human thought' (221).

Williams's emphasis on examining the 'structure of feeling' underlying texts, objects and cultural phenomena is especially valuable for ecocriticism. Williams's phrase – which makes its first appearance in *A Preface to Film* (1954) and which thereafter forms a central part of his critical vocabulary – combines a complex and sometimes amorphous set of ideas. When 'confined' to a 'straightforward' definition, Williams remarks that 'structure of feeling' was 'developed as an analytical procedure for actual written works [...] with a very strong stress on their forms and conventions'. As Williams admits, however, the 'pressure of general argument' sometimes led him to expand the notion to cover larger areas of thought and history. In this broad application, 'structure of feeling' approached and understood 'works' as the 'articulate record of something which was a much more general possession. This was the area of interaction between the official consciousness of an epoch – codified in its doctrines and legislations – and the whole process of actually living its consequences'.[26]

In *Marxism and Literature*, Williams expands upon the 'structure of feeling' thus:

> The term is difficult, but 'feeling' is chosen to emphasize a distinction from more formal concepts of 'world-view' or 'ideology'. It is not only that we must go beyond formally held and systematic beliefs, though of course we have always to include them. It is that we are concerned with meanings and values as they are actively lived and felt, and the relations between these and formal or systematic beliefs are in practice variable (including historically variable), over a range from formal assent with private dissent to the more nuanced interaction between selected and interpreted beliefs and justified experiences. (132)

These remarks suggest the key concepts, as well as the animating spirit, of Williams's inquiry into the relations between texts and the cultures which produced them. At once a precise critical trope, a method of elucidating the 'forms and conventions' of written works, 'structure of feeling' was also intended as a hermeneutically open and flexible term, a way of thinking about the social history contained in texts (in both its 'codified' and unarticulated forms).[27] A poem, in this sense, could be approached according to its literary merits (with attention to its formal patterns, for instance, or its use of imagery) but also as a particular document of an historical era (with attention to the dominant features of that society, as well as to its marginalised ones). Indeed, in the contrast between 'official' and 'codified' (definitive and defining terms) and the more ambiguous phrase, the 'whole process of actually living', Williams's term gestures towards the many forms of life that are not expressed and sometimes actively displaced in a text. To look at a text's 'structure of feeling', then, actively involves a hermeneutics of engagement and sympathy, as well as one of suspicion and irony. As Williams remarks, 'a dominant set of forms or conventions – and in that sense structures of feeling – can represent a profound blockage for subordinated groups in society, above all an oppressed class'.[28]

Extended to *The Country and the City*, Williams's interpretative method resulted in some searching modes of social and environmental analysis. Not only was the text concerned to investigate the diversity of human relations with the natural world (from the experience of the court poet to the rural labourer), it also presented a sustained critique of the many ways in which we mis-see the natural world, usually in ways that suited those in positions of privilege. This mis-seeing often involved misrepresenting and exploiting those in less privileged positions, and central to the opening chapters of *The Country and the City* is its examination of the pastoral mode, a critique of the various 'images' writers projected onto the country. For instance, Williams observes that Sidney's *Arcadia*, while giving a 'continuing title to English neo-pastoral, was also written in a park which had been made by enclosing a whole village and evicting tenants. The elegant game was then only at arm's length – a rough arm's length – from a visible reality of country life' (22).

The observation on *Arcadia* is a terse and cutting example of Williams's hermeneutics of suspicion and gives a rough idea of the fault-lines of his investigation in *The Country and the City*. He expands upon this mode of criticism at length in his discussion of Ben Jonson's and Thomas Carew's 'country house' poems. As Williams writes of these texts, not only were they connected to centres of privilege and wealth (as in Jonson's celebration of the Penshurst country estate), they also fashioned idealised images of rural labour that became dominant images in pastoral writing. Such poems championed husbandry and farming, celebrated nature's bounty, and praised the simplicity and beauty of rural life, but crucially involved little or no personal experience of agricultural work. They extolled rural life because they abstracted what such a life involved: 'Jonson looks out over the fields of Penshurst and sees, not work, but a land yielding of itself. Carew, characteristically, does not even look' (32–3). As Williams goes on to say, the poems are not documents of 'country life but social compliment', full of the 'familiar hyperboles to the aristocracy and its attendants' (33). This sceptical approach underpins Williams's reading of country literature, from Georgian poetry to the Roman pastoral genre. The cumulative effect, Ryle writes, is to expose 'country writing' as forming an 'ideological mirage' which conceals 'real historical processes behind a nostalgic cultural fiction' (49).

Williams strongly influenced the terms of the debate in Britain, but it should be pointed out that the pastoral continues to be redefined. Terry Gifford, for instance, argues that the pastoral requires a more complex delineation, and proposes the terms 'pastoral', 'anti-pastoral' and 'post-pastoral'.[29] That latter phrase, Gifford remarks, offers a 'term for writing about nature that outflanked the closed circle of the pastoral and its opposite, the anti-pastoral', a space, in other words, between those who simplified country life and those who opposed the simplifiers (21). This category is important, as it avoids one of dangers implicit (if not actualised) in Williams's critique of the pastoral were it developed uncritically: an outright rejection of the impulse to 'connect' with the natural world. As Dominic Head writes, Gifford's post-pastoral 'represents a challenge to contemporary alienation from the non-human world, as well as an enlightened engagement with the Real' (194). It accommodates environmental writing that arises from a pastoral impulse, but which elaborates that impulse in more sophisticated forms.

It should also be pointed out that the 'pastoral' has many different valences in the North American context. For at the same time Williams 'finally put the nail in the coffin of the term 'pastoral' in any other than a negative, pejorative way', as Terry Gifford puts it, other scholars with ecological commitments – such as Lawrence Buell and Leo Marx in the United States – were critiquing traditional and uncritical forms of the pastoral while advocating more considered and radical variants of the same genre.[30] In *The Machine in the Garden* (1964), for instance, Leo Marx makes a distinction between 'sentimental' and 'complex' pastoral – and argues that whereas the former expresses an 'inchoate longing for a more "natural" environment' and sets up a uncritical distinction between the country and the city, the second actively interrogates these notions, acting as a '*counterforce*' against the image of the simple life.[31] Complex pastoral works, Marx continues, 'manage to qualify, or call into question, or bring irony to bear against the illusion of peace and harmony in a green pasture' (25). As with Gifford in the British context, Marx freights the pastoral with an ambiguity and self-awareness that help us go beyond certain limitations in Williams's critique of the genre.

As critical as Williams was of pastoral writing, it seems that he would have been sympathetic to the more positive aspects that Marx and Gifford detect in the mode. In the work of the writer W.H. Hudson, for instance, Williams finds 'a strong and genuine simplicity, an intensity of vision […] always modulated by thought' (254). That qualifier – 'modulated by thought' – is central to Williams's understanding of what sophisticated country writing might look like. Hudson's observations of the country, Williams continues, are not only 'convincingly recorded', they are also 'reconsidered' and 'modestly weighed' so that 'instead of uncritical surrender, or uncritical rejection and parody, we find ourselves making connections with experiences many of us have had and can recall' (254). Williams also singles out the work of John Clare, and underscores the poet's ability to respond to the particularities of nature in a clear and unsentimental manner. As Williams writes, what 'we find in Clare is not [Ben] Jonson's idealisations of a landscape yielding of itself' (133) but rather direct and concentrated attention. His is a poetry of 'prolonged, rapt, exceptional description', characterised by 'an intricate working of particularity' (144). As for Thomas Hardy, a writer discussed at length in *The Country and the City*, his 'major novels [are centred] in the ordinary processes of life and work' (203). Thus he could 'run the whole gamut' of describing rural life, from 'external observation of customs and quaintness [...] to the much more impressive but also much more difficult humane perception of limitations, which cannot be resolved by nostalgia or charm or the simple mysticism of nature, but which are lived through by all the characters, in the real life to which all belong' (211).

Williams's method of reading – of which 'structure of feeling' is an interpretative tool – offers an approach to literary texts that is at once historical, political, literary and environmental, and that tries to understand the intricacy of what it examines through an appropriately broad and intricate methodology. Ecocritics who are suspicious of theory, and who envision an ecocriticsm founded primarily on 'the accrued analysis of literary works' (Robisch), might learn from this integration of environmental issues with politico-literary ones; just as, on the other hand, ecocritics drawn to theory might see how their theoretical concerns can be channelled into particular texts and debates, a move which can make theory more relevant but also (and importantly) open to revision as it is moulded by the practical issues it both addresses and is addressed by.[32]

Many ecocritics will disagree with Williams's politically charged readings of literature and others will find a perhaps all too human focus in his writings, as Ryle notes, with too little attention given to our relations with the nonhuman world. Another criticism is that Williams's preference for realist literature can sometimes weaken his evaluation of other writers. For instance, Williams takes the writer and poet Edward Thomas to task for his lack of engagement with the social realities of rural England, and for developing an 'uncritical, abstracting literary anthropology, within which folktales and legends became part of an unlocalised, unhistorical past' (258). As with other Georgian poets – a group which includes Lascelles Abercrombie and John Drinkwater – Thomas succumbed to an all too literary approach to rural life: 'The observation is so often clear and intense, but as the mode forms there is an inrush of alien imagery: that set of ideas about the "rural" and the "pastoral", filtered through a version of the classical tradition' (255). But Williams's remark evidently measures Thomas's work against a realist criterion and, while it is true Thomas was prone to romanticising the landscape and the conditions of rural life, Williams's account seems less able to respond to the interiorised and even spiritual elements of Thomas's writing. Thomas's *Pursuit of Spring* (1913) may not be a complex work of social realism, for instance, but as a descriptive catalogue of the English landscape – the book records a bicycle journey from Clapham to the Quantocks – and as a highly personalised account of Thomas's moods and thoughts as he completes his journey, the book sensitively portrays the excitement of exploring the English countryside, an excitement which it draws the reader into sharing and which cannot be simply dismissed as pastoral. Not all writing about the country, that is to say, need involve Hardy's complex communities, or Clare's finely observed externalities, and room should be made for other approaches to country writing that extend beyond the realist mode.

These disagreements with Williams are important, as there are particular limitations in his Marxist-inspired reading of literature whereby political and social issues can take precedence over the aesthetic and imaginative elements of literary works. But even here disagreement with Williams might provoke conversation about how far ecocriticism can and should develop from its roots in literary studies and embrace the insights of other disciplines. To what extent, that is, might ecocriticism aspire towards a total form of criticism, in its integration of aesthetics, politics and the sciences? But on the other hand, what is lost in this outward expansion towards other disciplines? Can ecocriticism draw so many fields together without becoming a superficial conglomeration of different forms of knowledge?

However those particular questions are answered – and however particular disagreements with Williams are negotiated – *The Country and the City* seems increasingly relevant for ecocriticism. For the cascading effect of Williams's criticism is to draw attention to how deeply we are involved in the natural world and to sensitise us to connections and relationships not always visible to us, but in which we may nevertheless participate through our economic, social and environmental activities. In contrast, Birkin's thought experiment (imagining a pastoral sublime in which humans are absent) is really a disengagement from the problem of modernity. Against Birkin's apocalyptic absenteeism, Williams proposes a more detailed engagement with the actual processes of our relations to the environment. This means a resistance to 'singular abstractions' and a commitment to elucidating the complex ways by which we interact with (and are enmeshed in) nature. The following passage is from Williams's essay 'Ideas of Nature' and is worth quoting in full:

> In this actual world there is then not much point in counterposing or restating the great abstractions of Man and Nature. We have mixed our labour with the earth, our forces with its forces too deeply to be able to draw back and separate either out. Except that if we mentally draw back, if we go on with the singular abstractions, we are spared the effort of looking, in any active way, at the whole complex of social and natural relationships which is at once our product and our activity.[33]

Michael Malay

This line of thinking, with its insistence on examining 'the whole complex of social and natural relationships', firmly rejects the sublime in its various manifestations. Against the nostalgia of the pastoral mode, or the fatalism of catastrophic thinking, it suggests a careful and lucid response to our dealings with the environment (and our hand in causing environmental problems). It also compels an understanding of 'nature' as inextricably linked to culture and society, not as something 'out there', separate from 'Man', but as woven into the texture of human life and activity.

There is a practical as well as ethical force behind this insight. To understand how deeply our 'labour' is mixed in with the earth – economically, culturally, politically – is to confront the material consequences of that labour. Thus if we find our environment in a state of trouble, and our society in a state of inequality, we must accept it as mirroring, in some sense, the unsustainability and unfairness of our practices. Yet, as Williams pointed out in *The Country and the City*, this acknowledgement is often never made, or is qualified in such a way as to diminish what that acknowledgement would commit us to. Thus one could celebrate the simplicity of rural life from a country estate and at the same time inveigh against the corruption of the city. As Williams remarks of Jonson's 'To Penshurst' or Thomas Carew's 'To Saxham':

> The greed and the calculation, so easily isolated and condemned in the city, run back, quite clearly, to the country houses, with the fields and their labourers around them. And this is a double process. The exploitation of man and of nature, which takes place in the country, is realised and concentrated in the city. (48)

Privilege and the pastoral, then, are closely interlinked elements – part of a structure in which privilege is able to denounce the city while simultaneously drawing on its resources. These privileged centres, moreover, establish legitimacy by describing themselves as part of the 'traditional' or 'natural' order. Thus the rural folk enjoyed their lot as much as the aristocrat enjoyed his estate. Or the rural folk did not exist at all:

> The actual men and women who rear the animals and drive them to the house and kill them and prepare them for meat; who trap the pheasants and partridges and catch the fish; who plant and manure and prune and harvest the fruit trees; these are not present; their work is all done for them by a natural order. (32)

As Williams remarks, such 'mystification [...] requires effort' (31). And since privilege constantly seeks to perpetuate itself, it must create and sustain dominant images that make it seem part of a 'natural order'. This gives it the flexibility to praise life in the country and criticise 'greed' in the city, but not see how those judgements rely on double standards, since the urban centres one inveighs against are precisely what sustains one's life in the country.

Williams's critique of 'country house' literature provides a partial model for how ecocriticism might connect with questions of social and environmental justice.[34] This is a quickly growing field in what is called 'second-wave' ecocriticism, albeit one Williams was engaged in decades ago.[35] Every rich city, the philosopher Val Plumwood wrote in 2008, has its 'shadow place in the world', and communities 'should always be imagined as in relationship to others, particularly downstream communities, rather than as singular and self-sufficient'.[36] Or as Williams remarked in *Politics and Letters*:

> I feel the weight of those country houses. Who has not admired the admirable architecture or furniture to be found among them? But if we acknowledge them as a contribution [to Western culture], we must also at the same time acknowledge them as an obstacle [...] the country houses are not just buildings of elegance. They are constantly presented to us as 'our heritage', including a particular way of seeing and relating to the world, which must be critically registered along with our acknowledgment of our value. (309)

If every document of culture is also a document of barbarism, then part of the task of criticism, it seems, or at least of the kind initiated by Williams, was to show the various manifestations of that dialectical relationship – to describe the relations between the 'official consciousness of an epoch' and 'the whole process of actually living its consequences' (*Politics and Letters*, 159). Nevertheless, an acknowledgement of culture's shadow places does not mean a wholesale rejection of that culture's 'value'. One may be suspicious of 'elegance' and at the same time appreciate the craftsmanship behind elegant objects (as when we express astonishment or surprise at certain levels of cultural ingenuity). The point is, rather, that separating the rich from the poor, the country estate from the rural labourers is inimical to a proper understanding of the totality of that culture. As Plumwood writes, strongly echoing Williams: 'An ecological re-conception of dwelling has to include a justice perspective and be able to recognise the shadow places, not just the ones we love, admire or find nice to look at' (139).

To see the 'actual world' as 'at once our product and our activity', as Williams suggests, is to alter the nature of our response to social and environmental problems. The remark compels us to see those problems not as tangential to our ideological attitudes, but as *direct* embodiments of them. This requires us, in turn, to reflect upon the processes and practices that underpin our economic relations with the natural word, as well as the grammatical distortions that help us avoid thinking about these issues. I use the word 'grammatical' quite deliberately here, as Williams's insights often operate at the level of language (and the various ways we use and abuse it to suit our needs). Consider, for instance, the following passage from 'Ideas of Nature':

> In our complex dealings with the physical world, we find it very difficult to recognise the products of our own activities. We recognise some of the products, and call others by-products; but the slagheap is as real a product as the coal, just as the river stinking with sewage and detergent is as much our product as the reservoir. The enclosed and fertile land is our product, but so are the waste moors from which the poor cultivators were cleared, to leave what can be seen as an empty nature. (83)

The issue, then, is partly one of description. How we name our activities reflects our attitudes towards the natural world, and also legitimises them. By calling 'coal' a product and the 'slagheap' a by-product (83), we separate the benefits of mining from its consequences.[37] This separation is to the advantage of our current economic practices, since it allows us to ignore (and thus continue) the destructive implications of our labour. By refusing to see the good and the bad as structurally enmeshed, language effects a kind of magical separation between the benefits and 'side-effects' of our activities. Moreover, this strategy works on a sliding scale. As on the local level we disconnect sewage from the reservoir, or fertile land from the waste moors, we disconnect, on the macro scale, the goods of capitalism from its discontents. In many ways, the survival of the system depends on just this kind of separation.

In contemporary culture, this estrangement between products and by-products is still a common feature of our economic system. Just as common is how this estrangement is disguised or obscured by the overarching narratives of technological 'progress'. We are yet to understand, for instance, the full implications of IT waste on the environment. On one hand, it is surely a good thing that emailing and scanning helps minimise our use of paper. On the other hand, abandoned and 'junked' computers have had devastating effects on environmental and human life – usually elsewhere. Ghana, for instance, is one of the largest dumping grounds of electrical waste from the EU. While there are real advantages in this relationship for Ghana – recycling Western waste becomes a source of local employment – and while the EU has strict laws on what kinds of waste can be exported, there is little regulation over working conditions on these sites. There is also little oversight on how technological waste can be managed so as to protect the local environment from contamination. This is where the divorce between our patterns of consumption and our patterns of waste obscures the effect of our practical activities on the world. For functioning computers and rotting ones are both the 'real products' of our consumption. To isolate one from the other is not only false, but leads to the outsourcing of environmental problems and social inequalities. The links between throwing away a computer in England and the contamination of water supplies in an African village (by heavy metals such as lead, mercury and arsenic) are not always fanciful and exaggerated. Sometimes they are directly connected, even when – or precisely when – those networks are largely invisible to us.[38]

IV

In 'Ideas of Nature', Williams's identifies Marx as a key figure in his methodological approach.

> We have to look at all our products and activities, good and bad, and to see the relationships between them which are our own real relationships. More clearly than anyone, Marx indicated this. (84)

But affinities should not be taken as identifications and Williams was alert to many conceptual weaknesses and problems in the Marxist approach. As Williams goes on to say, Marx also wrote 'in terms of quite singular forces' and critics had to 'develop this kind of indication in more refined and thoughtful ways' (84).

Although much of Williams's work has been oriented towards just this task, labelling his work as 'Marxist' is reductive. Not only does it fail to cover the full range of his thinking but Williams himself probably would have had reservations about such categories.[39] As Williams warns, Marxist criticism can sometimes be simplistic, particularly when it unthinkingly accepts the governing terms of its dialectic:

> the practice can degenerate into what I have precisely called a formula. At that point it becomes an obstacle. Take the example of the famous slogan of the mastery of nature. Of course anyone who views history in a materialist way must see the processes of understanding and working within nature as the central founding element of any civilisation. But to describe these as *mastery* was to treat nature as if it was just material to dominate [...] Marx's innocent use of the phrase, or of the terms 'produce' and 'productive', is comprehensible in his time. But its unthinking repetition today, when

we have reason to be aware of the consequence of the formula, is really inexcusable.[40]

This is a helpful caveat for the burgeoning field of 'eco-Marxisim' and ecocriticism in general.[41] 'Mastery' and 'production' may have an explanatory power in traditional Marxist criticism, but they also assume, and perpetuate the assumption, that 'production' and 'mastery' are settled ways of speaking about the world, rather than themselves part of a 'structure of feeling' that allows us to 'dominate' the environment. As they stand, these terms are fundamentally incompatible with current ecological thought and any synthesis between Marxism and ecocriticism would require major theoretical intervention.

Nevertheless, as Williams remarked, Marxism 'indicated' the methodology an ecological approach might adopt. This would involve a continual interlinking between patterns of privilege and subordination, rich places and their shadow zones, and an analysis of how our economic activities are related to material problems in the world. At the same time, however, this method requires greater subtlety lest it become simplified by its own dialectical procedures. And this, indeed, is part of the value of Williams's methodology, which not only pinpointed the various deficiencies of Marxist criticism, but which developed a mode of reading that continued (in a critically refined form) the central insights of Marxist thought. As Gifford has shown with 'pastoral' and 'post-pastoral', and as I tried to suggest briefly with my defence of Edward Thomas, ecocritics drawn to Williams's work will need to elaborate upon his thought whenever his terms seem restrictive or out-dated. Seen in this light, Nirmal Selvamony's observation that 'ecocritics are not agreed on what constitutes the basic principle in ecocriticism' is potentially a virtue, as it allows a constant revision of modes of thinking we have inherited. Williams's suggestion that Marxist lines of thought should be supplemented and reconfigured applies no less strongly to how we read Williams today.

Ecocriticism might benefit from a re-reading of Williams's central texts, not because it will be sympathetic to all of his work, but because his insistence on unearthing the connections between diverse but related practices compels a recognition of the variety of phenomena that ecocriticism might potentially address, from pastoral poetry to electronic waste. This is not to suggest that ecocriticism should dispense with its primary strengths: its aesthetic sensitivity to literary texts, for example, or its ethical appreciation of environmental 'Others'. But it is to say that ecocriticism could be strengthened by vigilantly appropriating other methods of reading literary texts – Marxist criticism being one of them – and by becoming more intimate with the technology, economics and politics of globalisation. To adapt an earlier quotation from Williams, ecocriticism requires 'a more radically honest accounting than any we now have'. The challenge, in short, is for ecocriticism to supplement itself with other concerns in a manner that concentrates rather than dilutes its commitments.

In *New Historicism and Cultural Materialism* (1998), John Brannigan writes:

> Williams marked a radical break from humanist conceptions of literature and was crucial to the development of a critical practice which would analyse the way in which culture both reflected and acted upon the society of which it was a part.[42]

This evaluation is basically correct – only I would query the idea that Williams marked a 'break' from humanist thinking. If anything, Williams's methods of analysis – his engaged readings of culture, literature and politics, and his balance between sympathy and critique – are a continuation and enlargement of humanist forms of thought. For there is nothing more humanistic than a refusal of the apocalyptic mode, and a determination to offer 'resources of hope' in the face of various environmental, social and economic problems.

Notes

1. Slavoj Žižek, *Living in the End Times* (London: Verso, 2010), x. Žižek then describes capitalism's 'four riders of the apocalypse', a group 'comprised by the ecological crisis, the consequences of the biogenetic revolution, imbalances within the system itself (problems with intellectual property; forthcoming struggles over raw materials, food and water), and the explosive growth of social divisions and exclusions' (x).
2. D.H. Lawrence, *Women in Love* (London: Penguin, 1989), 187–8.
3. The ecocritic Greg Garrard quotes the same passage in his essay 'Worlds Without Us: Some Types of Disanthropy', *SubStance* 41, no. 1 (2012): 40–60, 40. 'Lawrence's disanthropy', Garrard writes, 'is terminal and total' and reflects a 'crushing moral verdict upon humanity' (42).
4. For a longer discussion of 'scale' in relation to climate change, see Timothy Clark's 'Some Climate Change Ironies: Deconstruction, Environmental Politics and the Closure of Ecocriticism', *Oxford Literary Review* 32, no. 1 (2010): 131–49 and 'Scale: Derangements of Scale', in *Telemorphosis: Theory in the Era of Climate Change*, Vol. 1, ed. Tom Cohen (Ann Arbor: Open Humanities Press/University of Michigan Library, 2012), 148–66.
5. For extinct species, of course, the 'end' is a truism rather than a literary device. The same is true for species (and landscapes) nearing extinction. In these cases, 'catastrophe' is a legitimate term. My suggestion, however, is that the term is misapplied when used in phrases such as a 'global catastrophe' or 'environmental catastrophe'.

6   Damian Thompson, *The End of Time: Faith and Fear in the Shadow of the Millennium* (London: University Press of New England, 1996), 13–14.
7   Donna Haraway, 'Staying with the Trouble: Becoming Worldly with Companion Species', Women's Studies Program, 5th Annual Feminist Theory Workshop, 18 and 19 March 2011.
8   Raymond Williams, *Keywords: A Vocabulary of Culture and Society* (London: Fontana, 1983), 219.
9   Raymond Williams, *Problems in Materialism and Culture: Selected Essays* (London: Verso, 1980), 67.
10 Williams, *Problems in Materialism and Culture*, 84.
11 Cherryl Glotfelty, 'Introduction' to *The Ecocriticism Reader*, ed. Cherryl Glotfelty and Harold Fromm (Athens, GA: University of Georgia Press, 1996), xviii.
12 Richard Kerridge, 'Introduction' to *Writing the Environment: Ecocriticism and Literature,* ed. Richard Kerridge and Neil Sammells (London: Zed, 1998), 5.
13 From William Rueckert's 1978 essay, 'Literature and Ecology: an Experiment in Ecocriticism', reprinted in Glotfelty's *The Ecocriticism Reader*, 105–23, 107.
14 Nirmal Selvamony, 'Introduction' to *Essays in Ecocriticism*, ed. Nirmal Selvamony, Nirmaldasan and Rayson K. Alex (Chennai: OSLE-India, 2007), xix. For an interesting discussion of the difficulty of defining the relations between ecocriticism and environmental literature, see Ralph Pite, 'How Green Were the Romantics?', *Studies in Romanticism* 35, no. 3 (1996): 357–73.
15 Private correspondence.
16 S.K. Robisch, 'The Woodshed: A Response to "Ecocriticism and Ecophobia"', *ISLE* 16, no. 4 (2009): 697–708.
17 Kate Soper, *What Is Nature?* (Cambridge, MA: Blackwell, 1995), 151.
18 Dominic Head, 'Beyond 2000: Raymond Williams and the Ecocritic's Task', in *The Environmental Tradition in English Literature*, ed. Richard Kerridge and Neil Sammells (Aldershot: Ashgate, 2002), 24–36, 27. For other perspectives on Robisch's article see Garrard's brief remarks in 'Ecocriticism: Review of 2009', *The Year's Work in Critical and Cultural Theory* 19 (2009): 46–82, and Louisa Mackenzie and Stephanie Posthumus, 'Reading Latour Outside: A Response to the Estok–Robisch Controversy', *ISLE* 20, no. 3 (2013): 1–21.
19 Dominic Head, 'Raymond Williams and Ecocriticism', *Green Letters: Studies in Ecocriticism* 1, no. 1 (2000): 7.
20 Head gives a fuller treatment of Williams's novels – particularly *Border Country* (1960), *Second Generation* (1964) and *The Fight for Manod* (1979) – in 'Beyond 2000: Raymond Williams and the Ecocritic's Task'.
21 Martin Ryle, 'Raymond Williams: Materialism and Ecocriticism', in *Ecocritical Theory: New European Approaches*, ed. Kate Rigby and Axel Goodbody (Charlottesville, VA: University of Virginia Press, 2011), 43–54, 48 and 49.
22 This is the charge that is sometimes levelled, for instance, against 'first-wave' ecocriticism. As Lawrence Buell explains, first-wave ecocritics typically focused on 'nature writing, nature poetry and wilderness fiction'. *The Future of Environmental Criticism* (Malden, MA: Blackwell, 2005), 138. For first-wave ecocritics, 'environment effectively meant 'natural environment' (21), whereas second-wave ecocriticism

elaborates a '"social criticism" that takes urban and degraded landscapes just as seriously as "natural" landscapes' (22). In this expanded framework, then, a 'pastoral' poem – besides being an object for literary analysis – also invited other forms of inquiry, among them postcolonial studies, environmental justice issues and feminism. Buell notes, however, that his 'first-second distinction should not [...] be taken as implying a tidy, distinct succession' (17), and suggests that 'palimpsest' would be a better metaphor than 'wave'.

23 Raymond Williams, *Marxism and Literature* (Oxford: Oxford University Press, 1977), 145.

24 For a study which *does* integrate Hopkins's poetry with broader environmental and cultural issues, see John Parham's *Green Man Hopkins: Poetry and the Victorian Ecological Imagination* (Amsterdam: Rodopi, 2010).

25 As Greg Garrard writes, a Marxist interpretation may have 'impressive explanatory leverage' when it comes to certain kinds of historical analysis, but elsewhere its reach is severely limited. 'A deterministic account of how the advent of iambic pentameter reflected the demise of the feudal economy [...] can easily be exposed as historically naïve and dismissive of the internal dynamics of prosodic development.' 'Literary Theory 101', *ISLE* 17, no. 4 (2010): 781. Garrard's example is deliberately far-fetched, but it nevertheless shows up the problem of subsuming a heterogeneity of practices and activities into a single framework, even if that framework has both the breadth and 'explanatory leverage' of the Marxist critic. On the other hand, Garrard remarks that ecocriticism could be buttressed by adopting some elements of Marxist thought, although a 'proper definition of the "base" of human society in socio-ecological terms is likely to prove bewilderingly complex' (782). In any case, and however that relationship is to be configured, he observes that ecocriticism should be 'a great deal more difficult than it presently is' (782).

26 Raymond Williams, *Politics and Letters: Interviews with 'New Left Review'* (London: New Left Books, 1979), 159.

27 Williams, *Marxism and Literature*, 133.

28 Williams, *Politics and Letters*, 164.

29 Terry Gifford first articulated these terms in his article on Ted Hughes: 'Gods of Mud: Hughes and the Post-pastoral', in *The Challenge of Ted Hughes*, ed. Keith Sagar (Basingstoke: Macmillan, 1994), 129–41. See also Gifford's 'Post-pastoral', in *Pastoral* (London: Routledge, 1999), 146–74, and 'Towards a Post-pastoral View of British Poetry', in *The Environmental Tradition in English Literature*, 51–63.

30 Gifford, 'Pastoral, Anti-Pastoral and Post-Pastoral as Reading Strategies', in *Critical Insights: Nature and Environment*, ed. Scott Slovic (Ipswich: Salem Press, 2012), 42–61.

31 Leo Marx, *The Machine in the Garden* (London: Oxford University Press, 1964), 5 and 25.

32 Robisch, 'The Woodshed', 700.

33 Williams, *Problems in Materialism and Culture*, 83.

34 For a discussion of the developing relations between ecocriticism and environmental justice, see Lawrence Buell, *The Future of Environmental Criticism* (Oxford: Blackwell Publishing, 2005), 112–27.
35 Buell discusses 'first-wave' and 'second-wave' ecocriticism at length in *The Future of Environmental Criticism*. See also Buell's 'Ecocriticism: Some Emerging Trends', *Qui Parle: Critical Humanities and Social Sciences* 19, no. 2 (2011): 87–115.
36 Val Plumwood, 'Shadow Places and the Politics of Dwelling', *Australian Humanities Review* 44 (2008): 148.
37 As Williams writes in *Marxism and Literature*, language is 'positively a distinctly human opening of and opening to the world: Not just a distinguishable or instrumental but a constitutive faculty' (24).
38 See Steven C. Hackett, *Environmental and Natural Resources Economics: Theory, Policy and the Sustainable Society*, 4th edn (New York: M.E. Sharp, 2011), 330. For a photographic illustration of Agbogbloshie, an infamous 'electronic' dumping ground in Ghana, see Pieter Hugo's *Permanent Error* (London: Prestel Publishers, 2011).
39 As Cornwell West explains, 'what also attracted me to Williams's work was his refusal to sidestep the *existential* issues of what it means to be an intellectual and activist – issues like death, despair, disillusionment and disempowerment in the face of defeats and setbacks [...] His preoccupation with vital traditions and vibrant communities, sustaining neighborhoods and supportive networks, reflected his sensitivity to how ordinary people in their everyday lives are empowered and equipped to deal with defeats and setbacks'. 'The Legacy of Raymond Williams', *Social Text* no. 30 (1992): 7.
40 Williams, *Politics and Letters*, 311.
41 As a starting point, see Ted Benton (ed.), *The Greening of Marxism* (New York: The Guilford Press, 1996). This collection of essays brings together a number of scholars who discuss the complications (as well as the enriching possibilities) of bringing ecology and Marxist thinking together.
42 John Brannigan, *New Historicism and Cultural Materialism* (Basingstoke: Palgrave Macmillan, 1998), 39.

'A Specific Contemporary Sadness': Raymond Williams and the Speculative Socialist Tradition
Rosalind Brunt

Abstract: This article derives its title from an interview Williams gave to *New Left Review* (1979). Here, discussing ideas behind his novels, Williams notes a 'specific contemporary sadness' based on comparing 'a wholly possible future' with 'the contradictions and blockages of the present'. This quotation frames the ensuing analysis of Williams's two 'future' novels, *The Fight for Manod* (1979) and *The Volunteers* (1978), discussed in terms of a tradition of 'speculative socialism'. Two earlier examples of this tradition are then considered: Tressell's *The Ragged Trousered Philanthropists* (1914), a novel strongly championed by Williams, and Bellamy's *Looking Backward* (1888), which imagines a socialist utopia achieved by 2000. The conclusion discusses Williams's own aims for the millennium in his treatise, *Towards 2000*. Throughout, the article addresses the persuasive strategies each text employs to engage its readers and convince them of the significant 'blockages' to developing socialism and, notwithstanding, the potential 'resources' for future collective action.

*

In the late 1970s the *New Left Review* editorial board conducted a series of extended conversations with Raymond Williams.[1] These ranged over his life history and how this meshed with his political activism and major writing. Their final session featured the four novels Williams had published by then.

In this session, Perry Anderson, Anthony Barnett and Francis Mulhern, operating as one joint *NLR* questioner, discussed the recently published final novel of Williams's Welsh trilogy, *The Fight for Manod*,[2] set in the near-future. This book brings together two of the main characters from the previous novels, Matthew Price from *Border Country*,[3] now a middle-aged industrial historian, and Peter Owen from *Second Generation*,[4] now a radical young sociologist. The novel narrates how both are invited to live in the mid-Wales valley community of Manod to work as consultants on a government proposal to develop a visionary new city based on existing dispersed communities and advanced communications technology. In the course of their consultation they learn what Manod means for its current inhabitants whilst uncovering a web of local and global corporate interests which could wreck the scheme.

Commenting on the plot of the novel, the *NLR* interlocutors refer to its title and note that despite the plot's emotional and political tensions, 'there is surprisingly little actual fight demonstrated in the novel itself'. They go on to comment on the lack of collective action in the novel, especially when compared with the two earlier novels, which both featured scenes of industrial solidarity, and suggest this creates 'an undercurrent of sadness' to the book. Replying, Raymond Williams said: 'The eventual shape was indeed a certain sadness: not the retrospective sadness of so much rural fiction, but a specific contemporary sadness: the relation between a wholly possible future and the contradictions and blockages of the present.'[5]

In this article I will explore some of the dimensions of this 'sadness' in relation to both *The Fight for Manod* and Williams's other future novel, *The Volunteers*.[6] I then want to consider them in the light of two earlier exemplars of a speculative socialism, Robert Tressell's *Ragged Trousered Philanthropists*,[7] a novel championed by Williams, which also conveys a pervasive sense of the elegiac and raises important questions about the possibility of collective action during the early part of the twentieth century. Then, via a popular American novel that influenced Tressell's vision, Edward Bellamy's *Looking Backward*,[8] which imagines a fully-realised socialist utopia in the year 2000, I return to Raymond Williams to consider his own dystopian version of the millennium, *Towards 2000*.[9] I am interested in what persuasive strategies these three writers employ to engage their readers in their speculations; how they understand and negotiate contradiction, and how they resolve the question of agency raised by the *NLR* interviewers.

Williams sums up the stark intractability of the problem for his times as he expands on the 'sadness' of most of a twentieth century that neither Bellamy nor Tressell were actually to experience. While he points to the socialist writer's aim of restoring confidence in the future, he then produces a list of the century's 'contradictions and blockages'. These range from the global devastation of war and 'the terrible disintegration' of national labour movements, to the local and the personal, such as 'the quite specific sadness of rural Wales' and the experience of ageing.[10]

Much of the tension of the times that Williams outlines here is embodied in Matthew Price, the central protagonist of *Manod*. He is a sick man and suffers his second heart attack just as he and Peter Owen are outlining to a Whitehall ministerial meeting their discoveries of international corruption that could destabilise the new city plan. When he recovers he learns that Owen has resigned his own consultant position and plans to expose the corruption through media publicity. Price admires Owen's stance – 'He's fighting what he thinks the real cause. And I expect he's right'[11] – but decides to take a different line. He will stay on to complete the year's consultancy, but hold public hearings so that local people can decide for themselves on the merits of the plan with full knowledge of the speculative interests it has attracted.

Although 'fight' and 'fighting' crop up towards the end of the novel to describe possible future action, it is not clear that anything much will ensue. The narrative introduces a range of sympathetically-realised inhabitants of Manod whom Price and his wife Susan meet and like. Subsequently they are all bought off by the local property developer who turns out to be connected with the international corporate interests that Owen will expose. But Price recognises that, for the present at least, this very 'incorporation' has given them material and financial security for the first time in their lives.

So it is left uncertain how the positive aspects of the city plan could ever be implemented. Price is sticking with it because he can still see its potential for a desperately-needed new kind of rural-urban renewal based on exploring 'new social patterns, new actual social relations …'.[12] Just at that point comes Price's collapse at the meeting and the novel never subsequently elaborates what these new aspects could be, nor who might provide the local opposition to the corruption already attendant on the plan – especially when it has already appeared in the benign guise of spreading affluence.

As the *NLR* team remark, the only actual opposition in the novel happens off-stage and comes from outside the community. On the penultimate page of *Manod* there is brief mention that members of the radical group who first helped Owen with his international research are visiting Price 'tomorrow'. That apart, there appears to remain only the personal choice of individual stoicism. The novel ends with Susan asking Price both literally and metaphorically, 'Are you ready to go on?' And he replies, 'Yes love, yes we must'.[13]

Although *Manod* was completed in 1978 while a minority Labour government was heading for defeat, it originated in the mid-1960s when Williams was actively collaborating in political initiatives associated with the *May Day Manifesto*.[14] Many authorial revisions later, the novel's conclusion is clearly indicative of a 'sad' consciousness of present blockages as the dutiful imperative of just carrying on carrying on is presented in a near-future landscape mainly lacking in collective political action.

In his 1978 lecture 'The Tenses of Imagination', Williams describes 'the whole point' of *Manod* as being 'the relation between necessary and desirable plans for the future and at once the ways they get distorted and frustrated'. Describing *Manod* as a speculative novel set around a 'plan', he goes on to contrast it with his other future novel, *The Volunteers*, which is 'deliberately and discontinuously' set 'as an action'.[15]

Written quickly and published in 1978, a year earlier than *Manod*, *The Volunteers* adopts the more immediate, faster-paced format of a first-person thriller narrative. Set in 1987, it envisages the complete collapse of the Labour Party as an independent electoral force. The UK government is now a National Labour-Conservative coalition. When the novel opens, there has been a recent burst of industrial militancy from the rail and coal unions that power-workers have supported by occupying fuel depots to prevent the movement of stocks. At one such occupation in Wales, police have been withdrawn and the army sent in to force an opening. One power-worker has been shot dead attempting to drive a lorry to reinforce a barricade.

At the start of the story, the UK minister widely believed to have authorised the army's shoot-to-kill order has himself just been shot while opening a new Folk Museum for Wales. Although the assailant has got clean away, the setting for the shooting and the non-fatal wounding suggest a deliberate ultra-left attempt at reprisal-as-spectacle.

The narrator, Lewis Redfern, is a journalist and 'consultant analyst' with an international satellite broadcaster. Because of his extensive knowledge and former involvement with radical groups, he is sent to Wales to investigate and report on the minister's shooting. The narrative recounts Redfern's investigation and how it comes to link both shootings. The story works through a series of his encounters: with local Welsh trade unionists who are gathering evidence for an enquiry into their comrade's death; with a former Labour minister and erstwhile radical intellectual, Mark Evans, now head of an American-funded NGO; and his son David and colleagues who are in the clandestine group who shot the minister. Through these encounters, Redfern pieces together evidence of the minister's involvement in the army shooting and the novel concludes when he resigns his broadcast job and presents this information to the enquiry.

The two most powerful pieces of writing in the novel come first from a pamphlet Redfern reads, 'Death of a Loader', a compelling, minutely-detailed account compiled by the Gwent Writers' Group of what led up to the army shooting; and secondly, Redfern's own savage critique of the new Folk Museum for its depiction of a rural past that serves as a denial of Wales' more recent industrialisation. But unlike the Welsh trilogy novels, the characterisation of the very laconic Redfern and some of the key actors in the plot is underdeveloped and their actions unclear. Such plot weaknesses remove many of the conventional narrative hooks that would allow readers to insert themselves into the story and so become involved in its outcomes.

At the end of the novel it emerges that Redfern has abandoned some of his earlier hard-boiled cynicism and rediscovered his earlier radicalism. But the novel leaves it unclear which way he might now jump: towards the clandestine group, the trade union movement, or neither? Thus, when he is offered lift to the station after the enquiry by the brother-in-law of the dead power worker Redfern replies, 'No thanks Bob, I'll find my own way back'.[16]

Again, there is both the literal and metaphorical ending: Redfern remains 'his own man'. For all the novel's prescience about many of the political directions of the 1980s, it is as if the political imagination of the author is exhausted by the frustrating 'blockages' to radical thinking and action at the end of the 1970s. The novel seems to imply that, given the actual circumstances of the period, there may indeed be very little room for manoeuvre – apart from the same sort of personal radical integrity that Matthew Price showed in *Manod*.

Invited in the *NLR* interviews to compare himself with the character of Matthew Price in *Manod*, Williams commented: 'I feel a coarse hard bastard beside him, but more able, I think, or hope, to work and push through.'[17] Working and pushing through into the early 1980s, an angrier Williams with a more direct and stark political voice emerges. In May 1982 halfway through a Falklands War that was to give a shaky Tory government the electoral confidence to take on the trade union movement after the Argentinian government, Williams delivered a speech in Hastings. He spoke in the following terms about the need to address the oppression and, effectively, the 'imprisonment' of working people through ideological mystification, material deprivation and lack of actual power:

> It is terrible to live like this, to be this vulnerable to the whims of others, to be this vulnerable to the accidents of trade and the imbecilities of the system. It is terrible also, however, to be vulnerable not only to the propaganda and the self-justifications of others who have an interest in perpetuating ignorance, but to an ignorance that gets built in, inside people themselves – an ignorance that becomes their common sense. Being a prisoner can come to seem common sense, or can be made to seem what is human.[18]

The language here is cogent and terse. This is indeed a 'hard' statement of position and Williams concludes by referring to the confrontational value of political writing which squares up to the ideologies of 'common sense':

> But there is another way, still an original and lasting way. And that is to say: 'You are a prisoner, and you'll only get out of this prison if you'll admit it's a prison. And if you won't call it a prison, I will, and I'll go on calling it a prison come what may.[19]

The prison analogy here anticipates the shockingly dystopian vision of contemporary political tendencies which Williams was to publish the following year in *Towards 2000*. However, although the language and tone have a particular 'hard' resonance with the context of the early 1980s and chime especially with Williams's own continuing political project against the odds, he is actually referring in these passages to Tressell's *The Ragged Trousered Philanthropists* [hereafter *RTP*], which was written probably between 1906–10 and first published, posthumously, in a heavily cut and re-arranged form in April 1914.

The full uncut version, with some editorial help from Williams, only appeared in 1955. The first full-length study of *RTP*, to which Williams contributed a generous, if nuanced, preface, was written by Jack Mitchell in 1969.[20]

Mitchell's argument here chimes with that of Williams in his Hastings speech. For Williams, Tressell's stark-eyed ability to render an entire social and economic formation as a prison, is 'this strength, this challenge', that gives the novel its 'lasting quality'.[21] Similarly, Mitchell understands that the very bleakness that the novel represents is a necessary stripping of the decks before any meaningful collective socialist action can ensue in the world outside the novel. He suggests that the book offers a very full inventory of the actual impact of the current stage of monopoly capitalism, providing an acute demonstration of how an Edwardian imperialist economy comes to invade and destructively shape all aspects of everyday life, from working conditions to the apparently most intimate spaces of family and sexual relations. As Mitchell points out, Tressell's own manuscript title page described the novel as 'Being the story of twelve months in Hell, told by one of the damned'.[22]

The Ragged-Trousered Philanthropists outlines the many layers of this Hell using two main narrative drives. First, detailed reportage of the daily lives of a group of decorators both at work and out of it, together with satirical depiction of the employing classes in a small town (modelled on Hastings), and how their interests interlink with the local council and are sanctioned by the press and religious denominations. Secondly, descriptions of the propaganda efforts of the two key socialists in the book, the protagonist, Frank Owen, a master-craftsman painter and decorator and his colleague, George Barrington, a middle-class activist and funder from outside the town who is working with the group as a temporary labourer.

The propaganda of Owen and Barrington takes the form of both explaining how capitalism works in broadly Marxist terms and also how conditions could be different under socialism. Resorting often to parables, or inviting his workmates to 'suppose' a particular situation, Owen, especially, is frequently met with jeering challenges and interruption from his audience. This is a typical response after Owen has attempted to explain the causes of poverty by asking two men to 'suppose' they'd been shipwrecked on a desert island, one with a thousand sovereigns, the other with a bottle of water and tin of biscuits:

'Make it beer!' cried Harlow appealingly.
   [Owen:] 'Who would be the richer man, you or Harlow?'
   'But then you see we ain't shipwrecked on no dissolute island at all,' sneered Crass [the site foreman]. 'That's the worst of your arguments. You can't never get very far without supposing some bloody ridiclus thing or

other. Never mind about supposing things wot ain't true; let's 'ave facts and common sense.'
"Ear, 'ear,' said old Linden. 'That's wot we want – a little common sense.'
'What do you mean by poverty, then?' asked Easton.
'What I call poverty is when people are not able to secure for themselves all the benefits of civilization; the necessaries, comforts, pleasures and refinements of life, leisure, books, theatres, pictures, music, holidays, travel, good and beautiful homes, good clothes, good and pleasant food.'
Everyone laughed. It was so ridiculous. The idea of the likes of *them* wanting or having such things![23]

The scene ends after there has been further challenge to Owen, with strong objections to his describing their lives as worse than slaves – only for everyone to panic thinking they hear the footsteps of the boss four minutes after the lunch break should have ended. Throughout the novel the viewpoint of Owen about the intractability and lack of critical reflection of his fellow workers is endorsed by the third person narrator. It is reinforced by representing Owen's speech as being similar in style to that of the narrator and in marked contrast to the oral style and grammar of the 'commonsensical' workers. As the narrator sums it up here:

Some of them began to wonder whether Owen was not sane after all. He certainly must be a clever sort of chap to be able to talk like this. It sounded almost like something out of a book, and most of them could not understand one half of it.[24]

The challenge *RTP* sets itself is to present the 'blockage' of the most unpropitious circumstances for socialism in a town beset by regular unemployment, slump and often abject poverty where working people are presented as having very little sense of themselves as a cohesive class and do not appear to engage in any of the many current forms of collective action. Then to counterpose this closely-realised 'prison' and 'Hell' against a fully worked-out articulation of a possible socialist future as expounded by Owen and Barrington.

Hence, the book's ending, invoking 'the glorious fabric of the Co-operative Commonwealth' and 'the rays of the risen sun of Socialism',[25] is no glibly tacked-on reassurance. Indeed it follows an accumulation of some of the most unpropitious episodes in the book. The chronicled year has come full-circle and it is nearly Christmas. Barrington, who has earlier earned some grudging respect from the workers for delivering the most comprehensive account of what a socialist society might consist of in his 'Great Oration' lecture, is listening to some street electioneering for the Tories and Liberals. He meets the

Rosalind Brunt

'Renegade Socialist' who has developed complete contempt and cynicism for the workers and asks Barrington why he wastes his time with them. Barrington is deeply dispirited by his words and fails to find an adequate response.

Barrington then encounters Owen being threatened with a beating from a hostile audience – which would seem to prove the Renegade's views. Later, he witnesses evangelical Christians preaching and compares their pious hypocrisies with the actual words of Jesus. Owen, meanwhile, is threatened with job loss for standing up for another worker; from the opening chapter the reader already knows that he has a premonition of early death, has coughed up blood and contemplated different forms of suicide. Revealing himself to Owen as wealthy, Barrington plays Santa Claus to the children, gives money to Owen to tide his family over for the winter and promises to return in the spring with the socialist propaganda van.

Barrington's intervention at the close of the chronicle could be seen in the light of Raymond Williams's notion of 'the magic resolution' proposed in his well-known analysis of the 1840s English novel, whereby an element of narrative 'cheating' like a legacy or discovery of a long-lost relative enables the fictional resolution of actually irresolvable contradictions in the lived culture of the period.[26] However, Williams himself doesn't read the ending of *RTP* in these terms, acknowledging in his Hastings lecture the contribution well-off socialists did indeed make, both in time and money to contemporary radical movements.

But the temptation that *RTP* most radically and powerfully refuses is a magical resolution whereby the 'supposings' of Barrington and Owen actually achieve the desired effect: the scales drop from their hearers' eyes; they get the point of the need for socialism and become converts. That this resolution so manifestly does not happen, and that Williams's 'blockages and contradictions' remain so massively present throughout the book, does indeed provide *RTP* with 'a specific contemporary sadness'. So, given that the book concludes with the message that *nevertheless* socialism is both achievable and inevitable, it throws out a challenge to the readers themselves to find socialism convincing. Indeed, we know from much anecdotal evidence recorded in various prefaces to the book, and throughout Dave Harker's recent study of Tressell,[27] that readers of *RTP* have repeatedly responded to this challenge.

Thus *RTP* has appealed to readers, as it were, over the heads of its characters. Its title alone encapsulates Marx's central thesis about the motive forces of capital: the exploitation of labour power and the extraction of surplus-value. At the same time it provides the ironic perspective that frames the whole of the ensuing action. If the readers 'get' that from the start they can then make a contract with the book to learn how the capitalist mode of production works itself out in daily life and to be open to the arguments for a socialist alternative.

But then the question arises, how might that alternative be achieved? Clearly an appeal to the reasoning abilities of random readers will not of itself bring about the necessary change. What I think makes *RTP* a well-loved, as well as admired, socialist text is that readers take from it more than the overt message signalled by its title. For the book's 'other' narrative, the reportage that composes what Tressell calls in his Preface 'a readable story full of human interest and based on the happenings of everyday life',[28] serves as a counter-commentary on much of Owen's and the narrator's repeated despair at the apparent conservative quietism of the workers. Thus while the book features not one incident of conscious collective action, like union and party activity or any radical self-organisation, its closely observed daily 'happenings' repeatedly demonstrate acts of solidarity, kindliness, courageous ingenuity, quick-fire mocking wit and practical resilience against the worst depredations of the boss class. The novel's explicitly ironic framework enjoins readers to 'see through' the surface appearances and effects of capitalism. But the text also contains an implicit critique of both its own narrator's, and Owen's, superior reasoning powers, showing up their somewhat sectarian understanding of the workers' mystified 'philanthropy'. For instance, the frequent episodes of the workers' outmanoeuverings of the bosses and their spirited and earthy rejoinders to Owen's speculations repeatedly indicate a latent untapped energy and experience that the novel's overall irony cannot adequately encompass or acknowledge. Against the grain of the dominant arguments in the book, there is a subtextual reading of the 'philanthropists' that could render them the possible future 'gravediggers' of capitalism.

Tressell died in 1911. An active, widely-read socialist throughout his adult life, he organised his own penny library for fellow progressives. He probably knew Marx's and Engels's work primarily through his extensive knowledge of William Morris.[29] He was also familiar with much of the rich vein of popular utopian writing that had emerged in Britain and the United States during the last two decades of the nineteenth century. This would have included the work of the Danish-American socialist, Laurence Gronlund,[30] whose ideas inform the utopian set-pieces of *RTP*. It is not known whether Tressell had read Gronlund in the original; more likely he knew his ideas through Edward Bellamy's writing. But Gronlund's vision of 'the Cooperative Commonwealth' which Tressell adopted was a significant attempt to translate ideas derived from German social theory into a mainstream Anglo-American context whereby socialism could be represented as 'a logical, compact system'.[31]

A key aim of Gronlund's very influential treatise was to demystify socialism and remove its 'red scare' and 'alien' associations, by insisting on its innate rationality and potential to produce a felicitous future. In a preface, 'To the Reader', he states: 'I hope to show you that Socialism is no importation, but a home-growth, wherever found; to give you good reason to suppose that this New Socialist Order will be indeed a happy issue to the brain-worker as well as to the hand-worker, woman as well as man ....'[32]

Four years later, Edward Bellamy produced a fictional utopia that completely concurred with these sentiments and drew largely on Gronland's theories. Published in 1888, *Looking Backward* imagines a socialist mode of production fully achieved across Europe and America by the year 2000. This is based on a national industrial army that produces and distributes all necessary goods and services equitably to each citizen via the ingenious inventions of modern technology that have rendered a money economy obsolete.

Such a rapid achievement is explained in the novel by two key factors. Firstly, the contradictions of nineteenth-century competitive capitalism have played themselves out in the twentieth century. The result is a monopolistic state command economy which now, by the millennium, has lost any profit-motive and orders a society based solely on rational planning. Secondly, given this new material circumstance, a superstructural consciousness has inevitably and rapidly arisen, developing a truly Christian humanism to infuse all aspects of social and cultural life.

The frequent biblical allusions in the novel, Krishan Kumar has suggested, help to anchor readers in an already-known moral universe. Kumar's analysis of the many familiarising associations in the novel emphasizes the point that Bellamy's utopia seeks continuities with previously established political and ethical ideas. Most notably, its rational universe is represented as the culmination of what both the enlightenment and the American Revolution had initiated.[33]

This argument forms part of Kumar's detailed rebuttal of the long-held charge that Bellamy's vision is hardly, or not 'really', socialist. The accusation originated with William Morris, who produced his own utopian fiction *News from Nowhere*[34] two years later in direct response to *Looking Backward*. It emerged recently in Matthew Beaumont's extensively researched examination of fin-de-siècle Victorian writing.[35] Here Beaumont draws a sharp contrast, setting the revolutionary Marxist vision of Morris against Bellamy's 'reformist' idea of a future. In Beaumont's view *Looking Backward* offers little more than a cleaned-up version of consumer capitalism – a model that would be comfortably reassuring to a middle-class readership because it is achieved entirely through the automatic development of current economic forces and by-passes class conflict. Hence Beaumont's polemical notion of 'Utopia Ltd' to describe what he sees as a prophylactic viewpoint based on the denial of human agency and an overweening determinism.

One of the problems with this line of argument is that it risks taking the detailed content of a particular utopian vision too literally. Its tendency to mark the polarities of 'reform versus revolution' may verge on the reductive and ignore the ways speculative writing of the period may draw on an eclectic mix of sources. Hence, for instance, *RTP*'s imaginative future can encompass a Gronlund-Bellamy totalising system that is also passionately infused with Morris's views on fulfilling labour and creative culture. Further, Beaumont's suggestion that Bellamy's evolutionary determinism induces passivity in a complacent readership cannot adequately account for what Kumar calls the immediate and 'astonishing' appeal of *Looking Backward*. A bestseller in the US, it spawned a host of 'Bellamy' clubs in the 1890s discussing a variety of progressive ideas. These led in turn to the establishment of several utopian communities and a 'Nationalist' movement – in terms of devising socialist programmes for particular nations. For, as Kumar also demonstrates, the novel had an international success, including in Asia and South Africa, and was particularly influential for Russian progressive thinkers.[36]

To account for such enthusiasm, I suggest, requires more than an analysis of the specifics of the utopian proposition in the novel. It needs some attention, also, to the way the plot of *Looking Backward* creates a persuasive fiction.

The novel is the first-person narrative of a wealthy young Bostonian, Julian West. Falling into a deep hypnotic trance in 1887, he is discovered and awoken by the Leete family to find he is now living in the Cooperative Commonwealth of Boston 2000. The story then proceeds episodically and dialogically as the head of the family, cultured Dr Leete, replies in detail and with social and economic evidence to West's bewildered and quaintly naïve questions.

This account is rarely expounded dogmatically or abstractly. West's wonderment evokes practical responses and his dialogue with Leete is frequently humorous. The episodes exemplifying West's gradual millennial enlightenment are full of ingenious 'modern' inventions, suspense and an element of romantic intrigue. In short, it contains many of the familiar conventions of an accessible 'good read'.

At the same time, Bellamy introduces the novel feature of time travel that was to become such a staple feature of early twentieth-century science fiction. The new significance of West as the first major time traveller protagonist is, precisely, that he is enabled to manipulate 'the tenses of imagination' in ways that create new and shifting perspectives. Through the multidimensional vision of the hero's journey, the past may comment on the present, the present reflect on the future, and back, and round, again. How this works in *Looking Backward* requires the initial location of West in the 'present' Boston of 1887 to be one of amply-resourced cultural ease. He is about to make a 'good' marriage and enter into a comfortably prosperous family life. It is only his unfolding experience of the 'future' Boston that subsequently enables him to recognise that, for all his 'past' privilege, his mental and physical horizons were severely limited, his attitudes complacent and turgidly conservative. With this continual past–present comparison, the time travel narrative can demonstrate the superiority of a utopian vision in a way that avoids abstract didacticism on the author's part. Instead, readers may participate in an active transformative process, seeing it through the protagonist's eyes as he gradually assimilates the change.

West's millennial conversion to the new order is sealed on the final page as he steps into the garden to marry Dr Leete's daughter. But just before the utopian conclusion there is a strange twist to West's story. It is one which threatens to destabilise any happy-ever-after future with a counter-narrative of a past–present dystopia. West falls asleep in 2000, dreaming happily of his forthcoming marriage – only to awake back in the apparently 'real' Boston of 1887. Millennial Boston now becomes the fantasy which enables him to revisit the present of 1887 and interpret it from a drastically different perspective.

West finds the morning paper his servant has left on his breakfast table and reads a vivid summary of that day's accumulated headlines of worldwide poverty, war and misery. He then goes onto the streets, now seeing with a stranger's eyes, as a result of his millennium 'dream', the full horror of all he'd taken for granted and enjoyed about 1887 Boston life just the day before. There follow ten pages of graphic detail and heightened rhetoric about 'the festering mass of human wretchedness' that West suddenly notices everywhere. He tries to make a speech explaining the 'hideous, ghastly mistake' that civilisation has made, but the unheeding crowd turn on him: "'Madman!" "Fanatic!" "Enemy of society!" … "He says we are to have no more poor. Ha! ha!"'[37]

These passages form by far the most intensely-wrought section of the novel. Although the plot is then suddenly and magically resolved when it turns out that West still actually resides in 2000 and his revisiting of the 'past' was only a nightmare, the newly envisioned Boston of 1887, with the underside of its wealth now hideously revealed, remains a troubling 'present'. It continues to haunt the utopian conclusion of the book and points to that very 'specific contemporary sadness' that capitalism may, in fact, prove far more intransigent and provide many more 'blockages' on the road to socialism than the overtly optimistic and rationalist tenor of the novel has been maintaining.

The intrusion of the 'nightmare' perspective and its impact on the narrative serves as a further reminder of the need to consider the latent function of any speculative socialist vision in addition to the manifest specifics and utopian organisational arrangements that its author has elaborated. Readers could certainly be impressed and become passively transfixed by the ingenuity and comprehensive detail of Bellamy's millennium. But they could also come away from the novel disturbed by the light his utopian vision has cast on the shocking realities of daily life in the present and aware, possibly, of a need to take combative action.

The point is well made in Kumar's account of the effect *Looking Backward* had on Tolstoy:

> 'An exceedingly remarkable book', noted Tolstoy in his diary on 30 June 1889. The English-language copy in his library is extensively annotated and the passage at the end of the novel recounting Julian West's nightmare return to nineteenth-century Boston is especially heavily marked. It was indeed Bellamy's searing criticism of capitalist society, rather than his prescriptions for a future society, that most moved Tolstoy, and led him to seek a Russian translator.[38]

The international impact created by *Looking Backward* testifies to the view that speculation about the future can be most effective when it serves to defamiliarise, and hence demystify, the present. The complex interplay of 'tenses' in the book and the unsettling discontinuities of utopian and dystopian visions suggest that the text of the novel, as with *RTP*, in a sense '*knows*' more about the contradictions of the present than its author either acknowledges or intends.

Given the nearly hundred years that separate Bellamy's and Williams's versions of the millennium, it is of course Williams, from his much closer viewpoint, who has the actual advantage of 'looking backward' at the trajectory of the twentieth century 'as it happened'. Indeed, much of *Towards 2000* is devoted to hindsight, reflection and review. It consists of a series of essays employing the modes of treatise, manifesto and personal observation and conveys a somewhat elegiac sense of a late reckoning of accounts. Thus the first section is given over to a comprehensive reassessment of Williams's own earlier political and cultural projects, particularly the dimensions of 'the long revolution' that he had been variously elaborating since 1959. Only when these have been adequately reworked and mapped for the present conjuncture, he insists, will it then be productive to offer for the millennium what the last chapter of *Towards 2000* calls 'Resources for a Journey of Hope'.

Such 'resources' will require a radical reordering and widening of political and cultural institutions. This is a familiar theme for Williams, but it is newly informed by an interest in systems analysis and work by Rudolf Bahro on democratic accountability and theories of 'the alternative',[39] together with new ways of thinking about non-market economics and how 'production' might be linked to 'a whole way of life'. Finally, hope is placed in the transformative agency of a potentially dynamic connexion between a revived labour movement and the 'new social forces' representing peace, ecology and feminism.

Mine is a necessarily cursory summary, but the book itself is emphatic that such resources present no quick-fix solutions or easy shopping-list demands.

Rosalind Brunt

The adjectives insisted on are, relentlessly, *hard, difficult, long*. The evident continuities here with earlier Williams's formulations make it abundantly clear that the 'journey' being proposed is still on the very stony road of the long revolution.

At the same time, the overall aim of *Towards 2000* is to make practical arguments *for present use*. That is, to envisage a socialist future that could resonate with people's lived experience and engage with subjective emotional realities and creative imagination. In this spirit, Williams, a writer critically engaged with utopian and SF throughout his career,[40] introduces a detailed exposition of the value of 'the utopian impulse' at the start of the book. He suggests that, because utopian writing has a significant heuristic aspect, it can offer 'an imaginative encouragement' for change given that 'its strongest centre is still the conviction that people *can* live very differently'.[41]

Alan O'Connor has described Williams's speculative writing, both fictional and critical, as 'a kind of subjunctive realism'.[42] I think this notion gets to the heart of Williams's political project by encapsulating both the creative envisioning of future possibilities together with a need for clear analytical observation of the present. All speculative writing about socialism requires some such combination – as I've tried to indicate in terms of some of the tensions, difficulties and, indeed, 'sadness', that earlier efforts have produced. But with the actual experience of an already very 'long' twentieth century behind him, Williams cannot construct the sort of 'innocently' optimistic utopias that it was still possible to write before, say, 1914 or 1917.

Furthermore, the actual 1980s present a new and dangerous 'blockage' confronting any hopeful road to the millennium. This comes in the form of what Williams labels as the politics of Plan X. It is a disturbingly dystopian vision that he constructs here, one which has been prefigured, but only fragmentarily, in his two late 1970s novels. Now the writing assumes a new urgency, adopting spare, harsh and angry tones. Plan X's economic system proves to be an extraordinarily prescient account of the ruthlessly full-blown neoliberalism that has, indeed, emerged in these recent millennium years. But more shocking is Williams's take on the consciousness of the X Planners. For theirs is the ideology of no-ideology, a belief in no belief. Or rather, they believe solely in the administration of the game plan and the techniques of gaining the competitive edge in every situation. Hence the Planners' 'objective is indeed X, a willed and deliberate unknown, in which the only defining factor is advantage'.[43] This is because they have already made their reckoning with the inevitability of a future 'non-future', the final dystopia when the ultimate contradictions of imperialism have been played out through war, ecological disaster and global human emiseration.

As Plan X consciousness begins to invade all spheres of the economy and culture, Williams identifies the biggest danger it poses for all potential agents of change. This consists in its ability to fascinate, transfix, and thus immobilise, all the resources for hope. This is the 'specific contemporary sadness' that the book's dystopian vision identifies. However, unlike the earlier speculative writing discussed here, *Towards 2000* cannot attempt to avoid or deny the question of how any political transformation might be effected. Given the present conjuncture, merely staring at an already incipient Plan X and adopting the consolatory stances of cynicism or despair can never, in Williams's view, be valid political options. He himself intends to go on going on, but not in the rather indeterminate fashion of the protagonists of his future novels.

In an undated credo published posthumously, Williams sums up in one page the position he expounds at length in *Towards 2000*. With a straightforward series of statements that begin 'I think' or 'I believe' and contain none of his familiar cautious qualifications, Williams offers a personal manifesto that also requires a general redefinition of politics.

Starting quite unambiguously with a central belief in the 'necessary economic struggle of the organised working class', Williams presents the struggle as 'still the most creative activity of our society'. A similar cultural-material linkage that calls for a new 'quite different kind of political activity' is invoked throughout. Hence, corresponding to the essential economic conflict, comes this statement: 'I believe that the system of meanings and values which a capitalist society has generated has to be defeated in general and in detail by the most sustained kinds of intellectual work.' The tradition of speculative socialist writing clearly belongs within this redefined political space. For, as Williams concludes, 'the task of a successful socialist movement will be one of feeling and imagination as much as one of fact and organisation'.[44]

Notes

1 New Left Review, *Raymond Williams, Politics and Letters* (London: New Left Books, 1979).
2 Raymond Williams, *The Fight for Manod* (London: Chatto and Windus, 1979).
3 Raymond Williams, *Border Country* (London: Chatto and Windus, 1960).
4 Raymond Williams, *Second Generation* (London: Chatto and Windus, 1964).
5 *Politics and Letters*, 294.
6 Raymond Williams, *The Volunteers* [1978] (London: Hogarth Press, 1985).
7 Robert Tressell, *The Ragged Trousered Philanthropists* [1914] (St Albans: Panther Books, 1973).
8 Edward Bellamy, *Looking Backward* [1888] (New York: Dover Publications, 1996).
9 Raymond Williams, *Towards 2000* [1983] (Harmondsworth: Penguin, 1985).
10 *Politics and Letters*, 295.
11 Williams, *The Fight for Manod*, 201.
12 Williams, *The Fight for Manod*, 194.

13 Williams, *The Fight for Manod*, 207.
14 Stuart Hall, Raymond Williams and Edward Thompson (eds), *May Day Manifesto* [1967] (Harmondsworth: Penguin Special, 1968).
15 Raymond Williams, 'The Tenses of Imagination': lecture, Aberystwyth University College, 1978. Reprinted in *Writing in Society* (London: Verso, 1983).
16 Williams, *The Volunteers*, 208.
17 New Left Review, *Politics and Letters*, 295.
18 Raymond Williams, 'The Ragged-Arsed Philanthropists': speech, Queen's Hotel, Hastings, 23 May 1982. Reprinted in *The Robert Tressell Lectures, 1981–88*, ed. David Alfred (Rochester, Kent: WEA S-E District, 1988), 33.
19 Williams, 'The Ragged-Arsed Philanthropists', 33.
20 Jack Mitchell, *Robert Tressell and The Ragged-Trousered Philanthropists* (London: Lawrence and Wishart, 1969).
21 Williams, 'The Ragged-Arsed Philanthropists', 33.
22 Mitchell, *Robert Tressell and The Ragged-Trousered Philanthropists*, 5.
23 Tressell, *The Ragged Trousered Philanthropists*, 29–30.
24 Tressell, *The Ragged Trousered Philanthropists*, 30.
25 Tressell, *The Ragged Trousered Philanthropists*, 584.
26 Raymond Williams, *The Long Revolution* [1961] (Harmondsworth: Penguin, 1965), 80–88.
27 Dave Harker, *Tressell: The Real Story of the Ragged Trousered Philanthropists* (London: Zed Books, 2003).
28 Tressell, *The Ragged Trousered Philanthropists*, 12.
29 Harker, *Tressell*, 14–15, 40.
30 Laurence Gronlund, *The Cooperative Commonwealth in its Outlines: An Exposition of Modern Socialism* [1884], ed. G.B. Shaw (London: Reeves, 1892).
31 P.E. Maher, 'Laurence Gronlund: Contributions to American Socialism', *The Western Political Quarterly* 15, no. 4 (December 1962): 618.
32 Gronlund, *The Cooperative Commonwealth in its Outlines*, 5.
33 Krishan Kumar, *Utopia and Anti-Utopia in Modern Times* (Oxford: Blackwell, 1987), 132–67.
34 William Morris, *News from Nowhere* [1890] (Harmondsworth: Penguin, 1994).
35 Matthew Beaumont, *Utopia Ltd: Ideologies of Social Dreaming in England 1870–1900* (Leiden: Brill, 2005).
36 Kumar, *Utopia and Anti-Utopia in Modern Times*, 133–7.
37 Bellamy, *Looking Backward*, 160.
38 Kumar, *Utopia and Anti-Utopia in Modern Times*, 135.
39 Rudolf Bahro, *The Alternative in Eastern Europe*, trans. David Fernbach (London: Verso, 1978).
40 Andrew Milner (ed.), *Tenses of Imagination: Raymond Williams on Science Fiction, Utopia and Dystopia* (Oxford: Peter Lang, 2010).
41 Williams, *Towards 2000*, 13–14.
42 Alan O'Connor, *Raymond Williams: Writing, Culture, Politics* (Oxford: Basil Blackwell, 1989), 124.
43 Williams, *Towards 2000*, 244.
44 Terry Eagleton, *Raymond Williams: Critical Perspectives* (London: Polity, 1989) [no page no.].

The Long Recuperation: Late-Nineteenth/Early-Twentieth-Century British Socialist Periodical Fiction

Deborah Mutch

Abstract: This essay posits some explanations of why the phenomenally popular fictions of two socialist authors from the late nineteenth and early twentieth centuries (Charles Allen Clarke (1863–1935) and A. Neil Lyons (1880–1940)) are now largely forgotten. The serial and short fictions written by these authors had a large readership as they were initially published through the two best-selling socialist periodicals of this era: Clarke through his own *Teddy Ashton's Journal/Northern Weekly* (1896–1908) and Lyons through Robert Blatchford's *Clarion* (1891–1934). The essay applies some of Raymond Williams's ideas and theories on the 'judgement' and hierarchy imposed on literature to discuss the reasons why these respected and popular authors have been buried by literary history. For Williams, 'judgement' separates the 'good', mainstream literature from the 'poor', dissident fiction and creates a hierarchy based on 'deviations' from the mainstream 'norms' of genre, community, shared history, global events and regionalism.

*

In 'The Ragged-Arsed Philanthropists', Raymond Williams praises Robert Tressell's novel, *The Ragged Trousered Philanthropists* (1914), for breaking out of the autobiographical genre, previously the most popular form for the working-class experience.[1] Williams sets Tressell's novel 'in the context of a growing body of working-class and socialist writing'[2] and since his 1983 article scholars have recovered a vast range of working-class and politically-motivated creative literature published in Britain during the nineteenth and early twentieth centuries. Martha Vicinus's *The Industrial Muse* (1974) had already brought literary criticism to bear on a range of working-class literature; since then scholars such as Brian Maidment, Michael Sanders and Anne Janowitz have anthologised and analysed Chartist poetry and the same attention has been given to Chartist fiction by scholars such as Ian Haywood, Rob Breton and Greg Vargo. H. Gustav Klaus covered two hundred years of working-class writing in *The Literature of Labour* (1985) and collected essays on the literature of the British socialist movement in *The Socialist Novel in Britain* (1982) and *The Rise of Socialist Fiction, 1880–1914* (1987). But despite this academic interest, much of the fiction produced by the British socialist movement remains hidden and Tressell's novel is still the visible tip of the iceberg.

Franco Moretti notes, in *Graphs Maps Trees*, the 'minimal fraction of the literary field' studied in academia when set alongside the tens of thousands of novels published during the nineteenth century,[3] and the literature published by the members of the British socialist movement remains submerged beneath the continuing popularity of canonical and mainstream literature. Even within socialist literature there is hierarchy. Literary giants such as George Bernard Shaw and H.G. Wells are read, remembered and appreciated over a century after they were published; the wide-ranging talents of William Morris have left a legacy far beyond his literature, including his textiles, furniture and ecological ideas.[4] Just as Morretti resituates the canonical nineteenth-century novels in the wider terrain of forgotten literature, so this essay begins to do the same for other socialist authors who were as popular as Shaw, Wells and Morris – and more so – and who have subsequently been buried by history.

Wim Neetens notes that Tressell's novel did not fall out of fashion or print as did the earlier socialist author John Law (Margaret Harkness),[5] whose *A City Girl* (1887) provoked Friedrich Engels's famous declaration on socialist realism,[6] but there were better-selling authors who have disappeared even further into history than Harkness. This essay will consider serial fiction written by two of the most popular of the socialist authors at the turn of the twentieth century: Charles Allen Clarke (1863–1935) and A. (Albert Michael) Neil Lyons (1880–1940). Both Clarke and Lyons reached a large readership by publishing their fiction in periodicals before (sometimes) republishing in book form: Clarke in his own periodical *Northern Weekly/Teddy Ashton's Journal* (1896–1908) which, during the height of its popularity, sold between 35,000 and 50,000 copies per week;[7] Lyons in Robert Blatchford's *Clarion* (1891–1934) which achieved similar sales figures, reaching a peak of 83,000 in 1910.[8] But today neither Clarke nor Lyons's fiction has the literary status awarded to Morris's much-studied *News from Nowhere* despite the latter's initial publication in the *Commonweal* (1885–94), which achieved weekly sales of only 2,000 to 3,000 copies.[9]

The work of Clarke and Lyons was both popular and respected during their lifetime. D.H. Lawrence considered Lyons's fiction equal to that of H.G. Wells's depictions of working-class life in *Tono Bungay*, *Love and Mr Lewisham* and *The History of Mr Polly*,[10] and C.F.G. Masterman quoted at length from *Arthur's* in *The Condition of England* when discussing London nightlife.[11] Tolstoy translated into Russian Clarke's *The Effects of the Factory System*, which was partly serialised in the *Clarion* (1895–96), and his dialect fiction was popular throughout Lancashire and Yorkshire.[12] There is no single, simple reason why the work of Clarke and Lyons disappeared while others survived. Chances such as that which led Tressell's manuscript to Jessie Pope not happening for Lyons or Clarke may be one of the reasons they fell by the literary wayside. That they are no longer accessible in print form – while other left-wing novels such as Tressell and Walter Greenwood's novel *Love on the Dole* (1933) are still in print – affects their recuperation today. As Graham Holderness has argued, until 'working-class novels from the nineteenth and early twentieth-centuries are reprinted and educationally mobilized on a much larger scale, there can be no effective general recovery to shift radically the political balance of the literary tradition'.[13] Changes in literary fashion may also have had a hand in their demise: Clarke's biographer claims 'some of his literature is undoubtedly dated'.[14] I would argue that while all these reasons would affect the longevity of Clarke and Lyons's fiction, the most important factor is the way they were and continue to be judged as literature.

In *Marxism and Literature* Williams recognises that it is 'difficult … to prevent any attempt at literary theory from being turned, almost *a priori*, into critical theory, as if the only major questions about literary production were variations on the question "how do we *judge*?"'[15] This sense of how literature is 'judged' through class-based aesthetics is evident today as, after decades of literary recovery, socialist fiction is still dismissed by some critics as 'poor' literature. For instance, when Elizabeth Carolyn Miller discusses Robert Blatchford's 'A Son of the Forge', which was serialised in the *Clarion* under the title 'No. 66', she does not question the contemporary criticism of Blatchford's work as 'inartistic' nor Blatchford's own defensive response.[16] But if bourgeois literature is set as the standard, as an Arnoldian touchstone against which all 'literature' is measured, that produced by the working class or dissident groups will inevitably fall outside this arbitrary standard and will be defined as 'poor'. Different experiences require different forms for expression, which in turn require a different approach by readers. Williams recognised this, acknowledging that Tressell's *The Ragged Trousered Philanthropists* and other working-class fiction 'set[s] quite new problems of analysis and content.'[17] This recognition readdresses his acceptance of literary hierarchy in *The Long Revolution* when he claimed 'the real relations within the whole culture are made clear: relations that can easily be neglected when only the best writing survives'.[18]

Book historians have long associated the rise of the novel with the growth of middle-class economic, political and cultural power. Ian Haywood notes the difficulty of conveying working-class experience through the novel as the genre 'was deeply biased against reflecting a working-class perspective on society',[19] associated as it was with 'bourgeois individual[ism] and … personal development'.[20] Socialist authors needed to find forms through which their experiences and alternative ideologies could be articulated and this was partly achieved by breaking down what Williams termed, in *Marxism and Literature*, 'the crippling categorizations and dichotomies of "fact" and "fiction", or of "discursive" and "imaginative" or "referential" and "emotive", [which] stand regularly not only between works and readers ... but between writers and works, at a still active and shaping stage'.[21] He reads the desire for distinct literary and non-literary categories as the desire to place a hierarchical structure on what he calls the 'multiplicity of writing' which prioritises the 'factual' over the 'fictional'.[22] The socialist authors' dismantling of the 'fact/fiction' binary created a literature which Haywood has described as 'hybrid', combining literary genres, commentary and journalistic techniques[23] and this hybridity in turn created an ideological distinction between socialist and capitalist perspectives.

One of the clearest examples of this literary hybridity, the dismantling of 'fact' and 'fiction', is found in Charles Allen Clarke's 'The Red Flag'. First serialised under the pseudonym Vernon Harvey Franklin in *Teddy Ashton's Journal* between November 1907 and February 1908 and reprinted in the Social Democratic Federation's *Justice* under his own name between May and December 1908, 'The Red Flag' opens with an acknowledgment to 'Mrs Higgs' and her book *Glimpses into the Abyss*. Mary Higgs was the Cambridge-educated daughter of a Congregational minister, wife of Reverend Thomas Kilpin Higgs of Oldham and Secretary of the Ladies Committee visiting the Oldham workhouse. The Board of Guardians dismissed her arguments for the improvement of inmates' conditions and she initially proved her point by dressing as a female tramp, spending time in the workhouse and reporting her experiences. She made further undercover excursions into homeless life and published a series of works on her experiences. *Glimpses into the Abyss* (1906) was an anthology of her investigations, including 'Five Days and Five Nights as a Tramp Among Tramps', which was originally published in 1904 and anonymously attributed to 'A Lady'.[24] 'Five Days' was used by Clarke as the template for his fictional characters Mrs Wilkinson and May, who spend the first eight chapters of the fiction closely following Mary Higgs's account.

Clarke's fictionalised version of Higgs's account begins with 'A Night in a Common Lodging-House', her second chapter rather than the first, 'A Night in a Municipal Lodging-House', presumably because the latter was not the harrowing experience of the former. Clarke's description of the communal room in the common lodging-house, the filth of the house, the verminous bedding and the dirt and degradation is almost exactly the same as that of Higgs. Where Clarke differs is in the description of the human inhabitants. Mary Higgs presents the inhabitants of the lodging house through a tone of barely suppressed horror while Clarke gives a positive image without sanitising the scene. The main focus of Mary Higgs's account is 'a huge negro with a *wicked* face',[25] while Clarke presents the reader with a well-read cobbler who quotes Shelley. Higgs questions the veracity of the wedding ring worn by two women in the room – one is with the 'negro' – while Clarke makes no such suggestion of the cobbler's wife or the mothers in the room. Higgs separates herself from the inhabitants by giving only a visual description of the people whereas Clarke's Mrs Wilkinson and May speak with some of the other lodgers, learning the cause of homelessness through Jim Campbell's story and the experiences of life on tramp from others. Both acknowledge that there is bad language, loose morals and alcohol swirling around the homeless but Clarke depicts a choice available to them, separating the 'respectable' from the less decorous but without imposing any moral judgement.

The literary genre of realism is the basis of Clarke's dismantling of fact and fiction and his interleaving of realist fiction with sociological survey exemplifies Williams's arguments for a broader approach to the definition of realism in *The Long Revolution*. Williams considers the association of the 'bourgeois' or 'domestic' with realism and argues for a wider, less judgemental perspective.[26] Like Williams, the unquestioned relation between form and ideology is rejected by H. Gustav Klaus, who suggests that: 'Form, whether as a narrative mode or technical device is doubtless a carrier of ideology. However, form is not the only (ideological) constituent of a text, and it is, above all, not some kind of cosmic, transhistorical category immune to change.'[27] As the boundaries of Clarke's fiction open and draw in Higgs's investigative work, so the amalgamation of the literary genre of realism and the non-literary concept of 'fact' are drawn together to shift realism away from its close association with the middle classes and to develop the socialist argument for the necessity of change.

The overlap of fact and fiction was not the only hybrid formula used to uncouple the association of realism, the novel and the middle-class experience. A. Neil Lyons dismantled the boundaries of fiction and journalism through the position of the narrative voice: the narrative voice is that of the journalist, situated within the frame of action but as an observer rather than a participant. Throughout his fictions, the narrator's identity is overlapped with the author, characters' direct references to the narrator-character and his references to himself suggest the conflation of narrative voice and author as journalist. In 'Little Pictures of the Night' (1903–04), the narrator refers to 'the acting-editor of the great newspaper by means of which I live';[28] in 'The Diary of a Loafer' (1904), Lyons opens Chapter XVII with a meditation on his next piece of 'copy' while looking at the homeless sleeping on the Thames Embankment and later, when addressed by the New Thinker, an extreme socialist who asks '"You write for the CLARION, sir?"', the narrator 'shyly admitted the charge'.[29] And in an early chapter of 'Little Pictures of the Night', written before the serial began in the *Clarion*, the narrator is challenged by Arthur, the coffee stall owner, for writing about him and his clients: 'And what is this I 'ear in regards to you 'avin' put me into print? Nice idea of friendship you *'ave* got, to be sure!'[30] The narrative perspective suggests the reality of the stories by placing the narrator in the same relation to events as the reporter in the surrounding journalism; it allows the characters to speak for themselves, albeit mediated through the sympathetic narrator/reporter; it encourages identification with the narrator who addresses the reader directly – 'We at Arthur's know better. We know that there is warmth at coffee stalls';[31] and it draws the reader into a sense of community with both narrator and characters.

Lyons's fiction has as its primary focus the most necessary part of realist fiction, according to Williams: a sense of community, 'a genuine community: a community of persons linked not merely by one kind of relationship – work or friendship or family – but many, interlocking kinds'.[32] Lyons's community of characters suggests both the communal nature of working-class life and the spirit of community support. For instance, 'Little Pictures of the Night' centres around Arthur's south London midnight coffee stall, its regulars and visitors, and presents the collective self-help of those gathered around Arthur's coffee stall: Arthur employs the tramp Beaky; Mr Honeybunn employs Miss Hopper, Beaky's female companion on tramp; Trooper Alfred greets arrivals at his father's coffee stall with the offer to ''Ave a corfee' and the narrator and Trooper Alfred join together to find Miss Hopper's wayward boyfriend.[33] The community is not static in any of Lyons's fictions: the regulars and occasional visitors to Arthur's coffee stall come together and disperse throughout the serial; in 'Sixpenny Pieces' (1907–08) the narrator lodges with Dr Brink and his daughter after a chance meeting and the fiction is a series of observations of Dr Brink's work with his Whitechapel working-class patients, creating a community of people across a borough of London; 'The Diary of a Loafer' initially follows the narrator's descriptions of people and communities encountered on a walking tour before this cohering theme is abandoned.

Lyons's communities were expansive; not only did he create communities of people who were tied by a multitude of connections but throughout his fictions characters moved through and between serials and short stories. Dr Brink, the General Practitioner of 'Sixpenny Pieces' (1907–08), appears as the GP of Mr Boyle in the story of the worker who survived an industrial explosion, entitled 'The Survivor' (16 October 1908) and delivers a baby in 'Simple Simon: The History of a Fool' (1911); Arthur's coffee stall, the focus of 'Little Pictures of the Night', is also the setting for the short story 'The Gentleman Who Was Sorry' (1908 Specimen Supplement); the narrator's formidable aunt, a stalwart of his short stories, makes an appearance in 'Little Pictures of the Night'. The narrator's gardener, his aunt and his aunt's gardener appear in multiple short stories as Lyons dismantled the boundaries, not only between 'fact' and 'fiction', but also between the fictions themselves to create a community of characters.

The position of Lyons's narrative voice – within the scene but not always a part of it – might be read as erring too much towards the 'social' end of Williams's scale of realism. The separation of 'social' and 'personal' raises the danger of imbalance: at the 'social' end of the scale by reducing the characters to 'illustrations of the way of life'[34] and at the 'personal' end by creating 'a highly personalised landscape, to clarify or frame an individual portrait'.[35] Lyons's fiction is 'socially panoramic'[36] as he avoids a focus on the family unit, or even a number of family units, through the positioning of the narrative voice as journalist/observer. Clarke's, fiction, on the other hand would often centre round a family or a number of families. Although Clarke would present romance within his fiction (for example 'The Cotton Panic' (1900–01) includes the lovers Nelly Milner and Sid Clifton, 'The Red Flag' has the relationship between May Marsden and Jim Campbell) the relationships are part of a wider social pattern and evidence of literary hybridity rather than the primary focus. Clarke creates a sense of community through his fiction, not only through a shared sense of social experience – in a way similar to that noted by Williams as the selection of 'community' through shared class position in Jane Austen's novels[37] – but also through a richly textured, shared history and geographical location.

The 'stranger' in Clarke's 'The Cotton Panic' who enters The Virgin's Inn in Preston sets out a Lancashire history of working-class organisation and voices. Preston is the origin of teetotalism; the 'Seven Men of Preston' formed the Preston Temperance Society in September 1832; the working-class journalist and reformer, Joseph Livesey, who edited the weekly halfpenny anti-Corn Law paper *The Struggle*, is one of the 'Seven Men'; the 'stranger' recounts the myth of Richard Turner's stutter as the origin of the word 'teetotal'; Rochdale in east Lancashire is mentioned as being where, in 1844, local weavers (or the 'Rochdale Pioneers') founded the cooperative movement. The 'stranger' is revealed as Edwin Waugh, the dialect author best remembered for his poem 'Come whoam to thi childer an me' (1856). The character of Waugh situates himself within a range of Lancashire dialect authors: Tim Bobbin, the pseudonym of John Collier and author of the first dialect publication, *A View of the Lancashire Dialect, or Tummas and Mary* (1746); Ben Brierley, the author of dialect character Ab-o'th-Yate; Samuel Laycock whose *Lancashire Lyrics!* (1864) was written during the cotton famine. By drawing working-class history into the serial and collapsing 'fact' and 'fiction' Clarke creates a community through class position, literary and historical knowledge wider than the immediate face-to-face community of the locality. But this sense of shared community is not limited to the characters: there is an assumption that the reader will also identify with this shared history and the popularity of Clarke's work indicates that this assumption must have been largely correct.

Clarke's fiction invariably takes a wider perspective on Lancashire life than the experiences of one or two families or a single class group. Class interaction – both positive and negative and particularly interaction between workers, factory and mill owners and the clergy – is presented as fully rounded, neither used to throw the other into relief, and the broad landscape of class relations is considered as a whole. In 'The Cotton Panic', though, Clarke widens the perspective further and places the individual characters and community at the heart of historic global events by humanising and individualising the devastating effects in Lancashire of the American Civil War. The sufferings of the Lancashire mill workers are personalised as American cotton imports ceased: Nelly Milner, her family and friends experience the poverty and starvation arising from the closure of the cotton mills and the resultant unemployment. But Clarke does not restrict his historiography to the passive receipt of global fortunes by working-class Lancastrians; he also tackles the division between Britons over the support for one or other of the American sides. While the character of Chartist Grimshaw speaks of the working-class Lancastrian support for the northern states and their anti-slavery stance – "'It's very hard times ... But we mustn't grumble. The war is a just war the Northern States of America are fightin to give freedom to shackled slaves, an we must bear up in the thought that we are helpin by our sufferin'"[38] – the Confederate cause is supported by British manufacturers eager for the cotton exports to resume. Support is not divided only along class lines, it is not as simple as workers empathising with slaves: the protagonist hero, Sid Clifton, finds employment on the Confederate warship, the *Alabama*, while the fugitive Ted Banister finds employment in the Black Country where 'all the blacksmiths were busy making contraband of war; making bullets for the Confederates'.[39] There was support for the Confederate cause in Birmingham and the Black Country from businessmen and leaders such as William Schofield, a manufacturer and MP for Birmingham, but also from workers who benefitted from the increase in trade as an effect of the war. Clarke's strong historical focus in this fiction provides an alternative history of the impact of the war and the complex working-class attitudes to it while simultaneously personalising global events through a working-class perspective.

The wide perspective both Clarke and Lyons bring to their fiction might appear to make the communities constructed within those fictions 'unknowable' in Williams's terms. In *The Country and the City*, he points to the opacity of the knowable community in the city as opposed to the transparency of that in the country: the larger and more complex social structure in the city made 'knowing' the community difficult and he points to George Eliot, who he reads as placing community value in the past and the value of the present reduced to 'the individual moral action'.[40] If the 'knowable-ness' of a community is restricted to face-to-face daily interaction then there is only a limited community in the fiction of each author. But shared experiences of work, poverty, hunger on the negative side, nationwide trade unions, local and national cooperation on the positive, reveal – or, to use Williams's phrase, force into consciousness – the nationwide community of the working class and socialism. The method of publication for both Clarke and Lyons itself creates a reading community, as Laurel Brake and James Mussell have argued: 'Each issue of a newspaper or periodical was located at the centre of a complex network of contributors who collaborated to produce an object that would be bought and read' and 'in which different groups of readers read the same things at the same time'.[41] Thus, shared political ideas and the accessibility of the periodical create a network of readers who have their own individual and communal experiences reflected back to them in the fictions.

This broader, national, sense of community might have been expected to attract a wide readership and therefore give the fiction longevity but it is this breadth that brings to bear literary judgement on the fiction and the dismissal of it as 'regional'. Williams notes the separation between 'region' and 'general' in *Writing in Society*, asking 'whether a novel "set in" or "about" the Home Counties, or "set in" or "about" Bloomsbury – would be described as "regional" in a way comparable to descriptions of similar novels "set in" or "about" the Lake District or South Devon or mid-Wales – or, shall we say, Dorset or "Wessex"?'[42] Philip Dodd notes that Williams defines 'region' in relation to the metropolis and that the close relationship between London and the Home Counties exempts the latter from 'regional' status.[43] This 'regionality' is obvious in Clarke's fiction, set in Lancashire and presenting the working-class Lancastrian as his primary focus, but Lyons's fiction is predominantly set in various areas of London. Nevertheless, Lyons's fiction is still marginalised as 'regional' in Williams's definition. Lyons situates his fiction in working-class areas of London (for instance, Borough in 'Little Pictures of the Night' and Whitechapel in 'Sixpenny Pieces'), 'a social area inhabited by people of a certain kind, living in certain ways' upon which a 'value-judgment' is imposed creating 'an expression of centralized cultural dominance'.[44] In these terms, both Clarke and Lyons are not only 'regional' for their geographical location but also for their rounded, positive and inclusive depictions of working-class experience and, as Williams recognises, this 'regionality' has been embraced by authors with class and left-wing political motivations:

> such novels have been valued in the labour and socialist movements, just because they declare their identity in such ways. The undoubted neglect

of majority working experience, and the majority of working-class people, within the bourgeois fictional tradition, seems to justify the simple counter-emphasis. A whole class, like whole regions, can be seen as neglected.[45]

Lyons's fiction works to reverse this sense of 'regionality', placing both the narrator and the reader inside the working-class experience and positioning the bourgeois characters – those who, in reality, have the power to marginalise not only working-class literature but working-class life – on the margins of his communities as figures of comical naivety and ridicule. For instance, the issue of philanthropy and its motivations are addressed in both 'The Diary of a Loafer' and 'Little Pictures of the Night'. In 'Diary' the narrator opposes the wealthy, sympathetic but arrogant American woman, who doles out money to the homeless on the London Embankment, with the joyful cunning of the poor as they disguise themselves by swapping clothes and seats, gathering a substantial amount of money as she moves uncomprehending along the promenade. The narrator is a part of the scene – and a beneficiary of the woman's charity alongside the wily unemployed – thus creating a sense of community within the fiction and between the fiction and reader as all join to criticise (and laugh at) the individual philanthropist who, in bourgeois fiction, would be the '*exceptional* person'.[46] Philanthropy, while originating in benevolence, places too much emphasis on the giver and not enough on the systemic causes of poverty, as the narrator notes of the American woman: 'Her object was not so much to relieve suffering and alleviate hunger as to jingle a moneybag and receive blessings. It was champagne, not pity, which had played upon her heart-strings.'[47] Similarly, the chapter entitled 'Concerning a Benevolent Idiot' in 'Little Pictures' presents the disconnection between the middle-class idea of working-class life and the reality.

The eponymous benevolent idiot is Mr Fothergill, MA, a sociologist who approaches the *Clarion* in order to get a closer view of the London night coffee stalls for his new book. In his description of Fothergill, Lyons recognises the general compassion of philanthropists – as he does with the wealthy American woman – but in Fothergill's case also the arrogance of attempting to judge one social group by the standards of another. An exchange between Fothergill and the narrator-character foregrounds the narrator's dominant perspective, juxtaposing the scene with its perversion through middle-class values. Fothergill is shown Arthur's late-night coffee stall and the customers:

> And there you have a picture of the whole assembly: two cheerful sailors; two futile, but contented, debaters; an exceedingly flattered and happy old tramp; a chivalrous and conversational drayman; a resourceful drayman's boy; Trooper Alfred and party; and a drab being comforted with coffee and

lies. Over all, a pervasive odour of hot coffee and fresh buns, the glitter of the urn, and the smiling face of Arthur.[48]

Fothergill's response is to bewail 'The misery! The want!! The sorrow!!! The pain!!!! The sordidness!!!!!'[49] as he sees, not the gathering of like-minded souls in a place of comfort, inclusion and harmony, but rather drunkenness in the sailors, prostitution in the drab, theft by the drayman's boy of his employer's coffee and industrial subversion in the debaters' discussion of trade unionism. The narration is directed to the reader who shares the narrator's sympathetic and inclusive attitude to the coffee-stall customers; by placing the narrating voice in the position of the journalist, Lyons emphasises the 'reality' of his narrative, separates alternative ideological positions and diminishes their influence. The reader may come to their own conclusion of the well-intentioned efforts of Fothergill and his like, but punctuation and vocabulary separates the philanthropist from the 'true' perspective of the narrator.

Clarke and Lyons both use non-standard English in their representations of working-class life to create a sense of community between the author/narrator, reader and working-class characters, rather than separating reader and character as Williams notes of Elizabeth Gaskell in *Mary Barton* (1848).[50] Both authors present the use of standard and non-standard English and the working-class ability to move between registers: an ability not shared by characters from other class groups. Clarke's characters move between Lancashire dialect and standard English, and in 'Little Pictures' Lyons normalises the democratic vocabulary of the *Clarion* group – described by Blatchford as '[h]orse-sense in tinker's English'[51] – as Fothergill's ornate language is re-phrased by the narrator:

> 'Dear! dear!' said Mr. Fothergill, as we approached the stall, 'this is really very interesting. I apprehended you to state that these institutions plied an exclusively nocturnal commerce?'
>
> 'You understood me to say that these stall-keepers only traded at night-time.'[52]

Fothergill is not only humorously re-phrased but is also contained within the narrator's general descriptions of the scenes surrounding the verbal exchanges. Thus the middle-class sociologist is doubly separated from those whom he intends to study – a representation on the page of Fothergill's psychological and ideological separation from those he studies – while the narrator, characters and reader share an understanding of the community and humour shared at the coffee stall.

Lyons and Clarke were among large body of socialist authors who published serials and short stories through the socialist press at the turn of the nineteenth century. In *The Long Revolution*, Raymond Williams considered the motivation of mainstream periodical publishing as the desire 'to control the development of working-class opinion'[53] and this is precisely what the socialist press aimed to achieve, but not in ways which would perpetuate the capitalist *status quo*. While the driving force of mainstream periodicals was the pursuit of profit,[54] most socialist periodicals barely broke even and the high sales figures for Blatchford's and Clarke's publications made them exceptional. The socialist press prioritised political education over financial acquisition and fiction was an important part of that education. However, sales figures and readers are not the basis for longevity; rather, the cultural dominance of a small section of society imposes standards by which literature is judged and work which fails to meet those standards – or worse, actively opposes them – has little chance of a long reading life. Thankfully, the last forty years have seen academic research recover a great deal of the literature of the period. Looking back at P.J. Keating's claim at the beginning of *The Working Classes in Victorian Fiction* (1971) that '[m]ost working-class novels are … usually written by authors who are not working class, for an audience which is not working class',[55] we can see how far the recuperation of working-class literature has come. But as we uncover the hidden literature of working-class life and politics we also see how much further there is to go.

Notes

1. Raymond Williams, *Writing and Society* (London and New York: Verso, 1991), 241.
2. Williams, *Writing and Society*, 239.
3. Franco Moretti, *Graphs Maps Trees* (London and New York: Verso, 2007), 3–4.
4. Phillippa Bennett and Rosie Miles, 'Introduction: Morris in the Twenty-First Century', in *William Morris in the Twenty-First Century*, ed. Phillippa Bennett and Rosie Miles (Bern, Switzerland: Peter Lang, 2010), 2.
5. Wim Neetens, 'Politics, Poetics and the Popular Text: *The Ragged Trousered Philanthropists*', *Neohelicon* 14, no. 2 (1987): 212.
6. Friedrich Engels to Margaret Harkness in London, April 1888, *Selected Correspondence* (Moscow: n.p., 1953), transcribed Dougal McNeill, 2000, *Marx & Engels Internet Archive*, http://www.marxists.org/archive/marx/works/1888/letters/88_04_15.htm (accessed 7 November 2013).
7. Margaret 'Espinasse, '(Charles) Allen Clarke', in *Dictionary of Labour Biography, Volume 5*, ed. Joyce M. Bellamy and John Saville (London: Macmillan, 1979), 64–70; Patrick Joyce, *Visions of the People: Industrial England and the Question of Class: c.1848–1914* (Cambridge: Cambridge University Press, 1991), 264.

8. A.M. Thompson, *Here I Lie* (London: Routledge, 1937), 100; Carl Levy, 'Education and Self-education: Staffing the Early ILP', *Socialism and the Intelligentsia 1880–1914* (London: Routledge & Kegan Paul, 1987), 135–210, 149.
9. E.P. Thompson, *William Morris, Romantic to Revolutionary* (London: Lawrence and Wishart, 1955), 488.
10. D.H. Lawrence to August de Wit, 1916, *The Letters of D.H. Lawrence, Volume 8*, ed. J.T. Boulton (Cambridge: Cambridge University Press, 2000), 18.
11. C.F.G. Masterman, *The Condition of England* (1909), ed. J.T. Boulton (London: Faber and Faber, 2012). See the last pages of Chapter V.
12. See Paul Salveson, *Lancashire's Romantic Radical, The Life and Writings of Allen Clarke/Teddy Ashton* (Huddersfield: Little Northern Books, 2009), *passim*.
13. Graham Holderness, 'Miners and the Novel: From Bourgeois to Proletarian Fiction', in *The British Working-Class Novel in the Twentieth Century*, ed. Jeremy Hawthorn (London: Arnold, 1984), 19–32, 19.
14. Salveson, *Lancashire's Romantic Radical*, 107.
15. Raymond Williams, *Marxism and Literature* (Oxford: Oxford University Press, 1977), 146.
16. Elizabeth Carolyn Miller, *Slow Print, Literary Radicalism and Late Victorian Print Culture* (Stanford, CA: Stanford University Press, 2013), 95.
17. Williams, *Writing in Society*, 239.
18. Raymond Williams, *The Long Revolution* (Oxford: Oxford University Press, 1977), 85.
19. Ian Haywood, *Working-Class Fiction from Chartism to Trainspotting* (Plymouth: Northcote House, 1997), 3.
20. Anna Vaninskaya, 'Theory or Myth? Labour and the Working Class in William Morris and George Orwell', in *Culture + the State*, ed. James Gifford and Gabrielle Zezulka-Mailoux (Edmonton, Alberta: CRC Humanities Studio, 2003), 98–117, 111.
21. Williams, *Marxism and Literature*, 146.
22. Williams, *Marxism and Literature*, 149.
23. Haywood, *Working-Class Fiction*, 16.
24. Rosemary Chadwick, 'Higgs [née Kingsland], Mary Ann', *Oxford Dictionary of National Biography*, Oxford University Press, 2004, http://www.oxforddnb.com/view/article/38523 (accessed 8 November 2013); Peter Higginbottom, Introduction to 'Five Days and Five Nights as a Tramp among Tramps' by 'A Lady', *The Workhouse: The Story of an Institution*, http://www.workhouses.org.uk/Higgs/TrampAmongTramps.shtml (accessed 8 November 2013).
25. 'A Lady' (M. Higgs), 'Five Days and Five Nights as a Tramp Among Tramps', *The Workhouse, The Story of an Institution*, http://www.workhouses.org.uk/Higgs/TrampAmongTramps.shtml (accessed 7 February 2013).
26. Williams, *The Long Revolution*, 304.
27. H. Gustav Klaus, 'Introduction' to *The Socialist Novel in Britain*, ed. H. Gustav Klaus (Brighton: Harvester, 1982), 2.
28. 'By the Author of "Arthurs"' (A. Neil Lyons), 'Little Pictures of the Night', *Clarion*, 22 January 1903, in Deborah Mutch, *British Socialist Fiction, 1884–1914, Volume 3* (London: Pickering & Chatto, 2013), 78.
29. A. Neil Lyons, 'The Diary of a Loafer', *Clarion*, 12 August 1904, 1.
30. A. Neil Lyons, *Arthur's* (London: John Lane, 1914), 95.
31. A. Neil Lyons, 'Little Pictures', *Clarion*, 22 January 1904, in Mutch, *British Socialist Fiction*, 82.
32. Williams, *The Long Revolution*, 312.
33. Lyons, 'Little Pictures', *Clarion*, 25 December 1903, *passim*, in Mutch, *British Socialist Fiction*, 61–4.
34. Williams, *The Long Revolution*, 306.

35 Williams, *The Long Revolution*, 308.
36 Williams, *Writing in Society*, 236.
37 Raymond Williams, *The Country and the City* (Oxford: Oxford University Press, 1973), 166.
38 Clarke, 'The Cotton Panic', 13 October 1900, in Mutch, *British Socialist Fiction*, 235.
39 Clarke, 'The Cotton Panic', 2 March 1901, in Mutch, *British Socialist Fiction*, 382.
40 Williams, *The Country and the City*, 180.
41 James Mussell, *The Nineteenth-Century Press in the Digital Age* (Basingstoke: Palgrave Macmillan, 2012), 40, 41.
42 Williams, *Writing and Society*, 230.
43 Philip Dodd, 'Gender and Cornwall: Charles Kingsley to Daphne du Maurier', in *The Regional Novel in Britain and Ireland: 1800–1990* (Cambridge: Cambridge University Press, 1998), 119–35, 120.
44 Williams, *Writing in Society*, 230, 234.
45 Williams, *Writing in Society*, 233.
46 Williams, *Writing in Society*, 241.
47 Lyons, 'The Diary of a Loafer', *Clarion*, 2 September 1904, 3.
48 Lyons, 'Little Pictures', *Clarion*, 22 January 1904, in Mutch, *British Socialist Fiction*, 81.
49 Lyons, 'Little Pictures', *Clarion*, 22 January 1904, in Mutch, *British Socialist Fiction*, 81.
50 Williams, *Writing in Society*, 98. Dialect is an important aspect of Clarke's writing and development of a working-class literature but a detailed consideration of Clarke's use of dialect is beyond the scope of this essay.
51 Laurence Thompson, *Robert Blatchford: Portrait of an Englishman* (London: Victor Gollancz, 1951), 97.
52 Lyons, 'Little Pictures', *Clarion*, 22 January 1904, in Mutch, *British Socialist Fiction,* 79.
53 Williams, *The Long Revolution*, 73.
54 See Williams,'The Growth of the Popular Press', in *The Long Revolution*, 195–236.
55 P.J. Keating, *The Working Classes in Victorian Fiction* (London: Routledge & Kegan Paul, 1971), 2.

'The Rich Harmonics of Past Time': Memory and Montage in John Sommerfield's *May Day*

Elinor Taylor

Abstract: This article examines John Sommerfield's 1936 novel, *May Day*, a work that experiments with multiple perspectives, voices and modes. The article examines the formal experiments of the novel in order to bring into focus contemporary debates around the aesthetics of socialist realism, the politics of Popular Front anti-fascism and the relationship between writers on the left and the legacies of literary modernism. The article suggests that while leftist writers' appropriations of modernist techniques have been noted by critics, there has been a tendency to assume that such approaches were in contravention of the aesthetics of socialist realism. Socialist realism is shown to be more a fluid and disputed concept than such readings suppose, and Sommerfield's adaptations of modernist textual strategies are interpreted as key components of a political aesthetic directed towards the problems of alienation and social fragmentation.

*

This article analyses the formal experiments of John Sommerfield's 1936 novel, *May Day*, and in so doing attempts to shed light on British Marxists' relationships with the heritage of literary modernism during the period of the Popular Front (1935–39). *May Day* has been compared to a modernist day book[1] and to a documentary novel of metropolitan working-class life,[2] while Ken Worpole has identified the influence of Soviet montage techniques in its dynamic shifts in perspective.[3] Although the modernist resonances of *May Day* have been noted, critics have tended to read this in terms of an assumed schematic opposition between realism (and especially the unclearly defined 'socialist realism') and modernism. Perhaps the most graphic example is Valentine Cunningham's assertion that in Britain, socialist realism 'helped to slow down literary experiment and to smash up modernism especially in the novel'.[4] The basis of such claims is the assumption that writers on the left were bound by anti-modernist orthodoxy, an orthodoxy usually taken to be exemplified by the Soviet critic Karl Radek's notorious denunciation of James Joyce at the Soviet Writers' Congress of 1934. From this angle, Nick Hubble argues that *May Day*'s 'overt usage of modernist techniques has to be seen as a deliberate act of defiance',[5] while Cunningham reads James Barke's experimental novel of 1936, *Major Operation* (which has many affinities to *May*

Day), as 'staring down Karl Radek and his British supporters' by experimenting with form.[6] I will argue here that these arguments are premised on an over-estimation of the impact that Radek's address had on British literary leftists in the 1930s, and an under-estimation of the importance of the Popular Front context in shaping British Marxists' relationships with modernism. From this perspective, I propose a reading of *May Day*'s innovative form not as a mark of aesthetic dissidence from realist orthodoxy, but instead as an attempt to identify and elaborate modernism's radical and progressive potential, while critically isolating its perceived reactionary tendencies, an attempt fully compatible with the ethics and aesthetics of the Popular Front.

I

The source of an assumed polarised opposition between socialist realism and modernism is Karl Radek's contribution to the Soviet Writers' Congress, and especially the part of his speech entitled 'James Joyce or Socialist Realism'. Radek's remarks include the claim that, 'A heap of dung, crawling with worms, photographed by a cinema apparatus through a microscope – such is Joyce's work'.[7] Although the texts of the Congress were published in English in 1935, there is little evidence that British writers took Radek's polemic to heart. In the pages of *Left Review*, the main forum for leftist literary debate, the few references to Radek's speech that appear are noticeably lukewarm: Montagu Slater half-heartedly praised 'Radek's shrewd survey of certain limited fields of prose literature', while Amabel Williams-Ellis, the British delegate at the Congress, though describing Radek's speech as 'very able', contended that his targets were waning in relevance and significance.[8] British Marxists were regularly critical of certain prominent modernists, but the source of this criticism should not be assumed to be Soviet texts; it must be understood as a partial attack expedited by the rightwards shift of some major Anglophone modernists (a factor more pronounced in Britain than elsewhere[9]), and motivated by anti-fascism. Chief among the modernists held up for criticism was T.S. Eliot, whose *After Strange Gods* was reviewed by Douglas Garman in the first issue of *Left Review* as the work of a writer whose 'graph of development is closely parallel with that of Fascism'.[10] But what is striking in Garman's attack – even before the Popular Front line had been formally adopted – is his broad acceptance of Eliot's investment in tradition; indeed, '[Eliot's] search for a system of thought which would, by again relating art to society, nourish the former and be of service to the latter' is read as potentially Marxist.[11] This is indicative of the Marxist critique of major modernists that may be seen not as an outright attack, but rather as a resistance to a certain turn in their development, the turn that Jed

Esty has called the 'Anglocentric revival' marking modernism in the 1930s.[12] Ralph Fox, a key proponent of socialist realism, made a comparable point, rejecting what he felt to be the morbidity of Eliot's attachment to tradition while expounding the importance of the writer's relations with the cultural past.[13] Although Valentine Cunningham has noted the shared significance of tradition for Eliot and the Marxists, his argument ultimately reiterates the assumption that this was in defiance of Marxist aesthetic orthodoxy.[14] The affinity between Marxists and modernists on the question of tradition must be framed within the Communist movement's turn towards the Popular Front strategy, codified in 1935, which encouraged Communists to form broad alliances against fascism.[15] In terms of the status of modernism, this had two crucial consequences: firstly, it encouraged writers to align themselves with their own national traditions at a moment when major modernists like Woolf and Eliot were also moving towards such reconsiderations.[16] Secondly, it isolated fascism as the strategy of the most reactionary section of the bourgeoisie, leaving open the possibility of a rapprochement with certain elements of bourgeois culture.[17]

In this light, the fact that *May Day* adopts an experimental form should not, therefore, necessarily be assumed to be in opposition to Sommerfield's declared commitments. Rather, Sommerfield's politics furnish a perspective from which to adapt certain aspects of the modernist heritage, while critically reflecting on others. The novel takes up a range of familiar modernist themes – exile, the work of memory, the significance of tradition and the experience of urban alienation – recasting them in materialist terms as symptoms of the dislocations and displacements wrought by capitalism. Modernist themes, but also modernist stylistics, are incorporated within an attempt to narrate social totality in a way that offers solutions to those subjective problems. This commitment to totality can be usefully elucidated in relation to Georg Lukacs's theorisation of realism during the 1930s but, crucially, Sommerfield expresses this commitment through the kind of form Lukács uncompromisingly rejected.

Sommerfield is a useful focal point for this discussion of Marxists' relationships with modernism as his own trajectory of development moved from a modernist preoccupation with interiority evident in his debut novel to the socially-oriented *May Day*. Moreover, he was central to the cultural formation of the Popular Front. He joined the Communist Party in the mid-1930s, wrote for the *Daily Worker*, the newspaper of the Communist Party of Great Britain, and *Left Review*.[18] He was active in Mass-Observation, conducting research and writing its 1943 publication *The Pub and the People*.[19] In autumn 1936, shortly after *May Day* was published, he travelled to Spain to fight with the International Brigade, and fought with the Marty Battalion in the Defence of Madrid; his record of his experiences, *Volunteer in Spain*, is one of the earliest first-hand accounts of the conflict.[20] But Sommerfield was not formed as a writer by the Party, but rather had already developed his literary abilities in a quite different circle. Malcolm Lowry admired his first novel, *The Death of Christopher*, published in 1930, and Sommerfield became part of Lowry's bohemian circle that included Nina Hamnett, Elsa Lanchester and Dylan Thomas. Despite Lowry's lack of interest in politics, he regarded Sommerfield as 'approximately the best man I've ever met'.[21]

Sommerfield's debut, *The Death of Christopher*, announces a preoccupation with alienation and division that would recur throughout his literary career. In *The Death of Christopher*, described by a reviewer as a text hoping to 'attract the modernist hangers-on',[22] alienation is figured as a division *within*, as the protagonist vainly pursues 'that most ungetatable thing – his real self'.[23] The elusive integration that the novel's hero pursues is individualistic, or rather narcissistic, but is nonetheless congruent with the politicised version that is the core emotional drive in *May Day*. In *The Death of Christopher*, the narrator finds himself returning to the country he left behind:

> Now each turn of the screw that pushed so many feet of the ocean behind the *Halcyon* brought him so many feet nearer home. This long-cherished return of his, for which he had so much hoped and despaired was actually going to happen: the remote and unbelievable would soon be near and actual.[24]

Sommerfield begins this novel with a description of Christopher's death in a car crash, to which he is propelled by his belief that he cannot overcome the breach with the past. As he drives towards his death he feels that '[s]wifter than light and thought he had freed himself from dimension and overtaken the trampling feet of time, so that the past yet lay in the future and he was once again the Christopher of two years ago'.[25] In this early novel, history and its traumas can only be managed through fantasy and escaped from in death. *May Day*, conversely, proposes a different solution. In a passage that strongly echoes the one above, the returning sailor in this novel feels that 'scenes, half-remembered, half-anticipated moved in his mind, of London in spring […] memories and dreams that were about to become realities again for him'.[26] Return has become a material possibility, and in this fusion of past and present is the prospect of redemption. In the earlier text, the mixing of past and present is a sign of Christopher's delusions, already rendered ironic by the revelation of his death at outset. It is clear, then, that Sommerfield's style, methods and preoccupations were not simply produced by his engagement with Communism; equally, he clearly did not feel compelled to abandon his earlier concerns as a result of his move towards political commitment.

May Day's montage form tracks a wide range of characters on the run-up to a May Day demonstration. The possibility of integration and the overcoming of alienation are central problems. The tone is set by the opening scene in which James Seton, a working-class Communist sailor returned to London from sea, awakens as his ship docks. This moment of return is figured as a fulfilment of something anticipated in a dream: '[a]n image floated in his drowsing mind [...] of a drifting constellation of lights seen across dark waters' (27). James's exile from London produces a temporal and geographic dislocation: '[t]hey had been away too long; they had been too far' (27), and he contemplates the 'coming break as if it were a new, strange thing' (28). This estrangement is mirrored in his brother John's state of displacement. He is re-entering work after a spell of unemployment, a change that he experiences as a decisive temporal break separating 'now' from 'then' (32). For James, this return from exile is figured as offering both personal and political redemption through his resolve to find his brother: 'it seemed to James as if that kind, honest solidity of his brother was a thing of which he had long been in need, a balm for the disquietude which he had suffered since he had left Spain, a fugitive from a revolt drowned in blood' (29). This announces the novel's preoccupation with the intricate intertwining of personal and political memory: James's involvement with a failed uprising (unspecified in the text, but suggestive of the Asturias revolt of 1934) can only be exorcised by a re-forging of a link to his past, a re-establishment of personal history. The interdependence of personal and political exile is expressed in humanist terms as an image of alienation from human fulfilment: '[b]eauty, the token of his exile, flowered from bricks and pavements' (74).

Sommerfield develops his earlier subjective preoccupations into a sustained, Marxist-informed exploration of alienation, and the politics of alienation are crucial to interpreting the novel's experimental form. Readings of the novel have tended to note that the structure privileges the reader, giving him or her a perspective to which characters do not have access within what Brian McKenna calls their own 'micro-stories'.[27] This is certainly suggested by the cinematic, voice-over-like narration of the early pages, '[*l*]*et us take factory chimneys, cannons trained at dingy skies, pointing at the sun and stars*' (25, emphasis in original), utilising what Rod Mengham terms 'the rhetoric of apostrophe', a language of power and privileged perspective Mengham associates with the Auden group.[28] But rather than ironically undercutting this synthetic panopticism with the limited perspectives of individuals, Sommerfield experiments with the ways that such a totalising perspective might in fact be achieved. This is chiefly done through his figurations of the connection-making process of memory. At the level of character, memory takes on what Walter Benjamin describes as the 'epic and rhapsodic' quality of 'genuine memory', which must 'yield an image of the person who remembers'.[29] James Seton returns to a city layered with memory, 'liv[ing] again the memory-changed scenes of childhood, from whose actuality his memory had travelled so long a journey that he recollected them half-uncomprehendingly, half with an adult stranger's sight' (71). The images that memory yields suggest a utopian function:

> And his mother gave him an orange. 'Share it with John', she said, and he did, amicably for once. Her worn face creased peacefully. This was the scene he now remembered, sweet with the overtones of remoteness, loaded with the rich harmonics of past time. The heavy blossom-scent and the evening's islanded quiet affected him now, not as if it was an image of a scene through which he had lived but the memory of some picture seen long ago. (72)

At one level Sommerfield is adapting a modernist emphasis on time and memory for different political ends. In Virginia Woolf's *Mrs Dalloway*, for example, Septimus Smith is driven to suicide by the traumas of memory, by an inability to come to terms with the past as past, so that he feels the past and present blend into an unbearable synchronicity: '[t]he dead were in Thessaly, Evans sang, among the orchids. There they waited till the War was over, and now the dead, now Evans himself.'[30] In Sommerfield's novel, however, memory maintains the vital link between past and present that is shown to be integral to political consciousness. Where in *Mrs Dalloway*, memory presages the break-up of identity, the fatal intrusion of the external into the integrity of Septimus's self, in *May Day* memory is integral to the recognition of the self as socially and historically constituted. The communist poet, historian and novelist Jack Lindsay described this narrative tendency, in a survey of socialist novels in *Left Review*, in terms of the classical dramatic principle of 'recognition':

> *Now* Recognition appears as the point where the shell of the old self cracks and the new self is born, breaking into new spaces of activity and achieving fullness of social contact.[31]

The 'new self' in *May Day* is expressed in the self-recognition that James finds in the mass demonstration: 'the dear familiarity of these surroundings and the deep meaning of my own life for this scene' (213). Integration of past and future selves is continuous with social integration.

II

May Day's narrative moves between different individuals, but also between different styles and genres in a montage form. There is a documentary-style section called 'The Movements of People in London on April 30th', and a passage called 'The Communist Leaflets', the rattling rhythm of which emulates the sound of typewriters and printing presses. In an essay in the leftist journal *Fact*, the novelist Arthur Calder-Marshall wrote in 1937 of the prospects for a new type of 'social' novel written through a 'composite method'.[32] Sommerfield's novel adopts such a 'composite' structure, and this montage principle is the means by which Sommerfield attempts an expression of the social totality. In asserting the interconnected nature of all individuals and world-historical reality, we may consider *May Day* as an experiment in the epic. The connection between epic and the montage form was made by Walter Benjamin in his review of Alfred Döblin's *Berlin Alexanderplatz*. Benjamin argued that Döblin's montage technique, in which documents, incidents, songs and advertisements 'rain down' in the text, 'explodes the framework of the novel, bursts its limits both stylistically and structurally, and clears the way for new, epic possibilities'.[33] Like Döblin, Sommerfield constructs a text in which documents and fragments 'rain down': 'The slogans, the rain of leaflets, the shouts and songs of demonstrators echoed in a million minds' (67). For John, the sight of a Communist leaflet serves to temporarily focalise his entire situation, giving him access not to a depersonalised aerial perspective, but through a grasp of social connections: '[h]e saw it with a sense of recognition, he knew it was connected with a whole group of feelings, associations and events' (180).

In his deployment of montage, however, Sommerfield is at important variance with one of the major theorists of the epic and of literary form in the 1930s more widely, Georg Lukács. Lukács developed Hegel's central category of totality into a vision of the social totality marked by 'the all-pervasive supremacy of the whole over the parts'.[34] In such a structure, all parts are 'objectively interrelated'.[35] This objective interdependence, however, may be experienced as its opposite – as the apparent autonomy of the parts. Lukács rejected the technique of montage and other modernist forms on the grounds that they merely reproduced this superficial fragmentation. Remaining 'frozen in their own immediacy', they 'fail to pierce the surface to discover the underlying essence, i.e. the real factors that relate their experience to the hidden social forces that produce them'.[36] The apparent incompatibility of Sommerfield's form with Lukács's version of realism has been noted by Gustav Klaus, but to argue as Klaus does that 'Sommerfield simply starts from different premises', so that Lukács's criticisms are 'irrelevant', is to overlook important points of correspondence.[37] In spite of Lukács's rejection of montage as fragmentary and incoherent formalism, Sommerfield's montage articulates a model of the relations between the parts and the whole that is essentially congruent with Lukács's version of totality. Sommerfield attempts to show both the appearance of reification and the actual 'objective' relations.

In the reified world of the bourgeois characters in the novel, power is a mystery: doors are opened 'by men who moved as if they were trying to be invisible' (63). This is a world of illusion in which labour is thoroughly disguised, in which phenomena do appear as independent. Indeed, through the wealthy young couple, Peter Langfier and Pamela Allen, Sommerfield seems to echo Lukács's account of the antinomies of bourgeois consciousness: Pamela's minutely descriptive perceptions make her a 'completely passive observer moving in obedience to laws which [her consciousness] can never control'; Peter, meanwhile, is paralysed by his freedom of choice and is thus unable to distinguish real life from fantasy.[38] But Sommerfield is anxious to acknowledge the progressive potential of bourgeois dissidence as part of the alliance-making of the Popular Front. Peter's flights of fancy, his romantic attachment to 'the heroics of technology' (55), are abruptly terminated when, visiting his father's factory after an accident in which a factory girl is scalped, he sees the grotesque evidence of the realities of exploitation: a 'tangle of blood and hair [...] wedged between the belt and the pulley wheel' (228). This encounter with the reality of technologised production deflates his earlier heroic fantasies, but his romantic temperament is shown to have its positive effect, enabling him to recognise the victim as 'a young girl who may have been looking forward to seeing a lover that evening' (229). While typifying Peter as bearing the modernist sensibility characteristic of polarised bourgeois consciousness, Sommerfield is also anxious to identify progressive tendencies; in this sense he exploits a critique of modernism not simply to reject or denigrate it, but rather to explore its political potential.

Through recurring references to a single commodity, the artificial leather product produced by Langfier's factory, Sommerfield links together the moments of the productive process, and thereby de-reifies the commodity, stripping it of its appearance of independence. If, in Adorno and Horkheimer's well-known formulation, 'all reification is a forgetting', Sommerfield's use of montage and juxtaposition engages the reader's memory to continually resituate the commodity in context, referring the product back to the productive process.[39] The commodity in circulation is seen from a range of perspectives: the artificial leather features in John's wife Martine's dreams of a better domestic life (128), on the seats of taxis, and in the study of the reactionary union leader Raggett (141). Each scene bears the legible trace of the economic mode. In one short, isolated scene, a destitute old woman is seen 'grubbing in Soho dustbins for scraps of food', carrying 'a shabby bag made of squares of artificial leather' (192). The detail gives the commodity concrete social significance that serves to emphasise the isolation of the character, who does not reappear in the novel. The montage therefore restores the link between commodity and labour that Lukács assumed could only be lost by the fragmentation of modernist aesthetic form. Such de-reification was essential to Lukács's sense of epic in the 1930s.[40] Once again, Sommerfield appears to be working towards the epic and totalising ambitions that define Lukács's programme – suggesting that those ambitions resonated for British novelists even if they were not fully theorised – but doing so through a modernist textual strategy.

Sommerfield indeed appears at one point to deploy the juxtaposition of montage to dramatise 1930s aesthetic debates over modernism and realism. Sommerfield narrates a scene set in a music hall, where a strike threatens to disrupt the opening of the appositely titled *Backwards and Forwards*, 'the musical comedy that is going to be DIFFERENT', and follows it immediately with an antithetical scene featuring a lone man who 'looked like an intellectual' (146–9). In the theatre, a bustling scene featuring a vast list of characters involved in the production of the musical resolves into a demand for a strike. This suggests that this collective – though commercial – form of art has affinity with collective forms of action. The succeeding scene concerns a lone intellectual who stands for the inadequate response of many of the intelligentsia to the demands of anti-fascism. Reluctantly and bitterly politicised, he regards the masses as to be 'alternately pitied and despised' (150). He loathes both mass culture, 'people sitting in the warm darkness of the picture houses, lapped with the sickly disgusting tide of drugging, lying thought', and a high culture in decay (151). His inability to meaningfully discriminate is encapsulated in a passage that presents images, theories and commodities as a jumbled, undifferentiated mass in a bookshop window: '[c]over designs abounded with romantic photomontage and abstract representations of the Workers, red flags, hammers and sickles, fasces, swastikas, a chaotic jumble of baggage dropped in the great retreat of bourgeois thought' (151). This is precisely the decadence Lukács identified in the bourgeoisie, an abdication of critical thought and discrimination, 'a sticking together of disconnected facts'.[41] What this character is unable to see is the strike being orchestrated behind the scenes in the music hall. He mistakes the product for the labour process that creates it, and thus is blind to the radical potential of popular culture. Sommerfield's use of juxtaposition here reflects a Lukácsian critique of bourgeois intellectual culture while asserting the revolutionary potential of the collective aesthetic labour that produces the mass cultural form. The innovative montage form is appropriated to isolate and critically examine a politically reactionary modernist tendency.

III

Sommerfield therefore shows that the personal, political and aesthetic aspects of alienation are related. I will suggest that the novel attempts to solve these problems not just through the formal procedure of montage but also through the thematic and structural work of myth and tradition. These are terms closely associated with modernism, and especially the 'mythic method', which T.S. Eliot considered Joyce's discovery in *Ulysses*.[42] But again we find them given materialist coordinates. The central myth in *May Day* is the General Strike, encompassing both the historical strike of 1926 and an ideal form of it. Tradition – the May Day tradition that is both a festival of springtime and a monument to the labour movement – mediates between individual memory and the totality of history. The practices of tradition give graspable and intelligible form to historical processes: '[a] revolution is not a fight between those on one side of the line and those on the other. But today things are artificially simplified' (203). Tradition was central to the Popular Front's most defining ambition of activating a progressive, popular consensus, drawing from the past the images of popular resistance from the Peasants' Revolt through to the anti-fascist struggle.[43] '[T]hings aren't the same in England', the narrator of *May Day* tells us, identifying in the English May Day traditions a possible way of staging resistance to the increasingly invisible, decentred and denationalised forces of capitalism. The temporary massing of the workers overcomes that dislocation, just as, more widely, the labour movement is figured as the 'home' of the alienated sailor James Seton.

Part Three, covering the May Day demonstration itself, is organised by a sustained performative metaphor that attempts to deal with the traumatic memory of the 1926 General Strike. The May Day celebrations of 1936, the month Sommerfield's novel was published, took up the tenth anniversary of the strike and attempted to incorporate its problematic legacy into the labour tradition. The General Strike that is imagined in *May Day* operates at two levels: at one level the actual historical legacy of the 1926 strike presents itself as a problematic legacy from which lessons can be learned, but which haunts the text as a failure (223). At a second level, however, one finds a myth of the General Strike in line with Georges Sorel's analysis of it in terms of myth. The prospect of a mass strike presents itself as an outpouring of possibility: '[e]verywhere the accumulated bitterness of weeks and months and years' is 'bursting forth' (160). These levels of history and myth, inglorious history and radical possibility, conflict in the characters' minds in order to recast the events of 1926 as a 'rehearsal', subsuming them to a greater, as yet unrealised event (204). The demonstration is therefore both production and reproduction: the reproduction of tradition and the production of a new situation, the 'new thoughts' in people's minds (211). James feels himself no longer a 'spectator', alienated from historical reality, but instead a participant and actor in a mass drama.

The power of the 'myth' of the General Strike is to augment the consciousness of a scheduled interruption of the labour process – the May Day holiday – with radical future possibilities. The strike, for Sorel, is a way of imaging to the proletariat its own history: 'appealing to their painful memories of particular conflicts, it colours with an intense life all the details of the composition presented to consciousness'.[44] Political consciousness arises *in* the strike, and the acquisition of such consciousness is described in epiphanic terms: '[w]e thus obtain that intuition of socialism which language cannot give us with perfect clearness – and we obtain it as a whole, perceived instantaneously'.[45] In Sommerfield's novel, both these aspects are suggested in James Seton's sense of unity with the crowd. He finds in the demonstration the solution to his 'painful memories' of the failed revolt in Spain: 'I sink my identity into the calm quietness of this waiting crowd, I am part of it, sharer in its strength ... and the solution of my conflicts is bound up with the fate of this mass' (213). Although the violent outcome of the novel delimits possibility, Arthur Calder-Marshall made the case that this narrative tendency in socialist fiction was in fact a way of managing and transforming the reality of political violence: '[t]aken in its wider context, it becomes an incident in the political education of the group, not the end of protest, but the beginning of militancy.'[46]

If this politicised commemoration is the expression of one of the two poles of the May Day tradition, that of political, rather than social, revolution, then Pat's feeling that there are 'new thoughts in people's minds' evokes the second possible meaning of the tradition: as a spontaneous community celebration of rebirth and renewal. This is a reading of the May Day tradition articulated in a *Left Review* editorial the following year: the deepest concept in art 'is the concept of struggle forged by men at work, by men and women joined in harmony in the struggle against Nature. It is the story of the death and re-birth of the Year'.[47] In May 1938, Jack Lindsay argued that the May Day tradition was part of the deep structure of culture itself, celebrating 'all that is joyous, vital, constructive in the tradition of human activity, cultural as well as productive'.[48] The redemptive and revitalising qualities of the tradition give a kind of mythic underpinning to the novel's political plot, but it is a myth that is both available and useful to the characters. In James Seton, the frustrated desire for rebirth and renewal, reminiscent, especially, of Eliot's *The Waste Land*, is explicitly redirected to a political goal: '[t]he trees had hung out flags of a foreign country to him, and he had got himself a new flag, the banner of a different spring, whose harvest would be plentiful – the spring of revolution' (74–5).

*

I have tried to show here that there is no reason to suppose that Sommerfield felt bound by an opposition between realism and modernism. He was clearly aware of the relationship between certain modernist techniques and a problematic politics, but the novel is dynamised by a confidence in the possibility of taking over and transforming those techniques, and the perspectives that underpin them. The warm reception of the novel by leftist critics suggests it was not viewed as the kind of formalist deviation condemned by Radek; Jack Lindsay, for example, regarded it as 'the best collective novel that we yet have produced in England'.[49] There are certainly moments when *May Day*'s confidence in its political messages drowns out its more subtle effects, but to read this, as Frank Kermode does, as a sign that Sommerfield was uncomfortable with his 'bourgeois' literary gifts and felt compelled to use them in the production of a kind of 'anti-bourgeois bourgeois novel', is to over-state the demands placed on writers during the Popular Front period in relation to the 'bourgeois' heritage.[50] Indeed, as Peter Marks argues, the 'spectre' of socialist realism never fully materialised in Britain in the 1930s.[51] Instead, significant spaces and possibilities for experiment were available to writers like Sommerfield, and indeed we might identify comparable Marxist inhabitations of modernist positions and strategies in the work of James Barke in his *Major Operation* (1936) and Arthur Calder-Marshall in his *Pie in the Sky* (1937).[52]

Notes

1. H. Gustav Klaus, *The Literature of Labour: Two Hundred Years of Working-Class Writing* (Brighton: Harvester, 1985), 117.
2. Andy Croft, *Red Letter Days: British Fiction in the 1930s* (London: Lawrence & Wishart, 1990), 221.
3. Ken Worpole, *Dockers and Detectives* (London: Verso, 1983), 89.
4. Valentine Cunningham, *British Writers of the Thirties* (Oxford: Oxford University Press, 1988), 299.
5. Nick Hubble, 'John Sommerfield and Mass-Observation', *The Space Between* 8, no. 1 (2012): 131–52, 140.
6. Valentine Cunningham, 'The Anxiety of Influence; or, Tradition and the Thirties Talents', in *Rewriting the Thirties: Modernism and After*, ed. Keith Williams and Stephen Matthews (Harlow: Longman, 1997), 17.
7. Karl Radek, 'Contemporary World Literature and the Tasks of Proletarian Art', in A.A. Zhdanov et al., *Problems of Soviet Literature* (London: Martin Lawrence, 1935), 153.
8. Montagu Slater, 'The Turning Point', *Left Review* 2, no. 2 (October 1935): 15; Amabel Williams-Ellis, 'Soviet Writers' Congress', *Left Review* 1, no. 2 (November 1934): 27.

9 Raymond Williams, 'The Politics of the Avant-Garde', in *Politics of Modernism* [1989] (London: Verso, 2007), 61.
10 Douglas Garman, 'What? ... The Devil?', *Left Review* 1, no. 1 (October 1934): 36.
11 Garman, 'What? ... The Devil?', 36.
12 Jed Esty, *A Shrinking Island: Modernism and National Culture in England* (Princeton: Princeton University Press, 2004), 12.
13 Ralph Fox, *The Novel and the People* [1937] (London: Lawrence & Wishart, 1979), 141.
14 Cunningham, 'The Anxiety of Influence', 12.
15 Kevin Morgan, *Against Fascism and War: Ruptures and Continuities in British Communist Politics* (Manchester: Manchester University Press, 1989), 195.
16 Esty's *A Shrinking Island* is a pioneering study of the turn towards national culture evident in the work of major modernists in the 1930s.
17 The key source for this sectional analysis of fascism is Comintern General Secretary Georgi Dimitrov's address to the Seventh Congress in August 1935, published as *The Working Class Against Fascism* (London: Martin Lawrence, 1935).
18 Andy Croft, 'Returned Volunteer: The Novels of John Sommerfield', *The London Magazine*, 1 April 1983: 62–3.
19 Mass-Observation, *The Pub and the People: A Worktown Survey* (London: Victor Gollancz, 1943). Tom Harrisson confirms in his 'Preface' that the project was mostly Sommerfield's work (11). Nick Hubble gives a thorough account of Sommerfield's M-O activities in 'John Sommerfield and Mass-Observation'.
20 John Sommerfield, *Volunteer in Spain* (New York: Alfred A. Knopf, 1937).
21 Gordon Bowker, *Pursued By Furies: A Life of Malcolm Lowry* (London: HarperCollins, 1993), 41.
22 Bowker, *Pursued By Furies*, 141.
23 John Sommerfield, *The Death of Christopher* (New York: Jonathan Cape, 1930), 30.
24 Sommerfield, *The Death of Christopher*, 345.
25 Sommerfield, *The Death of Christopher*, 12.
26 John Sommerfield, *May Day* [1936] (London: London Books, 2010), 30. Hereafter, page references are given in parentheses.
27 Brian McKenna, 'The British Communist Novel of the 1930s and 1940s: "A Party of Equals"? (And Does That Matter?)', *The Review of English Studies* 47, no. 187 (1996): 376.
28 Rod Mengham, 'The Thirties: Politics, Authority, Perspective', in *The Cambridge History of Twentieth-Century Literature*, ed. Laura Marcus (Cambridge: Cambridge University Press, 2004), 373.
29 Walter Benjamin, 'Excavation and Memory', in *Selected Writings: Volume 2, Part 2, 1931–1934*, ed. Michael W. Jennings et al. (Cambridge, MA: Harvard University Press, 2005), 576.
30 Virginia Woolf, *Mrs Dalloway* (London: Penguin Classics, 1996), 69. Keith Williams offers a thorough account of *May Day*'s intertextual relationships with canonical modernist works, especially Joyce's *Ulysses*, in 'Joyce's "Chinese Alphabet": *Ulysses* and the Proletarians', in *Irish Writing: Exile and Subversion*, ed. Paul Hyland (Basingstoke: Palgrave, 1991), 181–5.
31 Jack Lindsay, 'Man in Society', *Left Review* 2, no. 11 (January 1937), 840; emphasis in original.
32 Arthur Calder-Marshall, 'Fiction', *Fact* 4 (July 1937): 42.
33 Walter Benjamin, 'The Crisis in the Novel', in *Selected Writings: Volume 2, Part 1, 1927–1930*, ed. Michael W. Jennings et al. (Cambridge MA: Harvard University Press, 2005), 301.
34 Georg Lukács, 'The Marxism of Rosa Luxemburg', in *History and Class Consciousness*, trans. Rodney Livingstone (Pontypool: Merlin Press, 1971), 27.
35 Georg Lukács, 'Realism in the Balance', in Theodor Adorno et al., *Aesthetics and Politics* (London: Verso, 1980), 32.
36 Lukács, 'Realism in the Balance', 36–7.

37 Klaus, *The Literature of Labour*, 117.
38 Georg Lukács, 'Class Consciousness', in *History and Class Consciousness*, 77.
39 Max Horkheimer and Theodor Adorno, *Dialectic of Enlightenment* (Redwood City, CA: Stanford University Press, 2002), 191.
40 Georg Lukács, 'Essay on the Novel', *International Literature* 5 (1936): 74.
41 Georg Lukács, *The Historical Novel* (London: Penguin, 1976), 302.
42 T.S. Eliot, 'Ulysses, Order and Myth' [1923], reprinted in Vassiliki Kolocotroni et al. (eds), *Modernism: An Anthology of Sources and Documents* (Edinburgh: Edinburgh University Press, 1998), 371–3.
43 This project is exemplified in Edgell Rickword and Jack Lindsay (eds), *The Handbook of Freedom* (London: Lawrence and Wishart, 1939) and Jack Lindsay's *England My England: A Pageant of the English People* (London: Key Books, 1939).
44 Georges Sorel, *Reflections on Violence*, ed. Jeremy Jennings (Cambridge: Cambridge University Press, 1999), 118.
45 Sorel, *Reflections on Violence*, 118.
46 Calder-Marshall, 'Fiction', 43.
47 Randall Swingler, 'The Cultural Meaning of May Day' [Editorial], *Left Review* 3, no. 3 (April 1937): 130.
48 Jack Lindsay, 'The May Day Tradition', *Left Review* 3, no. 12 (May 1938): 963.
49 Jack Lindsay, 'Three Novels', *Left Review* 2, no. 11 (January 1937): 915.
50 Frank Kermode, *History and Value: The Clarendon Lectures and the Northcliffe Lectures 1987* (Oxford: Clarendon, 1988), 95.
51 Peter Marks, 'Illusion and Reality: The Spectre of Socialist Realism in Thirties Literature', in *Rewriting the Thirties: Modernism and After*, 34.
52 James Barke, *Major Operation* (London: Collins, 1936); Arthur Calder-Marshall, *Pie in the Sky* (London: Jonathan Cape, 1937).

Future Imperfect: Mass and Mobility in Williams, Orwell and the BBC's *Nineteen Eighty-Four*

Sean McQueen

Abstract: George Orwell's *Nineteen Eighty-Four* is the paradigmatic Anglophone dystopia, and its political inspiration has been widely contested, especially by Marxist and socialist critics. Fredric Jameson and Raymond Williams both critiqued Orwell's attitude towards the masses, and considered the novel a hostile critique of socialism. This essay will build on Andrew Milner's theorisation of dystopia and his renewed socialist reading of Orwell. Cinematic and televisual treatments of Orwell bear the impress of the novel's political indeterminacy. This essay will extend to these adaptations Milner's rereading of Williams, Jameson and Orwell, and his hypothesis that the subjunctive future perfect is 'the logically informing tense of dystopia'. With a shift from novel to television, Orwell's telescreens acquire a new relevance. Since Williams took exception to Orwell's representation of the masses, and conceived of television as a technology of mobile privatisation, I take special interest in the BBC's controversial 1954 televisual adaptation, with reference to his *Television: Technology and Cultural Form*. Drawing on historical evidence and textual analysis, I assess the BBC production's troubled political inspiration and reception.

*

> There is a moment in many cultures, and in many art-forms, when the concept of the mirror suddenly becomes exciting, and a wave of confusion and excitement suddenly breaks. Most people, within its area of confluence, start thinking of watching themselves in mirrors watching others watching others.[1]

George Orwell's *Nineteen Eighty-Four*[2] is the paradigmatic Anglophone dystopia. Two influential Marxist thinkers, Fredric Jameson and Raymond Williams, have criticised its representation of the masses and its lack of political ambition. In *Archaeologies of the Future*, Jameson considers the novel a reactionary, anti-socialist anti-utopia, while Williams was critical of its political fatalism on no less than three occasions.[3] This essay will build on Andrew Milner's theorisations of dystopia in 'Archaeologies of the Future: Jameson's Utopia or Orwell's Dystopia?'[4] and *Locating Science Fiction*,[5] which consider both Jameson's and Williams's readings. It will extend to cinematic and televisual adaptations of Orwell's dystopian novel Milner's hypothesis that the subjunctive future perfect is 'the logically informing tense of dystopia'.[6]

Since Williams took exception to Orwell's representation of the masses, and conceived of television as a technology of mobile privatisation, I take special interest in the BBC's controversial 1954 televisual adaptation, with reference to his *Television: Technology and Cultural Form*.[7]

Two authoritative readings of Orwell's novel concern us here. The first belongs to Raymond Williams, who considered Orwell's exploited class, the proles, a desperate but hopeless representation that ultimately betrays a low opinion of the working class as the 'masses'. In his first account of the novel, Williams notes the crippling paradox 'that the only class in which you can put any hope is written off, in present terms, as hopeless'.[8] The problem for Williams was in equal parts the fate of the protagonist, Winston Smith, and Orwell's own attitude, which projected 'an enormous apathy on all the oppressed', as he wrote in his second essay, '*Nineteen Eighty-Four*'.[9] Williams finds in Orwell a vindication of his own aphorism that 'there are in fact no masses, there are only ways of seeing people as masses'.[10] 'It needs to be said', he concludes, 'however bitterly, that if the tyranny of 1984 ever finally comes, one of the major elements of the ideological preparation will have been just this way of seeing "the masses"'.[11] In his final assessment, '*Nineteen Eighty-Four* in 1984', Williams finds a mixture of horrific exaggeration, parody and a general lack of foresight.

The second reading is Fredric Jameson's. What makes Jameson unusual is that he places Orwell within the dystopian tradition, but claims that the novel is not, strictly speaking, a dystopia. For Jameson (and other science fiction critics) dystopia designates something much more specific, a sub-genre within the broader dystopian imaginary. Jameson's task is thus to locate the novel within the 'entirely mass-cultural and ideological phenomenon' of the Cold War dystopia, a reactionary aversion to utopia as 'a perfect system that always had to be imposed by force on its imperfect and reluctant subject', practically associated with Stalinism.[12] Jameson considers the novel an attack on socialism and, more narrowly, a critique of Labour Britain.[13] He concludes that *Nineteen Eighty-Four* is not a dystopia, nor what Tom Moylan calls a critical dystopia[14] (which Jameson cites with approval), for it engages neither feminism nor ecology, nor Left politics in general. Rather, it is an anti-socialist, 'anti-Utopia' that 'warns against Utopian programs in the political realm'. 'Surely, the force of the text', Jameson writes, 'springs from a conviction about human nature itself, whose corruption and lust for power are inevitable, and not to be remedied by new social measures or programs, nor by heightened consciousness of the impending dangers'.[15]

So, Williams and Jameson charge Orwell with, at worst, political negligence and fatalism and, at best, being cripplingly dispiriting. Both offer defensible readings, but neither, as Andrew Milner notes, attend sufficiently to the novel's ending. For it does not end with the well-known lines that testify to Winston's successful indoctrination: 'But it was all right, everything was all right, the struggle was finished. He had won the victory over himself. He loved Big Brother.'[16] Rather, it ends with the Appendix, 'The Principles of Newspeak', an undated and unattributed essay that concludes with some speculation as to the intended, final adoption of Newspeak in 2050.[17] Both Margaret Atwood and Milner attribute great significance to the Appendix:

> [T]he essay on Newspeak is written in standard English, in the third person, and in the past tense, which can only mean that the regime has fallen, and that language and individuality have survived. For whoever has written the essay on Newspeak, the world of Nineteen Eighty-Four is over. Thus, it's my view, that Orwell had much more faith in the resilience of the human spirit than he's usually given credit for.[18]

> [T]he Appendix is internal to the novel, neither an author's nor a scholarly editor's account of how the fiction works, but rather part of the fiction, a fictional commentary on fictional events.[19]

Milner points also to a footnote in the first chapter that reads: 'Newspeak *was* the official language of Oceania.'[20] There are no other footnotes in the novel, so it is hard not to accord significance to this aberration, nor to the use of past tense, which clearly indicates that Newspeak endures no longer. For Milner, as for Williams and Jameson, Orwell's lack of socialist alternatives renders problematic the novel's politics, hence the need for 'something external to itself to inspire belief in the possibility of resistance'. As a framing device, or perhaps a rejoinder, the Appendix is indispensable because the tense employed is that of the subjunctive future perfect, which means, for Milner, 'that these events will not necessarily have eventuated'.[21] Whether Newspeak and, thus, the Party, fell by means of revolution, theodicy or hubris is not apparent; whether it represents the same revisionist history perpetuated by the Party or its successors is unlikely, but not unthinkable. It does not represent, as Williams and Jameson would wish, a proper description of socialist alternatives, but, rather, a return to Oldspeak, and thus normalcy. Just as Newspeak was ill-fated in its totalising aspiration 'to make all other modes of thought impossible',[22] so too the Appendix renders unsustainable the dystopian society elaborated in the novel. Milner's task is to read Orwell against Jameson's thesis which, if correct, has a broader significance not only for understandings of Orwell and dystopia in particular, but for science fiction in general. In so doing, Milner rescues not only *Nineteen Eighty-Four* but Orwell himself from Jameson and Williams, both of whom share the view that the novel and Orwell turn their back on socialism and the proles *qua* the working class. But Jameson and Williams are not alone in their critique. Indeed, the 'commonly held attitude [...] is that Orwell developed as a political thinker from a generalised socialist standpoint to a clear and unequivocal revolutionary socialism and finally to an intensely anti-revolutionary and largely anti-socialist individualism'.[23]

Briefly setting aside the significance of the Appendix, Orwell's descriptions of the proles is ambivalent. Winston writes in his diary that '[i]f there was hope, it *must* lie in the proles, because only there in those swarming disregarded masses, 85 per cent of the population of Oceania, could the force to destroy the Party ever be generated'.[24] But this very hope is also denounced as a 'mystical truth and a palpable absurdity'.[25] Unlike the members of the Outer Party, the proles need no direct coercion, leading an impoverished but nonetheless libertarian existence. There is something of a depressing paradox in this revelation: the measures taken to control the Outer Party speak to their potential for subversion, a potential that must be extinguished, whilst the proles, whose existence is a vulgar but easy one, require very little supervision by the Inner Party. The strength or weakness of Williams's account of Orwell is his emphasis on the proles. For though the proles constitute the vast majority of the population, they are not Orwell's primary focus. Rather, it is the Outer Party, to which Winston belongs, who live the most carefully administered and telescreen-supervised existence. So, for John Newsinger, the 'novel is very much an exploration of totalitarianism as experienced by Orwell's "middling" group'.[26] Williams's antipathy is, then, to some degree reducible to his sympathy for and faith in the revolutionary potential of the proles *qua* the working class, and Orwell's contrary view that it was not (just) the working class but, and perhaps more so, the managerial and bureaucratic echelon that 'were vital to the success of the social project'.[27] For Jameson, this is Orwell's own bourgeois fear of the working class,[28] more palpable in *Nineteen Eighty-Four* than elsewhere.[29] The problem is that Jameson and Williams charge Orwell with an attack on socialism in general. Stephen Ingle's comprehensive study finds that the novel bears the impress of Orwell's complicated relationship with socialism abroad and at home, so that Orwell criticises not socialism but, like many, the questionable socialist nature of the Soviet Union,[30] as well as socialist intellectuals.[31] In the final analysis, Orwell's own sense of socialism is better grasped as 'non-libertarian, non-ideological, non-utopian, non-progressive and non- (probably anti-) intellectual'.[32]

Returning to the Appendix, its significance clearly lies in the mutual discontinuity in form and content, the fact that it is an Appendix and it is not written in Newspeak. The formal dislocation of the Appendix itself is an insufficient rejoinder for Roger Fowler. Rather, its significance is revealed less through its structural opposition than its tone and style which, when read carefully – and Fowler supposes that it rarely is – have no affinity with the rest of the novel.[33] But Fowler's careful reading is vulnerable on its own terms. The primary insight in Arthur Eckstein's analysis is Orwell's considered use of style to adopt a particular position or political sympathy. The 'plain style' Orwell used elsewhere 'to confront, as candidly and directly as possible, the bleak realities of the modern world', for the edification of a working-class readership is, problematically, at odds with the style adopted in the Appendix.[34] For Orwell's '"good plain Saxon" […] dominates throughout totalitarian Newspeak', but the truthful nature of the Appendix, rendered in classical prose, suggests that 'plain language' could not have conveyed the truth therein.[35] Bracketing off the question of the truth, the most important question for me, as for Milner, remains that identified by Jameson, which is not 'did it get the future right?', but rather 'did it sufficiently shock its own present as to force a mediation on the impossible?'[36]

Prolefeed

To explore this question further, I will look to adaptations of *Nineteen Eighty-Four*. As we have seen, a convincing argument can be made that the Appendix is in fact the novel's true conclusion, and it is significant that the absence of systemic Newspeak curtails the dystopian vision. Newspeak and the verbal register are central to Orwell's dystopian vision. They dominate thought and expression, and most analyses foreground its role both in Winston's eventual indoctrination – the triumph of doublethink – and in its structuration of the novel.[37] Nonetheless, Richard Posner calls the novel's telescreen – a two-way television – 'a powerful metaphor for the loss of privacy in a totalitarian state. But it is inessential to the political theme of the novel', which is the monopolisation of possible thoughts and expression by means of propaganda and Newspeak.[38] There is little to disagree with in this assessment: the deprivation of language, and thus the attenuation of adversarial forms of expression and thought, is the primary method of control in Orwell's Airstrip One, with the panoptican telescreens a supplementary form of behavioural modification. What interests me is whether the same can be said for televisual and cinematic adaptations of *Nineteen Eighty-Four*; for a shift in medium from the verbal and linguistic register to the visual makes the telescreens less of a supplement, assuming a more sinister and authoritarian function than they do in the novel.

Orwell's *Nineteen Eighty-Four* was successful upon publication in 1949 and has never been out of print.[39] It has been adapted numerous times for the stage, opera, radio, television and cinema. The BBC's 1954 television adaptation was, as we shall see, a mixed success, while Michael Anderson's 1956 film adaptation was a wide departure – 'freely adapted from the novel', as the credits state at the outset – decried by Orwell's estate.[40] Michael Radford's 1984 adaptation was received well by critics and claimed Best Film and Best Actor (John Hurt as Winston Smith) in the *Evening Standard British Film Awards*. But Richard Grenier's review in *The New York Times* laments the loss of Orwell's Newspeak: 'What is missing in the movie, plainly, are Orwell's brilliant essays in the novel on "Newspeak," "doublethink," [and] "INGSOC"'.[41] These three adaptations have only recently become readily available, leading James Perloff to note with irony that their unavailability parallels Orwell's novel, 'where the past simply disappears'.[42]

Given the significance accorded to the novel's Appendix by both Atwood and Milner[43] it is interesting that two of the three adaptations retain this framing device in some fashion. The BBC version, produced and directed by Rudolph Cartier and adapted by Nigel Kneale, begins with a voice-over: 'This is one man's alarmed vision of the future; a future which he felt might, with such dangerous ease, be brought about.' It concludes with an intertitle: 'THE END.' Anderson's film makes more extensive use of the framing device. The film begins with an intertitle:

This is a story of the future–
Not the future of space ships and men from other planets –
But the immediate future.

It ends with the camera panning out to range over the city, far from an ecstatic crowd, whose cries of 'long live Big Brother!' fade out, to be replaced by a voice-over: 'This, then, is a story of the future. It could be the story of our children if we fail to preserve their heritage of freedom.' An intertitle then appears, proclaiming 'The End' of the film. Made in 1956, it would be safe to situate this film in the context of science fiction films of the same decade, such as Don Siegel's *Invasion of the Body Snatchers* (1956), which reflect American anti-communism and fit Jameson's account of the anti-socialist Cold War dystopia. But it is only in some editions of Orwell's novel that the chapter preceding the Appendix concludes with the words 'The End',[44] with the Appendix existing extratextually. Orwell died in January 1950, living long enough to contest the reception of his novel, but not long enough to see subsequent editions. A sceptical interpretation of the film's conclusion might suppose this voice-over to be that of the Party, rather than that of an objective voice-over, thus perverting the redemptive authority of the extratextual subjunctive future perfect. But it is more likely that, since both the voice-over and the concluding intertitle are not part of the film's diegesis, they work in a manner similar to

Orwell's Appendix. This also applies to the BBC production: both are bookended by non-diegetic Oldspeak. Indeed, it is only in the most recent film that the framing device is abandoned.

Tony Shaw notes that both American and British governments appropriated Orwell's books 'as they did no other [...] trading on [his] status as an independent-minded icon of the left who had definitively exposed Soviet-style communism, and "clarifying" his powerful rhetoric and vision for the masses'.[45] Orwell unequivocally contradicted the interpretation of *Nineteen Eighty-Four* as a critique of socialism, but this is, nevertheless, the most enduring interpretation, so much that Milner suggests Jameson's reading is likely to be 'unavoidably overdetermined by the novel's American Cold-War reception'.[46] But there are two aspects to this. Jameson laments Orwell's negative critique of socialism, which is the American intelligentsia's reception, determined by the Cold War era. But, on the other hand, Jameson's Cold War dystopia, as a mass cultural and overwhelmingly American phenomenon, hostile to socialism in general and taking Orwell's novel as an exemplary critique of socialism in particular, conforms to the enthusiastic anti-communist, anti-socialist interpretation of the first televisual adaptation of *Nineteen Eighty-Four*, an episode in CBS's *Studio One* series, directed by Paul Nickell. In this sense, '*Nineteen Eighty-Four* came to be used for the very purpose it warned against: propaganda for the maintenance of a super-state conflict'.[47] Williams too eventually observed that the novel was 'primarily used [...] ironically by some of the same propaganda methods which it exposes and attacks'.[48] This reactionary American political context, in fact, corresponds to Jameson's assessment of the novel: the CBS adaptation was received much as Jameson understands Orwell, as a critique of socialism. Indeed, as John Newsinger notes, that his novel was welcomed as an attack on socialism came as a shock to Orwell, and it was only his illness and death that prevented extensive efforts at repudiation.[49] Similarly, Milner points out that Cold War readings of the novel are produced less by readers than by 'precisely those institutionalised, politically and economically dominant, vested interests, both in the West and the Soviet bloc, that Orwell himself had so cordially detested'.[50] But it is also true that Williams's reading, correct or incorrect, 'sets the tone for much of the New Left's hostility to Orwell'.[51] While the reception of the BBC production was decidedly more varied, director/producer Rudolph Cartier 'intended his play to act as a warning against totalitarianism in all its forms, including fascism, communism and McCarthyism'.[52]

Milner says of Orwell:

> The political point of [his] own dystopia was becoming apparent. His book would need to be unremittingly horrible so as to expose the sheer ugliness of totalitarianism. But it would therefore need something external to itself

to inspire belief in the possibility of resistance. Which is why "THE END" could not actually be the end.[53]

This does not apply to Radford's film, hence Milner's broader hypothesis:

> The subjunctive future perfect is by no means always empirically present in dystopian [science fiction] [...] [B]ut, even when this is so, even where the tense fails to appear altogether, it remains nonetheless the logically informing tense of dystopia. For this is what dystopia future fictions recount: what *would have happened* if their empirical and implied readerships had not been moved to prevent it.[54]

I wish to focus on this question of implied audience, and on the change in emphasis from Newspeak to the telescreen, with special reference to Williams's work on television. For Williams, the direct means of repression – the coercion and torture of the Ministry of Love and Room 101 – were less interesting than Orwell's emphasis on communication.[55] Here, we can benefit from Philip Bounds, who notes that Orwell's own interest in mass communication was characterised by a contradiction, a 'combination of enjoyment and *Marxisant* despair':

> On the one hand he clearly believed that certain media texts reflected all the qualities which had attracted him to working-class culture [...] On the other hand, deeply influenced by Marxist approaches to culture, he consistently portrayed the media as one of the main means by which the ruling class disseminated its ideology.[56]

With this in mind, it will be useful to look closely at the argument in Williams's *Television: Technology and Cultural Form*.

With the exception of a number of pre-recorded segments of film telecined in, *Nineteen Eighty-Four* was performed and telecast live on 12 December 1954 in the prime-time slot of 8:35pm to 10:35pm. It was, at that time, the most expensive drama produced for television. The performance was repeated the following Thursday and was recorded on film, and this is the existing version.[57] So, the teleplay was ambitious both in the scope of its production and in its intended audience, both of which unfolded in real time. Here we can recall Williams's assessment of television as a technology of 'mobile privatisation', distinct from the physical mobility of public technologies of transport and communal city spaces; that which extends a presence into, and simultaneously out from, the home.[58] Mobile privatisation evokes viewers 'separate from yet coordinated with, in some remote sense, strangers doing the same thing in their little, shell-like worlds'.[59] The previous year, the BBC had broadcast the Coronation of Queen Elizabeth II, cementing television's 'increased visibility as a *national broadcasting* medium',[60] but also strengthening the BBC's role as a national broadcaster. The Queen herself had apparently 'thoroughly enjoyed' the BBC's teleplay of *Nineteen Eighty-Four* and Mark Guguid, writing for the British Film Institute, writes that '[t]his endorsement, and the publicity generated by its opponents, ensured that the programme attracted a massive audience – the largest since the Coronation – when transmitted a second time'.[61] Now the BBC is, of course, not Big Brother, even though licences are compulsory for owners of televisions. But on the issue of proximity, it is curious that it was forbidden to film the Queen in close-up,[62] while the glowering eyes of Big Brother that occupy the whole frame are a recurring visual motif in the teleplay. There is an irresistible irony between the illusory camaraderie endorsed by the Party and the 'nation-as-family' mentality television helped to foster in the 1950s, between representations and televised transmissions of pictures of national authority: 'If the Coronation proved that television had access to a mass national audience, *Nineteen Eighty-Four* demonstrated that television could also frighten and perhaps harm that audience. A new, less cosy, but more visually daring form of intimacy had been recognised.'[63]

Indeed, the forced intimacy of the telescreens is central to the teleplay's narrative and performance. It is only in the countryside, away from the telescreens and concealed microphones, that Winston (Peter Cushing) and Julia (Yvonne Mitchell) can first meet in private. The hidden telescreen in their love nest leads to their capture, but also reveals Winston's most intimate vulnerability – his dread of rats – which will ultimately break his spirit in Room 101. The authority of the telscreens effects a change from the novel's emphasis on thoughtcrime, where the verbal register and consciousness intersect, to facecrime, where facial expressions betray one's private mental world. This shift in emphasis from the verbal to the visual register is captured in excruciating close-ups of Winston's face, where a voice-over reveals that while his mind races, he must adopt a neutral expression. His countenance and those of the other characters come to assume the same blank malevolence of the telescreen, the default display of which is nothing more than luminous frosted glass. The telescreens even dictate the blocking of the characters within the *mise en scène*, so that when Winston talks to O'Brien (André Morrell), the latter suggests that they do so not face to face, but side-by-side, so as not to obscure one another from the telescreen's view, gazing offscreen at an implied monitor as they do so. The strength of this forced, denaturalised staging is that it mirrors the television audience's own perspectival relationship to the television, for they too assume a horizontal distribution in relation to a screen, blurring the line between voyeurism and observation.

To date there have been two analyses of the BBC's *Nineteen Eighty-Four*, Jason Jacobs's formal analysis of the teleplay and the technology used to broadcast it,[64] and Derek Johnston's broader examination of the gradual, though contested, Americanisation of Britain via television and other mass media, of which the BBC's adaptation is an example.[65] Clearly many of Williams's objections to Orwell relate strongly to his own views on class, mass culture and the 'masses'. I have already referred to Williams's aphorism, which suggested that the masses were less a political category than a projection of a particular mindset. He wrote in *Culture and Society* that this projection conferred on the masses 'gullibility, fickleness, herd-prejudice, lowness of taste and habit',[66] and he levelled a similar criticism at Orwell's proles: 'how does [he] see them? As a shouting, stupid crowd in the streets; drinking and gambling.'[67] But Williams's aversion to the term 'mass' has had a distinctive resonance. Tiziana Terranova notes that: 'The political category of the mass, or even that of the silent majority, is not very popular within media and cultural studies – which, from Raymond Williams onwards, has tended to identify it with a kind of conservative modernity, apopulist and thus implicitly anti-working class.'[68] For Williams, conceiving of people as masses precluded the interests of the working class, and it is this very preclusion he finds in Orwell's description of the proles. The proles are '"monstrous" and not yet "conscious"'[69] and the vague faith Orwell placed in the 'mighty loins' of the proles was, for Williams, an offensive, 'stale revolutionary romanticism'.[70] For Atwood, as we have seen, Orwell's Appendix, in its description of the failure of Newspeak, betrays more 'faith in the resilience of the human spirit' than critics like Jameson would care to acknowledge. Whether this faith in the human spirit extends to a faith in socialism is the more thorny point, and to conclude that it does not is clearly where Jameson and Williams fault the novel. But Nigel Kneale, who produced *Nineteen Eighty-Four* for the BBC, had a particularly polarised view of his audience, furthering Williams's sense that 'masses' is a divisive and potentially injurious concept:

> Viewers are already separating into two clear groups. The larger one is the happily habit-formed; demanding the Mixture as Before, the next series of quickies exactly like the last one. Then there are the others, the enquiring ones whose interest have actually been extended. The first group are the fodder, the second the only possible justification, of TV.[71]

Williams's *Television* is not futurology, but it often speculates as to the direction the medium might take. The generic narrative of versions of *Nineteen Eighty-Four* resolve many of these speculations, but in the ways Williams feared, mainly by depicting the telescreens as technologically deterministic causes, rather than engaged in a dialectic with the symptomatic effects of the social order.[72] Williams's basic, but powerful, insight is that television is, in its form, ideologically neutral. Competing theorisations of television, such as Marshall McLuhan's, took television as a cause, rather than, in Williams's view, 'at once an intention and an effect of a particular social order'.[73] Hence his faith that control over the modes of televised production might lead to the betterment of culture and society.[74] For Williams, McLuhan's was an 'ideological representation of technology as a cause', rather than a dialectical synthesis of cause and effect within the social order,[75] for there is always agency in Williams's conception, rather than McLuhan's technological determinism and privileging of form over content, crystallised in his 'the medium is the message' mantra. Setting aside McLuhan's immanent conservatism, his optimistic conception of the 'global village' is keenly rebutted by Williams: 'Most of the inhabitants of the "global village" would be saying nothing [...] while a few powerful corporations and governments [...] would speak in ways never before known to most of the peoples of the world.' Indeed, the direct analogy between a deterministic view of television and ruling ideology is the very logic that informs Newspeak in Orwell, but also the telescreens in the BBC's *Nineteen Eighty-Four*. The telescreen is, in fact, much closer to Williams's assessment of American broadcast television, a 'version of "public freedom"', that ironically 'came free and easy and accessible [...] planned [...] by a distant and invisible authority'.[76] But where Williams identified corporations, the BBC and Orwell had the Party.

Perhaps the most distinctive feature of the telescreen in *Nineteen Eighty-Four* is that it is a confusion of mobile privatised technology and mass communication. Williams considered these very different: to think of television as irrevocably 'mass communication' is to ignore the individualised point of reception.[77] Indeed, he notes that the only true 'mass' use of broadcast technology was in Nazi Germany, where public attention to broadcasts was either compulsory or inescapable.[78] Again, for Williams, 'community' and 'mass' are concepts and projections that aid commercial operators rather than counter-ideological independent programmers and networking authorities.[79] But the obvious point here is that the telescreen is both of these, simultaneously narrowcast to the point of the individual's receiver, yet 'mass' enough for the individual to be deprived of agency[80] – clearly not what Williams had in mind when he wrote in the final, more speculative, chapter, 'Alternative Technology, Alternative Uses?' that 'the most revolutionary technical developments are in the area of interactive television'.[81]

But it was precisely this elision of mass communication and private reception invoked by Williams's mobile privatisation that made the programme so powerful. Cartier said proudly:

> I could create suspense and fear amongst millions of people sitting at home and watching the terrifying image of Big Brother glaring at them. They were unable to find comfort and help [...] The essence of television [...] is that you can control the viewer's response to a much greater extent than other media permit.[82]

And:

> It was decidedly different in the TV viewer's own home, where cold eyes stared from the small screen straight at him, casting into the viewer's heart the same chill that the characters in the play experienced whenever they heard his voice coming from *their* 'watching' TV screens.[83]

Cartier is quite right. The production retains Newspeak, its horizon of 2050 and its aspiration to narrow the range of thought and vocabulary so that thoughtcrime itself will become impossible. But the most powerful moments of the broadcast occur when the distinction between the telescreen and the television is collapsed, turning the television set, a technology of mobile privatisation, into one of mass communication. At these moments, the telescreen occupies the entire frame, turning the television set into one of these sinister interfaces. The disembodied voice that issues commands and announcements thereby functions as a direct address to both the characters and the audience. The incessantly rotating light suggests less a consciousness behind the screen or belonging to the voice than a continuous, impersonal gathering and processing of information. This dialectic between the scope of a national broadcast and the private point of reception was also noted in the the way the broadcast was received. Editorials, commentators and politicians frequently referred to the teleplay as *coverage* rather than a *production*,[84] implying both the immediacy and accuracy of current-events reportage, as distinct from entertainment.

Pursuing the question of audience, we can place the production of the BBC's *Nineteen Eighty-Four* in the more specific context of BBC production history. It is difficult to speak of the BBC in other than general terms, since its history has been shaped not only by historical events, but also by the particular influence of its directors of programming. Nonetheless, it has been its longstanding mission 'to inform, educate and entertain'; 'to "improve" its listeners [and viewers] rather than provide the kinds of programmes that most of them wanted'.[85] Although both Orwell's novel and the teleplay were produced during the Cold War and considered as contemporary commentaries, the BBC production also bears the impress of preceding events and responses to class demands. Thus, although it first began conducting audience research in

1936, it was only during the Second World War that 'the BBC was forced [...] to learn a great deal about its audience'. Andrew Crisell notes that:

> Since the war effort depended so much on the workers in their factories, shipyards and mines, as well as upon thousands of ordinary servicemen and women, their tastes had to be discovered and catered for [...] [T]he populist tendency within the output became so strong that when the war ended it was irreversible.[86]

So, while the BBC was an independent corporation, even during war time, it was not immune to the democratic tendencies of populism.[87] Williams consistently championed the education of the working class, and *Television* demonstrates a faith in the educative and democratic potential of the medium. The BBC's demographic research in the early 1950s indicated that those with comparatively lower education were more likely to own a television, and while ownership of television sets was quite limited, research concluded that 'the typical viewer saw their television drama as escapism rather than food for thought'.[88] We can therefore make some observations about the reception of the BBC's *Nineteen Eighty-Four*.

An anonymous article published in *The Times* on 15 December 1954 offered three responses to the broadcast, tabled in the House of Commons:

1. The first was tabled by five Conservative MPs, and criticised 'the tendency, evident in recent British Broadcasting Corporation television programmes, notably on Sunday evenings, to pander to sexual and sadistic tastes';
2. the second was an addition to this motion, but was 'thankful that freedom of the individual still permits viewers to switch off and, due to the foresight of Her Majesty's Government, will soon permit a switch-over to be made to more appropriate programmes';
3. the third, tabled by five Labour MPs (with the support of one Conservative), criticised 'the tendency of honourable members to attack the courage and enterprise of the British Broadcasting Corporation in presenting plays and programmes capable of appreciation by adult minds'.[89]

These comments were made by political representatives, but they do seem to characterise accurately the mixed responses the teleplay received. Conservative members took exception to the more lewd aspects (and the claim that it pandered to public taste), and Labour members praised its sophistication. The broader public, at least those that voiced an opinion, were unamenable to its erudition. Indeed, many viewers took exception to it,[90] one viewer describing it as 'sadistically high-brow'.[91] It is hard not to draw a parallel between these responses and the Two Minutes Hate the Outer Party are forced to take part in. Here they hiss and screech Party slogans and hatred at telescreen footage of the socialist leader, Goldstein (Arnold Diamond), who informs them of their managed ignorance and enjoins them to revolution. Most detractors, like the Conservative members, objected to the broadcast's obscenity and deemed it 'unsuitable for a vast audience'.[92] One viewer allegedly died of a heart attack brought on by the torture scene,[93] while others telephoned in to register their complaints half an hour into the broadcast.[94] The irony, of course, is that in Orwell's novel the Party's Anti-Sex League is contrasted to the proles' consumption of Party-manufactured pornography. The 'obscenity' of the teleplay was in fact the illicit relationship between Winston and Julia. What is most depressing about this objection is that in Orwell's novel, sex is the genuinely subversive act Winston and Julia undertake, one of the few available to members of the Outer Party. As O'Brien explains to Winston, the 'sex instinct will be eradicated. Procreation will be an annual formality like the renewal of a ration card. We shall abolish the orgasm' (230). Unlike Winston, Julia is not interested in 'doublethink, the mutability of the past, and the denial of objective reality, and [...] Newspeak'; she is 'only a rebel from the waist downwards' (138). This is more or less the case here. Julia is content to confine the revolution to the bedroom, while Winston fantasises about a general uprising. Following Williams's critique of Orwell, the more urgent objection should of course be the managed liberation of the proles' libidos. As in the novel, the proles are captivated by the arcane novelty of pornography, which is, in fact, mass produced by the Outer Party's Pornosec division, ensuring the proles are both erotically stimulated and permanently distracted – what Herbert Marcuse famously called repressive desublimation.[95]

A second article appeared in *The Times* on 16 December. Unlike the above, it was not hostile in its interpretation, but it furthered the anti-socialist reception of the text. It approvingly identified in the broadcast a critique of communism and totalitarianism, praised the BBC's autonomy and the courage the teleplay displayed, and saw in the mixed reactions tabled in the House of Commons a vindication of television's capacity both to reach a large audience and to generate a range of public responses. While Williams was wary of the autonomy attributed to the BBC, since the government had an active role in appointing its authorities, he nevertheless praised television's ability to broaden public discussion.[96] 'Now and then', *The Times* article continues, 'there are events in world affairs and in the domestic news of other countries [...] which provide frightening echoes of ORWELL'S warning', and goes on to dismiss as foolish the assertion that the teleplay was 'too brutal and too painful for the masses'.[97]

Future Imperfect

Williams wrote that '[i]t is much more serious when what is offered as an arts programme gives currency to absurd confusions between a spectator and a voyeur'.[98] It would seem that this was one of the effects of the BBC adaptation of *Nineteen Eighty-Four*. When it was not condemned, it was praised as an anti-socialist commentary, and even its redemptive socialist features were decried as immoral: the proles did not attract any sympathy, while the torture and libidinal quasi-revolutionary activities of the Outer Party *qua* middle class were decried as sadistic and vulgar. The formal and aesthetic elision of the television and telescreen provoked outrage rather than contemplation, so that the overriding concern was the broadcast's appropriateness for the masses *qua* television owners. The royal endorsement and the controversy surrounding the first broadcast ensured a repeat performance, but one that, we can only conclude, reiterated and strengthened the overriding anti-socialist interpretation. Perhaps what is most crucial for us here is that the teleplay retained the framing device of the subjunctive future perfect tense, which Milner argues 'blunt[s] the force of dystopian inevitability'. But he also supposes that what 'we seek to avoid by negative example, will be the subjunctive future perfect'[99] *and not the example itself*, as many viewers clearly wanted to. Cartier's self-assessment suggests his production conformed to the most widely held interpretations of Orwell, while also taking aesthetic and technical advantage of the television and the more speculative nature of the telescreen. While the programme was exceedingly popular, particularly on second broadcast, public reception was overwhelming conservative and decried its high-mindedness. Williams's cautiously optimistic account of television led him to note that the variety of responses television invokes testifies to a wavering and potentially adversarial relationship between the interests of the public and the interests of the nation.[100] Try as we might to share Williams's optimism, or to rescue the BBC's production as Milner has done with Orwell, it is difficult not to see some truth in Max Horkheimer and Theodor Adorno's pessimism: 'The attitude of the public, which ostensibly and actually favours the system of the culture industry, is a part of the system and not an excuse for it.'[101]

Sean McQueen

Notes

1. Alan O'Connor (ed.), *Raymond Williams on Television: Selected Writings* (New York: Routledge, 1989), 119.
2. George Orwell, *Nineteen Eighty-Four* [1949] (Middlesex: Penguin, 1983).
3. While available elsewhere, Williams's essays on Orwell and *Nineteen Eighty-Four* are here taken from Andrew Milner's edited collected, *Tenses of Imagination: Raymond Williams on Science Fiction, Utopia and Dystopia* (Berlin: Peter Lang, 2010).
4. Andrew Milner, 'Archaeologies of the Future: Jameson's Utopia or Orwell's Dystopia?', *Historical Materialism* 17 (2009): 101–19.
5. Andrew Milner, *Locating Science Fiction* (Liverpool: Liverpool University Press, 2012).
6. Milner, *Locating Science Fiction*, 135.
7. Raymond Williams, *Television: Technology and Cultural Form* [1974] (London: Routledge, 2003).
8. Williams, 'George Orwell', in Milner, *Tenses of Imagination*, 41.
9. Williams, '*Nineteen Eighty-Four* in 1984', in Milner, *Tenses of Imagination*, 60.
10. Raymond Williams, *Culture and Society* (London: Penguin, 1963), 289.
11. Williams, '*Nineteen Eighty-Four*', 61.
12. Fredric Jameson, *Archaeologies of the Future: The Desire Called Utopia and Other Science Fictions* [2005] (London: Verso, 2007), 200 and xi.
13. A reading denied by Orwell himself: 'My recent novel is NOT intended as an attack on Socialism or on the British Labour Party (of which I am a supporter) but as a show up of the perversions to which a centralised economy is liable and which have already been partly realised in Communism and Fascism': *The Collected Essays, Journalism and Letters of George Orwell*, Vol. 4: *In Front of Your Nose, 1945–1950*, ed. Sonia Orwell and Ian Angus (Boston, MA: D.R. Godine, 2000), 564. Citing Orwell on this matter, Williams identified in Newspeak the political stance of the Labour government of the 1960s: Williams, '*Nineteen Eighty-Four*', 59.
14. Tom Moylan, *Scraps of the Untainted Sky: Science Fiction, Utopia, Dystopia* (Boulder, CO: Westview Press, 2000).
15. Jameson, *Archaeologies*, 198–9.
16. Orwell, *Nineteen Eighty-Four*, 256.
17. Orwell, *Nineteen Eighty-Four*, 268.
18. Margaret Atwood, 'Orwell and Me', *The Guardian*, 16 June 2003, http://www.guardian.co.uk/books/2003/jun/16/georgeorwell.artsfeatures (accessed 27 June 2014).
19. Milner, *Locating Science Fiction*, 122.
20. Orwell, *Nineteen Eighty-Four*, 9, emphasis added.
21. Milner, *Locating Science Fiction*, 126.
22. Orwell, *Nineteen Eighty-Four*, 257.
23. Stephen Ingle, *The Social and Political Thought of George Orwell: A Reassessment* (Hoboken, NJ: Taylor and Francis, 2006), 141.
24. Orwell, *Nineteen Eighty-Four*, 64.
25. Orwell, *Nineteen Eighty-Four*, 74.
26. John Newsinger, *Orwell's Politics* [1999] (Basingstoke: Palgrave Macmillan, 2001), 121.
27. Newsinger, *Orwell's Politics*, 121.
28. Jameson, *Archaeologies of the Future*, 201.
29. Arthur M. Eckstein, 'The Classical Heritage of Airstrip One', in *The Revised Orwell*, ed. Jonathan Rose (Michigan: Michigan University Press, 1991), 97–116.
30. Philip Bounds, *Orwell and Marxism: The Political and Cultural Thinking of George Orwell* (London: I.B.Tauris, 2009), 137.
31. Ingle, *The Social and Political Thought of George Orwell*, 143.

32 Ingle, *The Social and Political Thought of George Orwell*, 144.
33 Roger Fowler, *The Language of George Orwell* (New York: St Martin's Press, 1995), 211–25.
34 Eckstein, 'The Classical Heritage of Airstrip One', 101.
35 Eckstein, 'The Classical Heritage of Airstrip One', 102–3.
36 Milner, '*Archaeologies of the Future*', 117. Jameson considers this the more general nature of SF, to 'succeed by failure' by 'bring[ing] home, in local and determinate ways and with a fullness of concrete detail, our constitutional inability to imagine Utopia itself: and this is, not owing to any individual failure of imagination but as the result of the systemic, cultural and ideological closure of which we are in all one way or another prisoners' (289). The detached nature of the Appendix, while essential for Milner and Atwood, is, curiously, treated differently by Williams. On two occasions he wrote that its lack of attachment to the story was problematic and indicative of uncertainty on Orwell's behalf: '*Nineteen Eighty-Four*', 58; and '*Nineteen Eighty-Four* in 1984', 182.
37 This was the case too for Williams, who wrote of the Appendix: 'its central perception of the relation between linguistic and social forms is powerful'. '*Nineteen Eighty-Four*', 58.
38 Richard A. Posner, 'Orwell versus Huxley: Economics, Technology, Privacy, and Satire' in ed. Abbott Gleason, Jack Goldsmith and Martha C. Nussbaum, *On Nineteen Eighty-Four: Orwell and Our Future* (Princeton, NJ: Princeton University Press, 2005), 197.
39 Andrew Milner, *Literature, Culture and Society* [1996] (London: Routledge, 2005), 172.
40 James Perloff, '1984 Revisited', *The New American* 25, no. 9 (27 April 2009): 29.
41 Richard Grenier, 'Did the Heart of Orwell's "1984" Get Lost in the Movie?', *The New York Times*, 24 February 1985.
42 Perloff, '1984 Revisited', 29.
43 And by Thomas Pynchon in recent editions of the novel. Thomas Pynchon, 'Introduction' to George Orwell, *Nineteen Eighty Four* (London: Penguin, 2004).
44 The edition used here, for example, does not. The first edition, however, does.
45 Tony Shaw, *Hollywood's Cold War* (Edinburgh: Edinburgh University Press, 2007), 73.
46 Milner, '*Archaeologies of the Future*', 117.
47 Shaw, *Hollywood's Cold War*, 86
48 Williams, '*Nineteen Eighty-Four*', 197.
49 Newsinger, *Orwell's Politics*, 122.
50 Milner, *Literature, Culture and Society*, 174.
51 Erika Gottlieb, 'George Orwell: A Bibliographic Essay' in *The Cambridge Companion to George Orwell*, ed. John Rodden (Cambridge: Cambridge University Press, 2007): 195.
52 Shaw, *Hollywood's Cold War*, 87. Whilst the connection between American media networks and government agenda amidst the general paranoid miasma of McCarthyism substantiates this reading, 'there is no evidence of any collaboration between the [BBC] and government on *Nineteen Eighty-Four*' (86).
53 Milner, *Locating Science Fiction*, 126.
54 Milner, *Locating Science Fiction*, 135 (italics original).
55 Williams, '*Nineteen Eighty-Four*', 183
56 Bounds, *Orwell and Marxism*, 64 and 63.
57 Jason Jacobs, *The Intimate Screen: Early British Television Drama* (Oxford: Oxford University Press, 200), 90.
58 Williams, *Television*, 19, and Jim McGuigan, *Cool Capitalism* (London: Pluto Press, 2009), 120.
59 McGuigan, *Cool Capitalism*, 121.
60 Jacobs, *The Intimate Screen*, 22 (italics original).
61 Mark Duguid, 'Nineteen Eighty-Four (1954)', British Film Institute, Sceen Online, http://www.screenonline.org.uk/tv/id/438460/index.html (accessed 27 June 2014).

62 Jacobs, *The Intimate Screen*, 133.
63 Jacobs, *The Intimate Screen*, 155.
64 Jacobs, *The Intimate Screen*, 110–55.
65 Derek Johnston, 'Genre, Taste and the BBC: The Origins of British Television Science Fiction' (PhD diss., University of East Anglia, 2009), 126–44.
66 Williams, *Culture and Society*, 288.
67 Williams, '*Nineteen Eighty-Four*', 61.
68 Tiziana Terranova, *Network Culture: Politics for the Information Age* (London: Pluto, 2004), 135. Although the 'silent majority' is a common turn of phrase, it refers here to Jean Baudrillard's *In the Shadow of the Silent Majorities… Or The End of the Social and Other Essays*, trans. Paul Foss, Paul Patton and John Johnston (New York: Semiotext(e), 1983), a most literal appropriation of the term as there ever was.
69 Williams, 'George Orwell', 41.
70 Williams, '*Nineteen Eighty-Four*', 61.
71 Nigel Kneale, 'Not Quite So Intimate', *Sight and Sound* 28, no. 2 (1959): 88.
72 Williams's *Television* was published in the same year as one of the earliest attempts to bring the social relevance of the Orwellian dystopian model into relief with communications technologies, Hans Magnus Enzensberger's *The Consciousness Industry*, which essays a Marxist analysis of the media. Mass media are said to be 'making possible mass participation in a social and socialised productive process, the practical means of which are in the hands of the masses themselves', but production and distribution is controlled in such a way that television 'does not serve communication but prevents it. It allows no reciprocal action between transmitter and receiver […] [and] reduces feedback to the lowest point compatible with the system'. The Orwellian model is rejected as undialectical, obsolete and technically implausible, since 'blanket supervision would demand a monitor that was bigger than the system itself'. *The Consciousness Industry; On Literature, Politics and the Media* (New York: Seabury Press, 1974), 97–9.
73 Williams, *Television*, 132.
74 Williams, *Television*, 133 and 152. He writes that 'the extent of the repression but also of the consequent potential for liberation can be seen as remarkable' (46).
75 Williams, *Television*, 131–2.
76 Williams, *Television*, 136.
77 A more measured view than that of Horkheimer and Adorno in *Dialectic of Enlightenment* [1944], trans. John Cummings (London: Allen Lane, 1973).
78 Williams, *Television*, 17. Friedrich Kittler has also shown that production of print media, considered by Hitler and Goebbels to be a 'completely ineffective medium', remained relatively autonomous in Nazi Germany, whereas visual and aural media were entirely in the service of the state. Friedrich Kittler, *Optical Media: Berlin Lectures 1999* [2002], trans. Anthony Enns (Boston, MA: Polity, 2012), 214.
79 Williams, *Television*, 154–5.
80 Interestingly, Williams would later call mobile privatisation 'an ugly phrase for an unprecedented condition', *Towards 2000* [1983] (Harmondsworth: Penguin, 1985), 188 in McGuigan, *Cool Capitalism*, 120–21.
81 Williams, *Television*, 143.
82 *The Times*, 1 December 1958, 14.
83 Rudolph Cartier, 'A Foot in Both Camps', *Film and Filming* 4 (1958): 12, in Jacobs, *The Intimate Screen*, 138 (italics original).
84 Shaw, *Hollywood's Cold War*, 87, and Jacobs, *The Intimate Screen*, 154.
85 Andrew Crisell, *An Introductory History of British Broadcasting* (London: Routledge, 2002), 50.
86 Crisell, *An Introductory History of British Broadcasting*, 52–3 and 59.

87 Orwell himself was a BBC employee between August 1941 and November 1943, and while there is no shortage of speculation as to the influence this had on *Nineteen Eighty-Four*, '[i]t has to be recognised that while Orwell's period at the BBC provided much useful material, it would be inaccurate to infer a simple cause and effect relationship'. C. Fleay and M.L. Sandars, 'Looking into the Abyss: George Orwell and the BBC', *Journal of Contemporary History* 24, no. 3 (1989): 514.

88 Johnston, 'Genre, Taste and the BBC', 130, drawing on Robert Silvey, 'Viewers, Viewing and Leisure', *BBC Quarterly* 7, no. 1 (1952): 33.

89 *The Times*, 15 December 1954, 5. The irony here is that, as in Orwell, it is *The Times* itself that is subject to 'routine corrections' in light of its 'misreporting' of history.

90 Jacobs, *The Intimate Screen*, 156.

91 Johnston, 'Genre, Taste and the BBC', 129.

92 Jacobs, *The Intimate Screen*, 155–6.

93 Shaw, *Hollywood's Cold War*, 86.

94 *The Times*, 1 December 1958, 14.

95 Herbert Marcuse, *One-Dimensional Man: Studies in the Ideology of Advanced Industrial Society* [1964] (London: Routledge, 2007).

96 Williams, *Television*, 33 and 45.

97 *The Times*, 15 December 1954, 9.

98 Williams, *On Television*, 119.

99 Andrew Milner, 'Framing Catastrophe: the Problem of Ending in Dystopian Fiction', in Andrew Milner, Matthew Ryan and Robert Savage (eds), *Imagining the Future: Utopia and Dystopia* (North Carlton, Australia: Arena Publications, 2006), 336 and 353.

100 Williams, *Television*, 34.

101 Horkeimer and Adorno, *Dialectic of Enlightenment*, 122.

Sovereign Is He, Who Knocks: The Neoliberal State of Exception in American Television

Liane Tanguay

Abstract: The US 'war on terror' occasioned in the humanities a renewal of interest in the Schmittian concepts of sovereignty and the state of exception along with their biopolitical correlate, 'bare life'. Much of this scholarship focused initially on the suspension of civil liberties in the name of 'homeland security'; more recently, critiques have emerged identifying neoliberalism's biopolitical practices and those of the security state as both analogous and symbiotic. Yet little attention has been given to how the permanent exceptionality of neoliberalism generates a 'structure of feeling' discernible within contemporary cultural production. By way of example, this paper reads the popular television series *Breaking Bad* as the site of a cultural politics that both mediates and engages with this exceptionality.

*

Defining the 'State of Exception'

When Giorgio Agamben brought to contemporary Western philosophy the ancient Roman juridical category of *homo sacer*, a 'limit concept' of law that deems certain lives beyond legal status or protection through the logic of the sovereign ban,[1] none could have foreseen the global war that would make its rationality so extraordinarily visible. Many of the main biopolitical debates of the late twentieth century readily lent themselves to analysis in terms of the sovereign 'decision' on the state of exception, on the literal 'a*ban*donment' of certain individuals or populations to 'zones of indistinction' beyond the right of appeal. But the terrorist attacks of 9/11 and the emergency measures enacted in their wake made *Homo Sacer* and its sequel, *State of Exception*,[2] seem especially pertinent. Extraordinary rendition, indefinite detention, warrantless surveillance and 'enhanced interrogation' quickly became the 'new normal' for an America that saw itself confronted with an exceptional and existential threat, and the concepts of sovereignty, bare life and the state of exception quickly gained influence in humanistic discourse.

The 'culture industry', for its part, offered up a wealth of material that drew significant criticism for 'normalising' the practices of the new security state. The television series *24* (whose first season, importantly, was produced before the attacks) was the first of its kind to explicitly dramatise the extralegalities of the American war. Its famous ticking-time-bomb premise and corresponding breakneck pace nicely complemented the haste with which Congress passed the PATRIOT Act, authorised the invasion of Afghanistan and deemed the naval base at Guantánamo a permanent offshore detention camp for 'unlawful combatants', so deemed as to vitiate their status as rights-bearing citizens under international law. Most controversially, its depiction of torture as a viable and effective intelligence-gathering technique merged with and reinforced the official discourse of counterterrorism, making extralegal practices seem quite commonsensical[3] and any misgivings about suspending the law purely 'academic' matters to be addressed once the norm had been restored.

The Democrats were elected partly in the hope that they would do just this. Instead they further entrenched the exception *as* the norm, albeit favouring subtlety over spectacle. President Obama has replaced the 'War on Terror' with 'overseas contingency operations', adopted a 'disposition matrix' identifying persons to be dispatched without due process and shown a marked preference for extrajudicial drone strikes over the 'shock and awe' of invasion and occupation. As if in step with these developments, the slightly more nuanced series *Homeland* has succeeded *24* as counterterrorism drama *par excellence*, earning a reputation as '*24* for grownups'. Far from being dispelled under an apparently enlightened leader, the logic of the exception has become at once less visible and more pervasive.

To put it another way, scholars influenced by Agamben's insights will not soon run short of fresh material. However, while the policies of the post-9/11 security state quite clearly articulate the rationality of the 'state of exception', it is a mistake to identify the latter solely with the war itself, or indeed the US government as the locus of sovereignty, in isolation from the broader context of neoliberal capitalism. For representations of the 'war', whether as news or fiction, are themselves cultural mediations of a more fundamental state of exception that was already long becoming the rule – namely, that produced by neoliberalism as the 'latest' stage of late capitalism. Indeed if the historical uniqueness of our military state of exception is its indefiniteness – its refusal to point towards any return to the norm – this is surely less because of the existential nature of the terrorist threat than because neoliberalism presents itself as the 'end of history', self-perpetuating and permanent, with the security state a consequence of, and condition for, its rule. It is this broader understanding of the state of exception that the following analysis will foreground.

Liane Tanguay

Neoliberalism as Exception: The Biopolitics of Disposability

The structural linkages between neoliberalism and the military state of emergency have not gone unremarked. The staggering profits reaped through the wars in Afghanistan and Iraq, as well as the enduring corporate and geopolitical interest in control over the world's oil supply and the means of getting it to market, are well documented. But these represent only specific instantiations of a deeper symbiosis between what Sophia A. McClennen identifies as 'the hegemonic exercise of geopolitical power, the biopolitics of bare life and governmentality, and the free market doctrine of neoliberalism'. As McClennen points out, Agamben, though exposing the exception as constitutive of the modern state, 'misses an opportunity to elaborate on the force of capitalism' as the driver behind its normalisation, while Naomi Klein – correctly theorising neoliberalism's structural dependence on disaster and shock – 'misses the biopolitics of governmentality'. The critic's priority should be to 'put these theories into dialogue'[4] and illuminate the biopolitics of neoliberalism.

Henry Giroux and Zygmunt Bauman have led this endeavour, linking the neoliberal logic of what David Harvey calls 'accumulation by dispossession'[5] to the sovereign logic of the exception and its by-product, 'bare life'. For Giroux, neoliberalism implements a 'biopolitics of disposability' that is 'organized around the best way to remove or make invisible those individuals or groups who are either seen as a drain or stand in the way of market freedoms, free trade, consumerism, and the neoconservative dream of an American empire'; it thus '[denies] the sanctity of human life for those populations rendered "at risk" by global neoliberal economies'.[6] Bauman counts as bare life the 'unintended and unplanned "collateral casualties" of economic progress',[7] with '[t]he state [washing] its hands of the vulnerability and uncertainty arising from the logic [...] of the free market, now redefined as [...] a matter for individuals to deal and cope with by the resources in their private possession'.[8] Simon Springer sees neoliberalism as an 'ascendant form of sovereignty' that combines the '"roll-back" of certain state functions' with the '"roll out" of [...] an invasive social agenda centred on urban order, surveillance and policing'. The relocation of sovereignty in the market rather than the state enacts a 'ban' on 'those who fall outside neoliberal normativity',[9] excluding them (as 'valuable' life) from legal protection and reinscribing them (as 'bare' or 'disposable' life) in its relations of domination. Ultimately, then, the logics of the military/security state of exception and free market fundamentalism converge, a phenomenon starkly if unwittingly illustrated by texts that merge 'insurgents' abroad with the 'leftovers' of an increasingly rapacious capitalism at home. David Ayer's *End of Watch* (2012) is a case in point, a documentary-style cop drama that seamlessly transposes the gritty, embedded-reporting aesthetic of Iraqi urban warfare onto the lawless back alleys of South Central LA. The concept of what McClennen calls the neoliberal 'state of disaster exceptionalism' is thus a productive one for critical engagement with the new authoritarianisms to which neoliberalism gives rise.

Neoliberal Structure(s) of Feeling: A Task for Cultural Studies

As the above example suggests, popular culture is as valuable a site of public pedagogy[10] as ever, permitting engagement with both the ideological forces normalising the state of exception and their disabling tensions. Yet while cultural studies has engaged with both neoliberalism and the military state of exception as these respectively resonate through contemporary popular culture, less attention has been paid to the 'lived experience' of the state of exception *seen as intrinsic to* the neoliberal order. And attention to the 'structure(s) of feeling' this convergence generates is all the more critical given neoliberalism's 'official consciousness', which, in Wendy Brown's words, 'depicts free markets, free trade, and entrepreneurial rationality as achieved and normative' and 'casts the political and social spheres both as appropriately dominated by market concerns and […] organized by market rationality'.[11] For this ethos, as Lawrence Grossberg says, pits the free market 'against politics, or at least against a politics that attempts to govern society in social rather than economic terms'.[12] To discern the energies that would reassert the social, we must therefore look, as Raymond Williams did, beyond neoliberalism's 'formally held and systematic beliefs' to 'meanings and values as they are actively lived and felt, and the relations between these and formal or systematic belief'.[13] And the 'structure(s) of feeling' that neoliberalism generates should be approached with its particular biopolitics in mind.

For Grossberg, whose 'economy of affect' can be usefully integrated with Williams's 'structure of feeling',[14] affective 'investments', as he calls them, are more often vehicles of ideological reinforcement than potential empowerment.[15] A structure of feeling can certainly mediate the 'official consciousness' of an era, permitting a degree of consensus between the 'abstract of a dominant group'[16] and 'social consciousness', or what is 'lived, actively, in real relationships'.[17] Thus elsewhere, using Jameson's and Harvey's observations on the temporal and spatial dimensions of 'late' capitalism or 'flexible accumulation', I identified the 'feelings' associated with increasing fragmentation, ephemerality and insecurity as particularly conducive to the politics of fear that underwrote the imperial venture and resonated through the popular culture of the time (including, of course, *24*).[18] Yet, seen as a 'set of internal relations, at once interlocking and in tension',[19] the structure of feeling also suggests a certain dynamism or potentiality within the affective realm of social consciousness, a refusal to be semantically 'fixed'. For as a precondition for the meaningful articulation of 'received thought', the structure of feeling also necessarily exceeds it, encompassing its 'omissions and consequences as lived',[20] and it is precisely this excess that can be mined for the potentially counter-hegemonic tensions it poses between the abstract and the affective. From such tensions then arises the possibility of discerning 'not only a consciousness of history but a consciousness of alternatives and then [...] a consciousness of aspirations and possibilities',[21] or what we might call the 'still-Utopian' in an era that has been stripped of precisely such drives.

What makes the 'structure of feeling' so fruitful – its resistance to systematic interpretation – also makes it difficult to work with: in Williams's own words, structures of feeling are 'social experiences *in solution*, as distinct from other social semantic formations which have been *precipitated* and are more evidently and more immediately available'.[22] Mitchum Huehls aptly summarises the problem: 'if you can identify a nexus of social relations and experiences as a structure of feeling, you are either observing a historical configuration that has lost its indeterminate dynamism, or your observation will be imprecise and provisional because structures of feeling actually precede articulation'.[23] However, by focusing on those affective 'tensions' that energise the structure of feeling, it should be possible to draw certain inferences without sacrificing the idea of its dynamism. I will therefore opt for 'imprecise and provisional' in positing a structure of feeling in American television that invokes, through its tensions, the 'truth' of neoliberalism as the most pervasive, antisocial and lawless form of Western capitalism to date.

The Neoliberal Exception in American Television

Beginning with *The Sopranos* in 1999, a range of 'exceptional states' on American television have depicted life at the 'limit concept' of the law, at thresholds of indeterminacy between order and disorder, culture and nature, 'valuable' and 'bare' life. *Breaking Bad*, *Boardwalk Empire* and *Sons of Anarchy* join *The Sopranos* in the category of organised crime, of worlds embedded in our own that operate outside of, but in relation to, the law. The Western frontier sees new treatment in *Deadwood* and *Hell on Wheels*, which depict life in an 'exceptional' space traditionally associated with lawlessness while foregrounding the logic of free enterprise and its ambivalent relation to state sovereignty (as well as the exercise of market sovereignty within that space).[24] The recourse to extralegality becomes a routine feature of law enforcement dramas, with

The Wire confronting head-on the failures of neoliberal governance, *Justified* extolling the 'rogue' US marshal in a present-day midwest (not a new trope, to be sure), and *Dexter* presenting a serial killer who works for the police but channels his pathology into the sovereign exercise of 'justice' where the 'law' has failed. There are parallel worlds like the puzzling time-warp of *Lost*, and post-apocalyptic worlds depicting human societies in the ultimate state of exception – that of no legal order at all (*Jericho, Revolution, The Walking Dead*). The series vary widely in quality, and there is equal variation in the extent to which they either reinforce or challenge prevailing ideologies. However, while some are clearly more conservative, or pacifying, than others, it is counterproductive to deem any of them categorically supportive of or resistant to the neoliberal ethos – precisely because the structure of feeling they manifest remains 'in solution' and is always potentially both a vehicle for, and a site of resistance to, the 'abstract of [the] dominant group'. My contention is instead that our affective investments in these various analogues of the 'state of exception' speak to the 'truth' of the neoliberal ethos pressed to its direst extremes: namely, its exceptional biopolitics of disposability, completing capitalism's redefinition of citizens on the axis of exchange-value and precipitating an '*aban*donment' from which only society's very wealthiest would seem fully protected. These dramas 'mirror' the permanent neoliberal state of exception, and its dominant ideology – of an unfettered 'free market' set to 'free' us all from poverty through growth, and from terror through territorial expansion – is confronted with the 'feeling' that the state has lost control; that sovereignty resides with inscrutable powers that violate the law and the public interest with impunity; that such powers command a space of exception in which the only rule is that there are none; and that the sovereign decision demarcating 'valuable' from 'disposable' life is imminent and implicates us all. They thus present a zone of engagement with the anxieties and fantasies of a democracy under seemingly permanent siege and lacking the vocabulary for a genuine alternative.

Breaking Bad: A Case Study

This paper will focus, as part of a larger undertaking, on *Breaking Bad*,[25] the story of teacher-turned-methamphetamine-kingpin Walter White, with attention to how, in 'mirroring' the neoliberal order, it both engages its enabling fantasies and exposes its disabling truth. Indeed 'mirroring', or more specifically 'chirality', is the subject of one of Walter's lectures early in the series (1.2), describing a property of certain chemical compounds that form non-superimposable mirror images of one another and that, while identical, can have very different effects. The lecture is clearly a deliberate metaphor for the duelling personalities of Walter and 'Heisenberg' (his drug-kingpin pseudonym), but 'chirality' provides a useful figure for the show's more general mirroring function, its increasingly nightmarish displacement of the neoliberal state of exception.

Affectively, we are invested at the outset in Walter's all-too-common plight – a catastrophic illness that will bankrupt him and leave his family permanently on the losing side of neoliberalism's zero-sum game. Indeed he is already effectively on that side, working at a car wash to supplement a paltry teaching income, and having sold for a pittance his share in a now multibillion dollar company founded on his doctoral research. A politically 'liberal' American audience will quickly recognise the implied critique of American health care and education, but this is only the beginning of what becomes a far more substantial and at least potentially oppositional vision of neoliberalism more broadly. For, faced with these exceptional circumstances, Walter 'decides' on an exceptional and quintessentially neoliberal response – in Bauman's words, an 'individual [solution] to socially created problems', implemented 'using individual skills and resources'[26] where the social state has failed. It is precisely through personal ingenuity, innovation and entrepreneurialism – the ostensible prerequisites for success in the neoliberal order, and by its legitimating tenets equally available to all – that Walter, initially 'disposable' by the logic of that order, asserts himself against it.

The assertion undoubtedly pays off. Walter escapes 'disposability' by becoming the sovereign Heisenberg, presiding over a global drug trade that sees his signature product expanding into European markets. The evolution of the cooking and protective gear (from a run-down RV with stolen high-school lab equipment to a multimillion dollar underground superlab, to a more 'deterritorialised' operation migrating state-of-the-art equipment from site to site) serves as a visual register of his ascent. The superlab with which erstwhile sovereign Gus Fring presents Walter in 3.5 is thus the organised-crime analogue of what Walter lost by selling his share in his company; the sheer visual appeal of the high-tech equipment overrides, like the news networks' showcasing of cutting-edge military technology in wartime, any 'moral' misgivings about its use, thus endorsing (along with the ever-growing piles of cash) the neoliberal fantasy of success and riches attained through individual resources and skill. In other words, where the 'legitimate' business world has effectively robbed him, its illegitimate 'mirror-image' will compensate him handsomely.

This 'mirroring' is critical to the series' economy of affect, at once investing us in the ideology of the 'neoliberal solution' and setting in motion the energies that resist it. Its ideological function is not especially new. As Jameson says of the *Godfather* films,

> [w]hen indeed we reflect on an organized conspiracy against the public, one which reaches into every corner of our daily lives and our political structure to exercise a wanton ecocidal and genocidal violence at the behest of distant decision-makers, and in the name of an abstract concept of profit – surely it is not about the Mafia, but rather about American business itself that we are thinking, American capitalism in its most systematized and computerized, dehumanized, 'multinational' and corporate form.[27]

The insight requires updating to apply to how *Breaking Bad* mirrors a more specifically neoliberal capitalism, with its emphasis on financialisation and deregulation, its structural dependence on risk ('casino capitalism'), and its creation of a permanent underclass of 'disposable' humanity, but the basic premise holds. The drug trade of *Breaking Bad* is the mirror image of 'legitimate' business in the neoliberal world order, a highly visible analogue of the less 'mappable' neoliberal state of exception. But the show's revelation of the 'chiral' centre that conceptually joins the two worlds invokes an affective tension that it does not subsequently resolve. Instead, it is through this particular looking-glass that our affective investment in Walter's neoliberal solution becomes conflicted, revealing those 'internal relations, at once interlocking and in tension' that make up the series' structure of feeling.

David Simon's *The Wire* has already shown how the drug business mirrors 'legitimate' business in its power relations, including its CEO-to-lowest-wage-earner ratios – a structural inequality quickly grasped by Walter's beleaguered partner in crime, Jesse Pinkman. Challenged by Walter – 'You're now a millionaire and you're complaining? What world do you live in?' – Jesse replies, 'One where the dudes who are doing all the work ain't the ones getting fisted' (3.9) – a fantasy world, in short, given the increasing poverty and precarity among America's working poor (Walter and Jesse are not quite in this class, but street-level dealers are a readily disposable stand-in for Walmart's 'associates'). Somewhat more troubling is the show's depiction of the permanent underclass that both neoliberalism and the drug trade produce, reproduce and in different ways depend upon: the 'consuming' end of the business, as it were, depicted in several instances as a sprawling mass of poverty, addiction, and disease, of effectively 'disposable' humanity visually reminiscent of the infected in *The Walking Dead*. Like the 'walkers', the end-users are depicted as gaunt, unwashed, covered in sores, mental faculties effectively hijacked by a single, insatiable need; they have suffered a social death, an 'abandonment', and can be 'managed' only by containment or extermination, though as a class they will never be eliminated. (This is of course an extreme – the show ignores a large class of 'functional' users forced to work multiple low-wage jobs often while raising children;[28] yet in both instances it is the structural inequality perpetuated by neoliberalism that ensures there will always be a consumer base for the fictional Heisenberg's product.)

The chirality metaphor also applies to the interaction between legitimate and illegitimate business. While money-laundering fronts feature in many depictions of organised crime, *Breaking Bad* 'maps' out some decidedly more sinister interconnections, tapping into the paranoid/conspiracist anxieties of 'late' capitalism[29] by implicating a German-based multinational in the action. Madrigal Electromotive is the parent company of the fried chicken chain that Gus Fring, the face of sovereignty through seasons 3 and 4, initially set up in Mexico as a front; it produces or sources from global markets the equipment and chemicals for the superlab and owns the industrial laundry under which it is located, and one of its American executives introduces Heisenberg's product to European markets in the final season (5.8). The enterprise thus appears as almost incomprehensibly vast, networked and deterritorialised, much like the other multinationals that invisibly determine our fate – and, incidentally though not inapplicably, much like the RAND Corporation has portrayed Al-Qaeda, with Bin Laden as a 'CEO' applying 'business administration and modern management techniques [...] to the running of a transnational terrorist organization'.[30] The sense that Walter has 'arrived' when he sees the gleaming superlab is therefore undercut by the dread that such ethereal visions provoke, the implicit terror of unmappability that for Jameson infuses the affective experience of postmodernity. Indeed there is a spectral, quasi-omniscient quality about Fring as CEO that feeds directly into this sense of otherworldliness and terror. Hiding in plain sight, he passes effortlessly between the realms of organised crime, legitimate business and law enforcement, maintaining the same impassive, inscrutable demeanour in each. His power to decide on life and death and his almost supernatural ability to anticipate threats against him loom menacingly over the action through season 4, heightening our anxiety and realigning our affective investment with Walter despite any lingering 'moral' objections to the latter's transgressions thus far. Fring makes a compelling stand-in for the shadowy and obscenely powerful 1 per cent, everywhere and nowhere, occupying the sovereign position of exclusive-inclusion at the threshold of indeterminacy that constitutes the exception. Even upon his death he steps calmly into the hallway and adjusts his tie before the camera reveals the missing side of his head (4.13), a sequence that, while admittedly implausible and cartoon-like, reinforces the 'spectral' impression and with it a sense of the omnipotence and ineradicability of the sovereign free market.

Through this 'mirroring', *Breaking Bad* reveals how the logic of the individual, neoliberal solution both arises from and reproduces neoliberalism's attack on the social as such. Indeed what propels the narrative, progressively complicating our affective investments, is the fact that Walter's initial exception, meant to be finite, becomes, like America's military exception, self-perpetuating; there is no 'arrival', there is never 'enough' and there is thus no return to the 'norm'. Instead the vast enterprise in which Walter becomes entangled comes to pose an existential threat, thereby escalating the original emergency and imposing increasing demands on his (and the viewer's) moral code. Such a code is thus revealed as a deracinated legacy of an era in which the social contract still held meaning, and as insufficiently robust to withstand the biopolitical pressures of the neoliberal order, particularly when one's family is at stake. Indeed the extent to which 'family' serves as Walter's tireless justification for his increasingly monstrous transgressions shows the process by which a Darwinist and patriarchal ethos rushes in to fill the void of the suspended social contract and makes the recourse to the exception the only choice.

Ultimately, however, it is not family but sovereignty that is revealed as the real stakes in this neoliberal adaptation of the traditional rags-to-riches story that perished alongside the American dream. In 3.10, Walter explicitly locates his point of no return as the night he makes an unambiguously sovereign decision, namely, the decision to stand by while Jesse's girlfriend asphyxiates in a heroin overdose (2.12); while 'Walter' instinctively rushes to intervene, 'Heisenberg' stops short and makes the calculated decision that she is disposable in light of the exceptional circumstances he is always trying to keep tilted in his favour. It is as 'Walter' that he expresses a wish to have 'stayed home that night', even to have 'lived up to [the] moment' before leaving home and no longer (3.10). Yet it is fully as the sovereign Heisenberg that he later takes credit for the shooting death (by proxy) of unwitting rival chemist Gale Boetticher. (For context, there are two visitors to Boetticher's apartment in 3.13, both announced by a knock: the first is Fring, as sovereign, come to decide upon the timing of Walter's death; the second is Jesse, who, at Walter's behest, shoots Boetticher in the face.) Confronted by his wife, Walter/Heisenberg responds:

> Who are you talking to right now? Who is it you think you see? [...] Do you know what would happen if I stopped going to work? A business big enough that it could be listed on the NASDAQ would go belly up [...] You clearly don't know who you're talking to. I am not *in* danger, Skyler. I *am* the danger. A guy opens his door and gets shot and you think that of me? No. I am the one who knocks. (4.6)

In other words, to adapt Carl Schmitt's famous opening line to the present context, sovereign is he, who knocks; and Heisenberg's ascent will see him topple Fring and preside over many more deaths in the name of protecting his 'empire' and maximising his profits. His power, as sovereign, to 'decide' on the exception, to deem lives worthless and mete out death, is captured neatly in the title of the episode 'Gliding Over All' (5.8), which sees ten prisoners savagely murdered in a two-minute period, at his bidding. In keeping with the parallels already shown between the drug business and 'legitimate' neoliberal enterprise, the 'chiral' centre conceptually linking the two worlds can thus be seen to reside in the structure of exception, in the violence – physical, structural and symbolic – of the sovereign decision demarcating disposable from valuable life.

This neoliberal version of rags-to-riches that lays waste to everything in its path thus plays on an uncodified tension between the tenets (and fantasies) of neoliberalism and the 'truth' of its exceptionality. Walter's exceptional circumstances secure viewer sympathy as he implements the perfect neoliberal solution, in the form of free enterprise based on skill, ingenuity and a Darwinian ability to outwit and outlast the competition. But his transformation from Walter of 1.2, for whom the prospect of taking a single human life poses an insurmountable dilemma, to Heisenberg, whose increasingly cold, manipulative and self-serving logic leads him to unthinkably more cruel extremes, is the very condition for the success of that solution – for his rise from impoverished, apron-clad meth cook to a multimillionaire who describes himself as being neither in the meth nor the money business but the 'empire business' (5.6). There is undoubtedly more to be considered in discerning those elements 'at once interlocking and in tension' that make up the series' structure of feeling – a feminist reading, for instance, would identify certain other affective priorities, and I have not touched upon the show's aesthetics, or its rendering visible the productive forces that neoliberal capitalism tends to eclipse. But I do maintain that the show exposes, through 'chirality', the structural violence of the neoliberal exception, its ruthless, implacable logic and its biopolitics of disposability. It exposes that to take the side of the 'free market' system is also to accept and excuse that system's intrinsic brutality, its infliction of a violence that is not merely an occasional or exceptional necessity but a constitutive one. In exposing this compromise, our complicity with this system, it complicates our renunciation of the protagonist's extremes on merely 'moral' grounds. It does not offer a Utopian alternative: its sweeping desert vistas, though offering a certain freedom (e.g., to cook meth), suggest more the disorientation, vulnerability and exposure of the state of exception than the 'consciousness of aspirations and possibilities' evoked by the open landscapes in Williams's reading of the Welsh industrial novel.[31] But its structure of feeling, though by no means unequivocally negative and critical, does suggest an overall negative stance towards neoliberal rationality.

Such critical impulses are always subject to re-containment, much as the periodic uprisings against neoliberalism provoke a policing response from the state. Jameson identifies at work in mass culture a 'psychic horse-trading' or a trade-off between the arousal of such energies and the imposition of 'symbolic containment structures which defuse'[32] them. The 'containing' function of the Mafia narrative, for him, is its implication that 'the deterioration of daily life in the United States today is an ethical rather than an economic matter', its substitution of 'the vision of what is seen to be a criminal aberration from the norm rather than the norm itself'; Mafia movies thus 'project a "solution" to social contradictions – incorruptibility, honesty, crime fighting, and finally law-and-order itself – which is evidently a very different proposition from that diagnosis of the American misery whose prescription would be social revolution'.[33] Expressed in terms of the structure of feeling, this is equivalent to the smoothing out of the tensions evoked by the disarticulation of lived experience from the 'dominant abstract' or legitimating narratives of capitalism.

This applies to some extent in *Breaking Bad*. Complementing our uneasy investment with Walter is a much more palatable one, namely with his unlikely moral counterbalance Jesse Pinkman. Though certainly 'no Boy Scout' (4.13), Jesse secures viewer sympathy and acts as a voice of conscience. His aversion to killing and intolerance of harm to children makes him easier to identify with than Walter, who poisons a child (4.12) and is insufficiently moved by the shooting death of another (5.5). Yet as a dropout and drug addict he also occupies an ambiguous position that in 'real life' is typically at the margins of mainstream culture, including surely for a large component of the viewership. More importantly, this 'moral centre' is shown to take multiple beatings over the course of the show, and though he scores a minor symbolic victory over Walter in the finale, his own happy ending is anything but guaranteed. So the extent to which morality is co-opted, manipulated, used and bruised in the neoliberal 'success story' takes precedence over any more pacifying alternative that would see morality triumph unconditionally and thus 'contain' the tensions aroused by our investment with Walter.

It is equally hard to argue that 'law-and-order' serves a containing function. Saul Goodman, the archetypically sleazy lawyer who consistently gets his clients off on technicalities, seems to embody the neoliberal notion of 'legalisms' as 'bothersome mosquitoes flying around the execution of foreign and domestic policy' and thus neoliberalism's 'desacralization'[34] of the law; he occupies at best an ambiguous place, both profiting from the drug business and safeguarding, albeit mainly out of self-interest, the civil liberties enshrined in the Constitution. Walter's DEA brother-in-law Hank Schrader, who tenaciously 'maps out' the multinational network around Heisenberg's blue meth, does draw a fair share of affective investment, partly as a likeable character but also along a decidedly more conventional, even conservative narrative trajectory: namely, that of the law enforcement officer whose instincts are accurate but whose efforts are hindered by 'the bureaucracy' and 'the law' itself (often in the person of Goodman). Hank must consequently go 'rogue' and open up his own little space of exception to catch the villain – a familiar trope, at home with libertarianism and American exceptionalism alike, and easily adapted to the neoliberal ethos with its contempt for bureaucratic restraint on individual enterprise (this was the appeal of *24*'s Jack Bauer). But Hank also abuses our 'moral centre', Jesse, every bit as callously as Walter does. He savagely beats him (3.7) and is later more than willing to risk Jesse's life to get to Walter, using him, in other words, as a disposable means to an end (5.12). His co-optation of Jesse to help him get Walter (5.12) 'chirally' mirrors Walter's own co-optation of Jesse to help him get Fring (4.12): both take place in Walter's house, both involve inflamed tempers and a loaded gun, in both cases it is the child's poisoning that brings Jesse to the house in a rage (the first time on suspicion, the second on certainty), and both situations are defused in the same way, with an offer to collaborate in toppling a common enemy. So 'law-and-order' contains a lot less than it mirrors; and our 'easy' identification with a familiar trope and an affable character is therefore sharply undermined. Finally, lest we forget, the very reason the drug trade operates as viciously and violently as it does is a four-decades-old military and policing catastrophe known as the 'War on Drugs'; the law-and-order solution – increased militarisation and security, the main function of the post-welfare neoliberal state, feeds directly back into the problem, along with the increasing inequality generated by the same order.

Conclusion

There is no easy way out of the discomfort *Breaking Bad* presents in its mirroring of the neoliberal state of exception, and it does not re-contain that experience with easy symbolic or narrative resolutions. Walter does, arguably, triumph – evading capture, ensuring his wealth will be passed on to his family, scoring a titillating (and bloodless) victory over the obscenely wealthy proprietors of his former business, massacring the unsavoury neo-Nazis who took over his empire, saving Jesse and fighting off his cancer until all these loose ends are tied up. But he also leaves a trail of devastation behind him and loses the love of his family, admitting finally that 'I did it for me' (5.16) – acknowledging, if unwittingly, the inescapably antisocial nature of the neoliberal solution.

The manifestation of affective tensions in a television show, of course, falls short of what Benjamin saw as necessary to bring about the 'real state of emergency',[35] or a revolutionary upheaval against the constructed emergency of the ruling order. *Breaking Bad* is after all a commodity, and every bit as 'addictive' as its protagonist's blue meth. The ultimate containment is in the relative discreteness of the commodity-form itself, as would then be the case with all of the series that engage with states of exception: in our 'real' world, the neoliberal state of exception becomes the norm, while in the series, it is contained *as* exception; that is, the structural, physical and symbolic violence that constitutes our 'real-world' norm is refracted back to us as an aberration. To this extent Jameson is right, and such series, regardless of their creators' political inclinations, may finally serve a normalising function that makes our real state of exception seem more like 'business as usual'. What remains for the cultural critic, and for left politics in general, then, is to work continually to expose the violence and dispossession intrinsic to business as usual in the neoliberal order, to 'make power visible' within the circuitry of cultural production and take seriously the latter's role as a form of what Williams called 'permanent education'.[36] A text like *Breaking Bad*, giving visual and narrative form to the unspoken biopolitical commitments of neoliberalism, and tapping into reserves of affect that, despite its hyper-individualising tendencies, remain profoundly social, is a productive starting point.

Notes

1. Giorgio Agamben, *Homo Sacer: Sovereign Power and Bare Life*, trans. Daniel Heller-Roazen (Stanford, CA: Stanford University Press, 1998).
2. Giorgio Agamben, *State of Exception*, trans. Kevin Attell (Chicago, IL: University of Chicago Press, 2005).
3. Elspeth Van Veeren, 'Interrogating *24*: Making Sense of U.S. Counter-terrorism in the Global War on Terrorism', *New Political Science* 31, no. 3 (2009): 361.
4. Sophia A. McClennen, 'Neoliberalism as Terrorism: or State of Disaster Exceptionalism', in *Terror, Theory and the Humanities*, ed. Jeffrey R. DiLeo and Uppinder Mehan (Open Humanities Press, 2012), http://quod.lib.umich.edu/o/ohp/10815548.0001.001/1:4.3/--terror-theory-and-the-humanities?rgn=div2;view=fulltext (accessed 19 December 2013).
5. David Harvey, *The New Imperialism* (Oxford: Oxford University Press, 2003).
6. Henry A. Giroux, 'Reading Hurricane Katrina: Race, Class, and the Biopolitics of Disposability', *College Literature* 33, no. 3 (2006): 175–8.
7. Zygmunt Bauman, *Wasted Lives: Modernity and its Outcasts* (Cambridge: Polity Press, 2004), 39.
8. Bauman, *Wasted Lives*, 51.
9. Simon Springer, 'Neoliberalising Violence: Of the Exceptional and the Exemplary in Coalescing Moments', *Area* 44, no. 2 (2012): 137–41.
10. Henry Giroux, 'Resisting Market Fundamentalism and the New Authoritarianism: A New Task for Cultural Studies?', *JAC* 25, no. 1 (2005): 15.
11. Wendy Brown, 'American Nightmare: Neoliberalism, Neoconservatism, and De-Democratization', *Political Theory* 34, no. 6 (2006): 694.
12. Lawrence Grossberg, *Caught in the Crossfire: Kids, Politics, and America's Future* (Boulder: Paradigm Publishers, 2005), 117, cited in Giroux, 'Reading Hurricane Katrina', 183.
13. Raymond Williams, *Marxism and Literature* (Oxford: Oxford University Press, 1977), 132.

14. See Jennifer Harding and E. Deidre Pribram, 'Losing Our Cool? Following Williams and Grossberg on Emotions', *Cultural Studies* 18, no. 6 (2004): 863–83.
15. Lawrence Grossberg, 'Postmodernity and Affect: All Dressed Up with No Place to Go', *Communication* 10, nos 3–4 (1988): 285, cited in Harding and Pribram, 'Losing Our Cool?', 873.
16. Raymond Williams, *The Long Revolution* (Peterborough: Broadview, 2001), 78.
17. Williams, *Marxism*, 130–31.
18. Liane Tanguay, *Hijacking History: American Culture and the War on Terror* (McGill-Queen's Univeristy Press, 2012).
19. Williams, *Marxism and Literature*, 132.
20. Williams, *The Long Revolution*, 80.
21. Williams, *Problems in Materialism and Culture* (London: Verso, 1980), 223, cited in Josh Dickins, 'Unarticulated Pre-emergence: Raymond Williams' "Structures of Feeling"', *Constellations* (2011), http://www2.warwick.ac.uk/fac/arts/english/constellations/structures_of_feeling (accessed 19 December 2013): 1.
22. Williams, *Marxism and Literature*, 133–4.
23. Mitchum Huehls, 'Structures of Feeling: Or, How to Do Things (Or Not) With Books', *Contemporary Literature* 51, no. 2 (2010): 420
24. See Erik Altenbernd and Alex Trimble Young, 'A Terrible Beauty: Settler Sovereignty and the State of Exception in Home Box Office's *Deadwood*', *Settler Colonial Studies* 3, no. 1 (2013): 27–48, and Daniel Worden, 'Neo-liberalism and the Western: HBO's *Deadwood* as National Allegory', *Canadian Review of American Studies* 39, no. 2 (2009): 221–46.
25. *Breaking Bad* (DVD), Sony Pictures Home Entertainment (2013).
26. Zygmunt Bauman, *The Art of Life* (London: Polity, 2008), 88, cited in Henry Giroux, 'Neoliberalism and the Death of the Social State: Remembering Walter Benjamin's Angel of History', *Social Identities* 17, no. 4 (2011): 589.
27. Fredric Jameson, 'Reification and Utopia in Mass Culture', *Social Text* 1 (1979): 146.
28. See also Dylan Matthews, 'Here's What *Breaking Bad* Gets Right, and Wrong, about the Meth Business', *Washington Post* (15 August 2013), http://www.washingtonpost.com/blogs/wonkblog/wp/2013/08/15/heres-what-breaking-bad-gets-right-and-wrong-about-the-meth-business/ (accessed 19 December 2013).
29. See Fredric Jameson, 'Cognitive Mapping', in *Marxism and the Interpretation of Culture*, ed. Cary Nelson and Lawrence Grossberg (Champaign, IL: University of Illinois Press, 1988), 347–57.
30. Bruce Hoffman, *Lessons of 9/11* (Santa Monica, CA: RAND Corporation, 2002), 13. In Jan Nederveen Pieterse, 'Neoliberal Empire', *Theory, Culture & Society* 21, no. 3 (2004): 126.
31. Dickins, 'Unarticulated Pre-emergence', 1.
32. Jameson, 'Reification and Utopia in Mass Culture', 141.
33. Jameson, 'Reification and Utopia in Mass Culture', 146.
34. Brown, 'American Nightmare', 694–5.
35. Walter Benjamin, 'Theses on the Philosophy of History', *Illuminations*, ed. Hannah Arendt, trans. Harry Zohn (New York: Schocken Books, 2007), 257.
36. Giroux, 'Resisting Market Fundamentalism', 14–15.

Cultural Immaterialism:
Wallace Stevens in Virtual Paris

Tony Sharpe

Abstract: This essay explores the paradox in Wallace Stevens's life and career that, notwithstanding his interest in France and especially Paris, he stood out from nearly all other American Modernist writers by the fact that he never visited Europe, even though, more than some who did, he endorsed the significance of what the French capital could offer. The essay suggests that the Paris Stevens denied himself strangely became the 'Paris' he achieved, and that his identification with the city was one that by its own logic not only did not require him to pay a visit, but in time rendered it essential that he should not do so; this uncovers something central to Stevens's poetry, and also to his Americanness. A quotation from 'Tea at the Palaz of Hoon' ('And there I found myself more truly and more strange') offers terms helpful in discussing his attachment to 'virtual Paris': where and what 'there' is, and how the strangeness of being 'there' is connected with its truthfulness, for the 'I' engaged in finding itself.

*

> And there I found myself more truly and more strange
> ('Tea at the Palaz of Hoon')[1]

Close to the Seine and not far from the Grand Palais constructed for the 1900 Great Exposition, there is an equestrian statue of Lafayette by the American sculptor Paul Wayland Bartlett (1865–1925). Its full-size plaster precursor had first been exhibited at the Exposition, and the duly-completed bronze, its inscription saluting Lafayette as 'patriot of two republics', was given to France in 1908 by the 'schoolchildren of America', organised to that end by the Daughters of the American Revolution. By gratifying coincidence, in 1932 a bronze copy was erected in Hartford, Connecticut: the city in which Wallace Stevens had lived since 1916, where he wrote most of his poetry and where he headed the Surety Claims department of the Hartford Accident and Indemnity Company (rising to Vice-President in 1934). The issue of dual allegiance has often been raised in discussions of Stevens, referring to his careers as poet and as legal executive; but just as those apparently separate spheres can finally be seen to have exerted complementary rather than antagonistic influences, so a parallel occurs with the development of his attachments to the two republics of America and France.

Tony Sharpe

The Franco-American axis celebrated by America's schoolchildren and re-echoed by Lafayette's statue in Hartford extended beyond Enlightenment politics into the arts, where it was particularly influential in the closing and the opening decades of the nineteenth and twentieth centuries – Bartlett, for example, lived mostly in France and learned his craft in Paris. Before the Civil War, Emerson had tried to dissuade Americans from any notion of the European tour as indispensable to their personal or cultural development, but with limited effect: Europe continued to be where one went to 'find oneself' as an American artist, with Paris a particularly prominent destination. There was, however, an implicit tension between the required expatriation of a would-be American artist and allegiance owed to the republic left behind – despite or because of the fact that America's priorities at this period were felt by many to be at odds with those of art. Stevens was part of this intellectual climate; but the solution he found to the competing demands of America and France was that he managed simultaneously to 'go' and to remain at home.

*

Stevens was in the habit of jotting down aphorisms for himself in a commonplace book; most were composed during the 1930s, and several found their way into his poems. This dates from the late 1940s:

> Reality is a cliché
> From which we escape by metaphor
> It is only au pays de la métaphore
> Qu'on est poète. (*OP2* 204)

This probably recalls Aristotle's emphasis on the primacy of metaphor, but Stevens's particular formulation is resonant: setting up a contrast between 'reality' as imprisonment and the metamorphosing mind (what he habitually termed the 'imagination') as the realm to which we 'escape' from its constrictions, the crossing of that frontier is enacted in the change from English to French. In this opposition between reality (here) and 'pays de la métaphore' (there), the move into French signifies poetic authenticity, with metaphor as the means by which an ordinary universe is visited by what he termed the 'necessary angel' of transformation. That the contrast is less than absolute – that such an angel is 'of earth' (*CP* 496) not heaven – is unobtrusively signalled by the fact that 'cliché' is itself a French word domesticated in the English language.

One of the books in Stevens's personal library was the English translation of Paul Cohen-Portheim's *The Spirit of Paris* (1937), originally published in Germany seven years earlier. Discussing Sylvia Beach, Cohen-Portheim reminisced that 'her shop was the intellectual centre of young literary America when almost the whole of it lived permanently or temporarily in Paris'; reminding us that France, and supremely Paris, once seemed the authentic milieu for the apprenticeship of a modern American writer.[2] The young Stevens had subscribed to such notions; he would have been in full agreement with the implication in Hemingway's bitter-sweet retrospect, that '[if] you are lucky enough to have lived in Paris as a young man, then wherever you go for the rest of your life, it stays with you, for Paris is a moveable feast'. Stevens, however, denied the opportunity to accumulate such reserves in his youth, evolved strategies of surrogacy, by which for him too Paris preserved its value into his maturity. What sort of city was it, then, that he would 'remember'? Clearly, he could not furnish the particulars of rapture encountered in Hemingway's recounting of the routes he took, when hungry, that avoided unaffordable restaurants, or found in Malcolm Cowley's reminiscence of day trips, in *Exile's Return*:

> Paris was a great machine for stimulating the nerves and sharpening the senses. Painting and music, street noises, shops, flower markets, modes, fabrics, poems, ideas, everything seemed to lead toward a half-sensual, half-intellectual swoon. Inside the cafes, color, perfume, taste and delirium could be poured together from one bottle or many bottles, from square, cylindrical, conical, tall, squat, brown, green or crimson bottles – but you drank black coffee by choice, believing that Paris itself was sufficient alcohol.[3]

For Stevens, any such particulars tended to be disaggregated from their originating location and rendered discrete and consumable, in the form of books about Paris such as Cohen-Portheim's, catalogues of art exhibitions that he collected avidly, French periodicals to which he subscribed, and the books and paintings he caused his Parisian agent, Anatole Vidal, to send him. We might judge that this adds up to a singularly unreal city; except that for Stevens most cities were 'material without being real' (Fitzgerald's phrase from *The Great Gatsby*),[4] unless actively perceived. A passage in the earliest of his critical essays, 'The Noble Rider and the Sound of Words', suggests how a material city might become more real, in consequence of the act of poetic perception:

> If we go back to the collection of solid, static objects extended in space [...] and if we say that the space is blank space, nowhere, without color, and that the objects, though solid, have no shadows and, though static, exert a mournful power, and, without elaborating this complete poverty, if suddenly we hear a different and familiar description of the place [quotes lines 4–8 of Wordsworth's sonnet on Westminster Bridge], we know how poets help people to live their lives. (*NA* 31)

Tony Sharpe

There were other places that intrigued Stevens, from which he excitedly received postcards, books, and other representative items; other languages as well as French crop up in his verse: Latin, German, Italian, Spanish. But it was France, and within France Paris, that most consistently compelled his imagination, early and late.

*

At the outset of the twentieth century Stevens, having finished his Harvard education and newly-embarked on his attempt to become a newspaperman in New York City, was restlessly aspiring to some of the pursuits that might be thought more appropriate to his class and education. A journal entry for November 1900 strikes some familiar attitudes:

> I keep asking myself – Is it possible that I am here? And what a silly and utterly trivial question it is. I hope to get to Paris next summer – and mean to if I have the money. Saving it will be difficult – with all the concerts and exhibitions, and plays we are to have – not to mention the butcher, baker, and candlestick maker. But to fly! Gli uccelli hanno le ali – that's why they're not here. Whenever I think of these things I can see, + do see, a bird somewhere in a mass of flowers and leaves, perched on a spray in dazzling light, and pouring out arpeggios of enchanting sound. (*LWS* 48)

This already manifests a characteristic dissatisfaction with 'here' that leads to desire for a 'not here', initially specified as Paris: a destination so beset with practical difficulties in its attainment that Paris is by implication substitutable by a poetic image – mediated by the linguistic swerve into Italian – of a visionary bird. Rhetorically this closural image concedes the unlikelihood of his achieving geographical translocation, even as it camouflages it. It is as if Stevens foresaw the outcome of his meeting the following month with his father, who declined to fund any *Wanderjahr* and caused him to record in his journal that 'Europe is still on the other side of the ocean' (29 December 1900; *LWS* 49). On his side of the ocean was the America where 'modernity is so Chicagoan' (*LWS* 32), and where his father – who, he ruefully reflected in March 1901, 'always seems to have reason on his side' (*LWS* 53) – effectively enforced a masculinist ethic of self-sufficiency through work on his would-be wayward son.

Stevens had been dreaming about London as well as Paris, but it may be that his awareness of the French capital had been sharpened by the Great Exposition. Interest in the American presence there had been drummed up by the Commissioner-General, Ferdinand W. Peck, when emphasising the commercial advantages to accrue from showcasing American manufacturers. Urging an increase of federal funding, Peck assured fellow-citizens that 'the American sections will prove the "*clou*" of the exposition', drawing particular attention to Bartlett's statue: 'The unveiling of the Lafayette monument, on July 4, will make United States Day the most conspicuously resplendent of the national days.' He also promised that '[t]he National Building will be an oasis where Americans may find Americans, and rest from the weariness of the sight of strangers'.[5] This struck an unfortunate note; but even if Commissioner Peck envisaged Americans depending on the wearisomeness of strangers, there were others for whom strangeness was very much the point. For in the dynamic unfolding between himself and his father, the Paris Stevens felt himself obliged to renounce became the site of imaginative revolt, a counter-city of the spirit to which he could snatch illicit access.

This is evidenced in January 1909 in comments made in a letter from New York to his fiancée, Elsie, recounting his visit to the National Academy:

> Another sensation (one depends on them): one of the pictures yesterday had been exhibited in Paris. It had the number of the Paris exhibition on its frame and bore the 'Médaille' mark – an honor picture. By looking at that, and at nothing else I could imagine myself in Paris, seeing just what any Parisian would see – I laughed in my sleeve at New-York, far out on the bleak edge of the world. (*LWS* 117)

Although depicting an 'Oriental' scene, its connection with the French capital gave this picture power to abstract Stevens from the 'here' of his American city, in an experience akin to what Pierre Bourdieu has termed 'cultural consecration', which 'does indeed confer on the objects, persons and situations it touches, a sort of ontological promotion akin to a transubstantiation'.[6] Such power may have been augmented by its secrecy, depending on a detail likely to have been overlooked by more ignorant gallery-goers; but while his act of inconspicuous consumption might seem to differentiate Stevens's private experience from the more collective phenomenon Bourdieu is concerned with, the accrual of cultural capital implies exclusivity. Yet there was also embedded in this scene – as with the desire to visit Paris that had in 1900 engendered Stevens's image of the singing bird – recognition that, as an instigation for his imagination, Paris could function by proxy: the mark on a picture frame was a much quicker and less expensive mode of gratifying desire than transatlantic passage on an ocean liner.

What I call a 'strategy of surrogacy' in respect of Paris - by which books, pictures (whether high art or postcards), catalogues, periodicals and French food and wines all substituted for the place itself – became a feature of

Tony Sharpe

Stevens's recourse to the city that long outlasted his initial reason for accepting substitutes, because he could not have afforded the trip. Once safely installed at the Hartford he was not averse to taking quite long holidays, and for the final twenty-five years of his life (1879–1955) he earned enough to finance a family trip to Europe. That he did not do so may attest to the effectiveness of the alternative he had devised: as a stimulus to his imagination, Paris functioned more effectively as symbol than it could have done as an achieved actuality. Gatsby's 'green light' at the end of Daisy's dock lost its magic potency once he reacquainted himself with the woman it symbolised; and for Stevens the colossal significance that Paris held for him might have been fatally impaired by visiting a city which, as a fiction, therefore continued to be one of his enchanted objects, more 'real' *because* immaterial. When Daisy bursts into tears at the sight of Gatsby's 'beautiful shirts', she has just been told he has 'a man in England' who selects and sends them – in much the same way that Stevens would rely on the Vidals to choose French artwork for his Hartford home. Gatsby's sartorial profusion – 'the soft rich heap mounted higher – shirts with stripes and scrolls and plaids in coral and apple-green and lavender and faint orange, with monograms of indian blue'[7] – itself is reminiscent of the imaginative nightgowns disdained but nonetheless enumerated in Stevens's 1915 poem 'Disillusionment of Ten O'Clock': both might be thought to model a kind of extravagant consumerism as means to resist a deadening normality. Such a response was earlier glimpsed in Stevens's repulsion from New York in June 1900:

> I am beginning to hate the stinking restaurants that line the street and gush out clouds of vegetable incense as I pass. To-day I bought a box of strawberries and ate them in my room for luncheon. To-morrow I propose to have a pineapple; the next day, blackberries; the next, bananas etc. (*LWS* 39)[8]

For in Stevens's poem, the description of the fancifully multicoloured night attire *not* being worn directly derives from what he asserts to be the case ('None of them are strange'): the relation between reality ('white nightgowns') and imagination ('purple with green rings', 'green with yellow rings', 'yellow with blue rings', *CP* 66) is symbiotically causal. His 1943 paper 'The Figure of the Youth as Virile Poet' makes the following observations:

> It is easy to suppose that few people realize on that occasion, which comes to all of us, when we look at the blue sky for the first time, that is to say: not merely see it, but look at it and experience it and for the first time have a sense that we live in the center of a physical poetry, a geography that would be intolerable except for the non-geography that exists there – few people

realize that they are looking at the world of their own thoughts and the world of their own feelings. (*NA* 65–6)[9]

Leaving aside his suppositions about other people, Stevens's interlinkage of a perceived geography with a complementary if antiphonal 'non-geography' of thought and feeling suggests how, for him, 'Paris' as a non-geography, a 'there', achieved its effect within the context of a 'here' that was America. He once declared to a correspondent that 'I never feel that I am in the area of poetry until I am a little off the normal' (*LWS* 287), but in such a formulation 'the normal' remains as a necessary *point de départ*. It is in this way that his attachment to France, and in particular his imaginative appropriation of Paris, interlinks with his Americanness.

*

After his marriage (1909) and the birth of his daughter (1924), Stevens became clearer that he was less and less likely to achieve his goal of visiting Paris. Although in 1913 he would write to Elsie that 'tonight I'd like to be in Paris, sipping a bock under a plane-tree' (*LWS* 181), by 1925 he was declaring to William Carlos Williams that 'oh la-la: my job is not now with poets from Paris' (*LWS* 246) – where the ghost of a Parisian exclamation seems to intensify the receding of his fantasy. Yet during the 1930s he maintained contact with Anatole Vidal there (and after the war with Vidal's daughter Paule), from whom he acquired books and paintings by which he hoped to 'keep in touch with new French books and with life in Paris generally' (*LWS* 523). In fact, one of the high-water marks of Stevens's involvement with imagined Paris occurred during the World's Fair of 1939 and 1940 in New York; this coincided with his also coming into contact with Henry Church, co-founder in France (with Jean Paulhan) of the little magazine *Mesures* – to which Stevens had subscribed since its inception, through Vidal. Church, an American millionaire who lived at Ville d'Avray near Paris, in a house designed by le Corbusier, had found himself stranded in the USA by the impending war. These years therefore found Stevens stimulated by French concerns in two distinct aspects.

The World's Fair was the shorter-lived and more theatrical. We know of Stevens's interest in it principally through a memoir written much later by a colleague at the Hartford, Wilson E. Taylor. The published letters mention it briefly, although it is clear that the four-day visit Stevens had made with his wife and daughter in mid-June 1939 involved 'seeing the World's Fair until I could describe it in the dark' (*LWS* 341). Joan Richardson reports that in the autumn Stevens 'had one of the Hartford drivers take him down just for the day',[10] and Taylor outlines his particular enthusiasm:

> I am sure that I shall never know anyone who enjoyed the New York World's Fair of 1939–40 as much as Wallace Stevens did. Time and time again we would go there in the afternoon, walk for a few hours, and always end up in the French Pavilion, where, after taking in some of its exhibits and a vermouth-cassis or two for our jaded appetites, we would have dinner. This was his favorite building in the fair, and he spent many hours there among the works of art and the other exhibits.[11]

The Fair was constructed on a vast reclaimed dump in Queens' which 'once presented a scene of stagnant pools and muddy rivulets [...] Mountains of ash rose to a height of 100 feet; the topmost peak, waggishly named "Mount Corona", dominated the dismal panorama'.[12] It had been the original for the valley of ashes in *The Great Gatsby*.

While commemorating the 150th anniversary of Washington's inauguration in the city, the Fair was principally intended to celebrate a technological future which would be, in its important aspects, American in character. Dominated at its main entrance by the futuristic structures of the 700–ft high spire-like Trylon and the globoid Perisphere (200–ft diameter), the architectural code enforced was essentially modernist; major American business corporations erected appropriately-themed buildings, advertising the contribution they had made to the betterment of America and anticipating the future as a consumer's paradise. Such displays may have left traces in Stevens's poetry. Did the 'fat girl' revolving 'in crystal' at the end of *Notes toward a Supreme Fiction* (*CP* 407) – who, he told Henry Church, was 'the earth: what politicians now-a-days are calling the globe, which somehow, as it revolves in their minds, does, I suppose, resemble some great object in a particularly blue area' (*LWS* 426) – owe anything to 'Arctic Girl' ('Clad in an abbreviated bathing suit, a beautiful girl is entombed in a solid cake of crystal-clear ice', *Guide* 35), or to the Perisphere's external stage-effects?

> Here is the magnificent spectacle of a luminous world, apparently suspended in space by gushing fountains of liquid reds and greens [...] while at night powerful lights project cloud patterns on the globe, and wreathing it in color mist, create the startling illusion that it is revolving like a great planet on its axis. (*Guide* 27)

World's Fairs were occasions for such spectacular consumption: Nick Carraway pays Gatsby the ambiguous compliment that, garishly lit up, his house 'looks like the World's Fair', and, mingling admiration and disdain, recognizes that his friend is in 'the service of a vast, vulgar, and meretricious beauty'.[13]

Stevens explored the Fair fully with his family, and doubtless would have seen much that could be dismissed as '[a]nother American vulgarity' – to quote a poem whose title, 'Celle Qui Fût Héaulmiette' (*CP* 438), evokes a French connection through the poet Villon and the sculptor Rodin. The Amusement Zone, in particular, shifted the balance from educational to sensational, by such displays as 'Strange As It Seems': 'strange people from remote lands', 'black beings with enormous distended lips', 'headhunters', 'fierce savages from Masambo and the Congo; and here you may stare in awe at the giraffe-necked women from Padeung' (*Guide* 33). Elsewhere in the zone was 'Little Miracle Town' ('its one hundred and twenty-five midget inhabitants have their own tiny restaurant, their city hall'), together with, of course, 'Merrie England' ('a faithful reproduction of an Old English Village' (*Guide* 44)) and, nearer home – if such a concept retain validity – the 'Seminole Village', with its own jail and police force, 'where Indians wrestle with live alligators' (*Guide* 47). Such multiply-indiscriminate displacements and simulations suggest Baudrillard's later critique of Disneyland:

> Disneyland is presented as imaginary in order to make us believe that the rest is real, when in fact all of Los Angeles and the America surrounding it are no longer real, but of the order of the hyperreal and of simulation. It is no longer a question of a false representation of reality (ideology), but of concealing the fact that the real is no longer real, and thus of saving the reality principle.[14]

According to Taylor, Stevens's favourite area lay in the Government Zone, where the various national pavilions were situated. Neither the Canadian Pavilion ('a style of architecture typical of this young and virile country') nor the British Pavilion ('four large panels show how Britain's history has centered around her kings') nor the Irish Pavilion 'designed in the form of a huge shamrock' (*Guide* 97, 103, 105) are likely to have much delayed his progress to where, at 'the intersection of Rainbow Avenue and Constitution Mall, the French Pavilion [...] faces the Court of Nations. Its majestic curves form an immense glass bay with a wide terrace' (*Guide* 102). Because the dominant tone of the Fair was one of American affirmation, his preference would have placed him in a minority. Indeed, so would his ability to afford so many repeat visits, since a widespread view of the Fair was that admissions charges were discouragingly high. Lower-than-anticipated visitor numbers, as well as the darkening political climate that shortly produced a future calamitously different from the planners' optimistic vision, were a factor in its ultimate financial collapse; but for Stevens, visiting the French Pavilion enabled him to imbibe a commodified France in an American locale: he did not need to go to Paris, because France had come to him.

The guidebook description (evidently translated from French) suggests the Pavilion's distillation of a French ambiance:

> The first floor is dedicated to the scenic beauties of France and has a Bureau of Information for all touristic inquiries. Here dioramas show the charms of the country's Provinces accentuated by four interiors of homes from Alsace, Provence, Brittany and Savoie. An immense crystal map glorifies the French Spas.
>
> The mezzanine is devoted to Arts and Industries. The Fine Arts Exhibit includes works of sculpture, painting, tapestries, and applied arts. A vast hall, adorned with Gobelins tapestries and an imposing Sèvres vase, is used for official receptions. The remainder of the floor houses displays of the many Parisian specialties for which France is famous […]
>
> The second floor of the Pavilion is divided into three sections, 'French Thought', which includes displays representative of the country's literature, philosophy, education and music: 'Five Centuries of French History Illustrated by Five Centuries of French Art' […] On the terrace, overlooking the Lagoon, a Centre de Dégustation, French wines and food delicacies may be sampled. Close by, in a charming roof garden restaurant, native wines and provincial food specialties are served. (*Guide* 102–3)

His response to the French Pavilion in 1939–40 can be seen as a more extended version of what had happened with the Parisian mark on that picture in New York, years earlier: it transplanted him to his 'pays de la métaphore'. The Pavilion restaurant, showcasing great French chefs, introduced America to *cordon bleu* cooking and, like the younger Stevens's proposed regime of different daily fruits, enabled consumption as a form of resistance to the everyday: an acquisition of cultural capital connected with actual capital, because it was expensive to eat there. It possibly enabled Stevens to feel superior to the crowds milling about below, and doubtless also offered opportunity to display connoisseurship to Taylor, his subordinate – in much the same way that he would later impress his nephew John, by taking him to 'a very fine little French restaurant' in New York, where he 'just rattled off a lunch in French'.[15] But if there was an element of revolt against what the Fair was principally designed to celebrate, this was safely contained by the fact that finally it all took place on American soil, as part of a quintessentially American spectacle, and therefore involved no fundamental conflict of loyalties. This elaborate engagement with commodified France, occurring at the juncture when that nation faced its profoundest historical crisis, may actually mark the point at which Stevens understood more clearly that there was a separation between his idea of France and the actual country, which he could preserve only by not going there. If so, it is less a question of Baudrillardian 'hyperreality' abolishing distinction between 'real' and 'unreal', than of preserving a fiction from divergent actuality.

Alan Filreis has argued that, at this period, Stevens was a committed isolationist; he shared the national majority's desire for uninvolvement in the European conflict, which in June 1940 made America resist French pleas for military intervention. It is noteworthy that when, six months before Pearl Harbour, he gave his lecture 'The Noble Rider and the Sound of Words' at Princeton, he chose to exemplify outmoded nobility by an equestrian statue he cannot have seen (Verrochio's statue of Colleoni in Venice), rather than Bartlett's 'Lafayette', a perfectly good copy of which existed in his home town. This is the more striking given that its erection in Hartford may already have suggested to Stevens just such an obsolescence: for in his 1935 poem 'Dance of the Macabre Mice', those rodents swarm over the statue of a Frenchman on horseback who, like Lafayette, brandishes a sword. In May 1941, it might have seemed tactless to evoke the Franco-American axis Lafayette embodied, lest it suggest uncomfortable debts of gratitude or historical obligations undischarged. The unidentified 'American artist' cited in the same lecture, a reproduction (!) of whose painting 'Wooden Horses' Stevens cited to exemplify an art 'wholly favorable to what is real' (*NA* 12), was in fact Reginald Marsh, who had been born in Paris and had studied there. Despite this, Marsh was known as painter of kinetic, demotic American scenes: his 'High Yaller', where a smart young woman strides confidently down a Harlem street in long yellow dress, hat and gloves, had featured in the exhibition mounted by the Museum of Modern Art to accompany the World's Fair.[16] The iconographical move in Stevens's lecture, from immobile (European) armoured horseman to revolving (American) carousel where, as he noted, a man with jutting cigar embraces a sturdy-legged woman astride their wooden horse, almost prefigures the 1960s slogan 'Make Love Not War'.

The actual being-in-France could be done by others like Henry Church, whom Stevens described to a third party in 1943 in terms that bear closely on his understanding of his own position: 'Mr Church is practically a Frenchman, although, like most Americans who are practically something else, he is devoted to this country, and his chief pride is that he is an American' (*LWS* 438–9). Like Stevens's former Harvard acquaintance Walter Arensberg (also a millionaire), in whose New York apartment the poet had encountered the milieu of the European avant-garde in his earlier years, Church brought France to Stevens's door. Through Arensberg he had met Marcel Duchamp, offering another example of France in America, both in his own person and in the ampoule of Parisian air he brought as gift for his host; through Church he would meet Jean Wahl, and feel himself associated with Jean Paulhan and others. Church and Arensberg lived the life that Stevens aspired to, and in a way they lived it for him – or he lived it through them. Church's is the more relevant example, because he came into Stevens's acquaintance in circumstances emphasising France as a state of mind or transportable culture rather than as a fixed geography. If the French Pavilion offered a sort of theme-park presentation, Church brought with him the intellectual ambiance associated with *Mesures*; so when world events were making it impossible for Stevens to visit France even had he planned to, he was presented with encapsulations of the country reinforcing his own predilection for relating to it as virtual rather than actual place. Church also personified familiarity with the French cultural and political situation which, while furthering Stevens's grasp of what was actually going on, doubtless also had the allure of conferring insidership. It would shortly be the case that 'true' France would constitute itself outside the national boundaries, with de Gaulle in London rather than Pétain in Vichy; later, Jean Wahl's presence at Mount Holyoke was further evidence of the constitution of Frenchness abroad.

'Paris is the great luxury of the French, a thing of beauty that lies beyond the domain of the useful, in short, a work of art'; Cohen-Portheim also described it as the 'playground of the whole human race,' and paid tribute to the 'many-coloured, ever-shifting pageant of her streets'.[17] Such perceptions of the city may have heightened the contrast between Stevens's imagined Paris and the American civic setting where he worked: a 1935 letter described Head Office as 'a solemn affair of granite, with a portico resting on five [*sic*: there are actually six] of the grimmest possible columns' (*LWS* 283). But just as the World's Fair could create a microcosm of France in New York, so the spirit of Paris could be felt as far away as Hartford – and not just in the statue of Lafayette recently acquired. Like Wordsworth's sonnet, the 1939 poem 'Of Hartford in a Purple Light' (*CP* 226–7) concerns itself with metropolitan transfiguration, showing how the city where Stevens composed poems walking to and from work could have its granite lightened by a *jeu d'esprit*. It opens noting that the sun, apostrophised throughout as 'Master Soleil', has made the trip 'From Havre to Hartford' many times. So, too, 'the ocean has come with you' as rain-showers, like a 'poodle' shaking water off in prismatic droplets, 'Each drop a petty tricolor'. In the 'male light' of earlier sunshine the city's features had been boldly defined but now, with the softenings of sunset, 'as in an amour of women / Purple sets purple round', and the poodle is finally enjoined to 'flick the spray / Of the ocean, ever-freshening, / On the irised hunks, the stone bouquet'. Suffused in this glow of the setting sun, prosaic Hartford is modified by poetic France, in a many-coloured pageant where inessential houses melt away and you may stare in awe, as cityscape turns into a bunch of flowers.

But not everyone is awestruck, it seems; briefly, the poem has diverted from Connecticut to California, to evoke '[t]he aunts in Pasadena'. Thus identified, at a knight's move from sibling fertility and caught in the act of 'remembering', they are, inferably, ageing spinsters, whom this French light dismays: for in response they 'Abhor the plaster of the western horses, // Souvenirs of museums'. I take this to imply that, in recalling France, they heighten their own sense of cultural exile by disdaining locally-available copies of European statuary (a plaster replica of Bartlett's 'Lafayette' was prominently displayed at the 1915 Panama-Pacific International Exposition in San Francisco). But this poem repudiates their abhorrence, rather registering how near France now becomes than how distant its museums are. Their fixatedly 'remembering' the Grand Tours of their girlhood runs counter to its pronounced commitment to the present tense ('It is Hartford seen in a purple light'), and to its deictic insistence that we should 'Look' and 'See' 'this purple, this parasol', 'Now'. Playfully, the poem inserts French words like 'soleil' and 'amour' into its register; the phrase 'petty tricolor' aspires to the condition of *petit tricouleur* even as it evokes the French flag, alongside the French national dog. By ending on the word 'bouquet' it shows how, as with 'souvenirs', the presence of French in English is an achieved actuality – with the correct pronunciation enforced by the rhyme, which itself points up harmonies between the languages. 'Paris', nowhere named, keeps coming constantly near: Havre, alliteratively linked to Hartford, is its principal sea-port. Hartford might turn into 'Havre', and 'Pasadena' starts off as if it, too, might turn into the French capital, abetted by those museum horses, whose 'plaster of' potentially initiates the formulation 'plaster of Paris'. The word 'parasol' puns on the possibility of 'Paris-soleil', which is the poem's basic premise. The virile poet finds himself willingly entranced, as masculine America is enticed by feminine France; but the fundamental implication is that, therefore, you can have your taste of Paris without needing to leave Hartford. Those 'aunts in Pasadena' should have tempered their abhorrence of what California offered (after all, the Huntington Museum is nearby); for, as 'Prelude to Objects' notes, in a very Emersonian sentiment: 'he has not / To go to the Louvre to behold himself' (*CP* 194).

*

The years following the war showed Stevens continuing to avoid the Louvre, becoming increasingly disinclined to visit Paris and almost comically disposed to believe he had already done so. In 1950 he wrote to Bernard Heringman, a young acquaintance then visiting the city, 'I suppose that if I ever go to Paris the first person I meet will be myself since I have been there in one way or another for so long' (*LWS* 665). When a young writer charged with reviewing Stevens's *Parts of a World* called on him in the early 1940s, he 'assumed from the way [Stevens] talked about Paris that he had been there [...] at least several times'. Holly Stevens, musing on her father's failure to visit Europe, reported that 'he felt World War II had changed everything'.[18] It became characteristic of his post-war correspondence that evocations of Paris were accompanied by acknowledgements that it was impossible to consider going there. 'Certainly I should get the keenest pleasure out of a visit to Paris. But, alas, I have no expectation of ever visiting Europe', he wrote to Paule Vidal in 1950:

> [t]he other day I received from Europe a copy of No. 7 of Le Portique. Merely to read the names of book-binders, the names of publishers and book shops excited me. But I think that perhaps the excitement is more real at this distance than it might actually be (*LWS* 698).

In fact, the intensity of his desire to be in Paris seems to have been matched by the strength of his resolve not to go there; a subsequent letter makes this clear:

> There seems to be only one place left in the world, and that, of course, is Paris, in which, notwithstanding all the talk of war and all the difficulties of politics, something fundamentally gay and beautiful still survives. I rode in town to my office this morning with a man who has just returned from Paris. When he had finished telling me about it, I sighed to think that it must forever remain terra incognita for me. (*LWS* 755)

Later in the same letter (18 June 1952), however, Stevens told her that 'There is a possibility that I might have come to Paris this spring in connection with the Twentieth Century Work gathering but I was asked in such a peculiar way that I said no' (*LWS* 755). The tenses are intriguing: although the event referred to was, as he wrote, in the past, the possibility remains, as possibility – 'there *is* a possibility that I might have come'.

Thus the significance of Paris for Stevens largely depended on its remaining 'terra incognita'. If earlier that same year he had written to Henry Church's widow, Barbara, that 'Paris seems to be more than ever a centre, this spring, if there is a centre anywhere' (*LWS* 751), I am tempted to think it was a centre that could be everywhere, including Hartford, provided he never visited the actual city. Two years earlier he had written to Thomas McGreevy in Dublin, criticising Léon-Paul Fargue because too many of his poems concerned themselves with Paris: 'Paris is not the same thing as the imagination and it is because Fargue failed to see the difference [...] that he is not first rate' (*LWS* 697). This might seem surprising, unless we see that for Stevens Paris was capital city of the 'pays de la métaphore' in the abstract, not the concrete: only as an object of prospective longing or as the subject of retrospective regret ('I wanted all my life to go to Paris' is his last reference, *LWS* 845) could it compel his imagination. In his psychological and artistic economy, the 1952 conference he declined to attend had possibly presented more as threat than opportunity.

A 1953 letter to Paule Vidal uses vocabulary that makes explicit the value of the idea of Paris to Stevens, and the ways in which that idea connects to concerns central to his poetry:

> After waiting for FIGARO a long time, several numbers came at the same time. This has brought Paris close to me. When I go home at night, after the office, I spend a long time dawdling over the fascinating phrases which refresh me as nothing else could. I am one of the many people around the world who live from time to time in a Paris that has never existed and that is composed of the things that other people, primarily Parisians themselves, have said about Paris. That particular Paris communicates an interest in life that may be wholly fiction. But, if so, it is precious fiction. (*LWS* 773)

There is hardly a higher accolade to be bestowed, in Stevens, than that of 'precious fiction'; its describing a spiritual resource bears comparison with Hemingway's valediction at the end of *A Moveable Feast*:

> There is never any ending to Paris and the memory of each person who has lived in it differs from that of any other. We always returned to it no matter where we were or how it was changed or with what difficulties, or ease, it could be reached. Paris was always worth it and you received return for whatever you brought it. (192)

The difference, of course, is that for Stevens the key to the experience was *not* to have lived in Paris: to visit the city would be the spatial equivalent of the 'minor wish-fulfillments' that he associated with 'the romantic' in its debased form ('Imagination as Value', *NA* 139). This may be why, when places specifically associated with Paris occur in the poetry, they seem to be subject to criticism: 'They will get it straight one day at the Sorbonne' (*CP* 406).

If imagination has value, however, it is through interaction with 'reality'; the purple light of Paris is meaningful *because* it shines on Hartford, enabling perception of what 'The Bouquet' (1950) defines as 'The infinite of the actual', when '[t]he real' is 'made more acute by an unreal' (*CP* 451). It was such a moment of prosaic epiphany that informed the 1949 poem 'Angel Surrounded by Paysans', suggested by Pierre Tal-Coat's still life of a Venetian glass bowl amidst more humdrum vessels, acquired through Paule Vidal. This interaction justifies Stevens's assertion that 'French and English constitute a single language' (*OP2* 202): not that they are the same but that they are complementary; that awareness of French within an inhabitation of English is an enrichment that depends on recognition of difference, not identity. This is what emerges from later comments he made in his letter to McGreevy, following on from his judgement of Fargue's poetry, and thinking of the distinctiveness of the French:

> I mean what I say in the same sense that I would mean if I said that it means more to one to live in Paris than to live in New York. Both places are much alike, but the accents of one are not the accents of the other and, however much alike they may be, there is a difference and the difference is not to be bridged. (*LWS* 697)

The irony here is that it could only 'mean more' to live in Paris than New York (which Stevens had) if one actually refrains from doing it: because it is the imagined plenitude ascribed to Paris from an American perspective that produces the meaning, which bridging 'the difference' would destroy. As he explained to an early enquirer (1928): 'Another way of putting it is that, after writing a poem, it is a good thing to walk around the block; after too much midnight, it is pleasant to hear the milkman, and yet, and this is the point of the poem, the imaginative world is the only real world, after all' (*LWS* 251–2).

And this, finally, is how Stevens's Francophilia was so deeply involved in his being American, a patriot of the two republics of the USA and of the 'pays de la métaphore' so closely linked to Paris as 'terra incognita'. Earlier I quoted the question from his journal, 'is it possible that I am here?', to which the answer is: 'Yes; because the "there" you long for turns out to be a function of where you long for it from'. It is fitting, then, that the last piece of public prose he wrote was a paean to his adopted state, 'Connecticut Composed' (1955), which closes with these words: 'It is a question of coming home to the American self in the sort of place in which it was formed. Going back to Connecticut is a return to an origin.' Interestingly, however, the very last sentence generalises this experience beyond the state and beyond the United States: 'And as it happens, it is an origin which many men all over the world […] share in common: an origin of hardihood, faith, and good will' (*OP2* 304). Connecticut, too, turns out to be a 'moveable feast', in a vision which supposes the whole world to be in natural sympathy with Yankee values (this was written for the 'Voice of America' airwave). Yes, it was certainly possible that Stevens was 'here', having never been anywhere else, except metaphorically; but rather than end with a piece somewhat inflected by propagandist intentions, I prefer to acknowledge the truth and strangeness of his finding himself in 'Paris', by recalling the end of 'Crude Foyer' (another French word at home in English), which accepts that, as 'ignorant men incapable / Of the least minor, vital metaphor' we shall be 'content, / At last, there, when it turns out to be here' (*CP* 305).

Notes

1. The following abbreviations for references to Stevens's writing will be used: *CP* = *Collected Poems of Wallace Stevens* (London: Faber and Faber, 1955); *LWS* = *Letters of Wallace Stevens*, ed. Holly Stevens (London: Faber and Faber, 1967); *NA* = *The Necessary Angel: Essays on Reality and the Imagination* (New York: Vintage Books, 1975); *OP2* = *Opus Posthumous*, revised edition (London: Faber and Faber, 1990). Page references to these will be given in the text.
2. Paul Cohen-Portheim, *The Spirit of Paris*, trans. Alan Harris (London: Batsford, 1937), 40.
3. Ernest Hemingway, *A Moveable Feast* (London: Jonathan Cape, 1964), 6; Malcolm Cowley, *Exile's Return: A Literary Odyssey of the 1920s* (New York: Viking, 1956), 135.
4. F. Scott Fitzgerald, *The Great Gatsby* (Harmondsworth: Penguin, 1974), 168.
5. Ferdinand W. Peck, Commissioner-General for the United States to the Paris Exposition of 1900, 'The United States at the Paris Exposition in 1900', *The North American Review* CLXVIII (January 1899): 24–33. All quotations at 32 (accessed via Cornell University Library website, 22 October 2013).
6. Pierre Bourdieu, 'From *Distinction: A Social Critique of the Judgement of Taste*', in *The Norton Anthology of Theory and Criticism*, 2nd edn, ed. Vincent B. Leitch (New York and London: W.W. Norton & Co., 2010), 1664–70, 1669.
7. Fitzgerald, *The Great Gatsby*, 99.
8. *Wallace Stevens, New York and Modernism*, ed. Lisa Goldfarb and Bart Eeckhout (New York and London: Routledge, 2012) explores the impact of New York on Stevens. Especially relevant is Edward Ragg's essay 'Bourgeois Abstraction: Gastronomy, Painting, Poetry, and the Allure of New York in Early to Late Stevens', 144–62.
9. Stevens delivered this paper in the presence of Jean Wahl as part of the 'Entretiens de Pontigny' conference transplanted (with Henry Church's financial assistance) from wartime France to Mount Holyoke College. As Alan Filreis (see note 18 below) has shown, Stevens's contribution was emphatic in its Francophile orientation; he gives a detailed exposition of the poet's evolving awareness of French political realities during this period.
10. Joan Richardson, *Wallace Stevens: The Later Years 1922–55* (New York: William Morrow, 1988), 153.
11. Wilson E. Taylor, 'Of a Remembered Time', in *Wallace Stevens: A Celebration*, ed. Robert Buttel and Frank Doggett (Princeton, NJ: Princeton University Press, 1980), 91–104, 101–2.
12. *Official Guide Book, New York World's Fair 1939* (New York: Exposition Publications, Inc., 1939), 17. Further references will be cited in the running text as *Guide*.
13. Fitzgerald, *The Great Gatsby*, 88, 105.
14. Jean Baudrillard, 'Simulacra and Simulations', in *Selected Writings*, ed. Mark Poster (Oxford: Polity Press, 1989), 166–84, 172.
15. Doggett and Buttel, *Wallace Stevens: A Celebration*, 121.
16. See *Art in Our Time: An Exhibition [...] held at the time of the New York World's Fair* (New York: Museum of Modern Art, 1939), reprint edn (New York: Arno Press, 1972), 143.
17. Cohen-Portheim, *The Spirit of Paris*, 99, 20.
18. Alan Filreis, *Wallace Stevens and the Actual World* (Princeton, NJ: Princeton University Press, 1991), 103. Holly Stevens, 'Bits of Remembered Time', *Southern Review* 7 (1971), 651–7.

'A Smell of French Bread in Charlotte Street': Louis MacNeice Revisited

Stan Smith

I only bumped into Louis MacNeice once – literally, in 1963. He was standing talking in the gangway of the Cambridge lecture theatre after he'd given the first of his Clark Lectures, and we exchanged that mumbled mutual apology typical of English culture, in which both parties humbly accept responsibility for an accident, as a way of placating and moving on. The lectures were to be published as, so it turned out, his last, posthumous critical study, *Varieties of Parable*.[1] A few months later he was dead, aged 56, on the twenty-fourth anniversary of the outbreak of World War II, a premature and unnecessary death, having caught viral pneumonia caving in Yorkshire, collecting sound effects for what became his ultimate BBC radio play, *Persons from Porlock*, yet one more parable of poetic creation cut short by a gratuitous interruption. It's the kind of biographical irony that would have appealed to him. Fifty years on from that death, it seems an appropriate time to reconsider MacNeice's contribution to twentieth-century poetry and, in particular, his troubled relations with Irishness, and with the political enthusiasms of his day.

At the memorial service, his lifelong friend W.H. Auden, with whom he'd visited Iceland in 1936 and produced the following year that inimitable collaborative potpourri, *Letters from Iceland* (1937), spoke of MacNeice's writings in his last couple of years as 'among his very best'. The slim volume published only a few days after the funeral, *The Burning Perch*, has been widely cited as a key influence by many present-day poets in both Britain and Ireland, particularly the North, and his work has in recent years been the subject of a major campaign to reappropriate him to a specifically Northern Irish identity, not only by poets from a Northern Protestant background such as Derek Mahon, Michael Longley and Tom Paulin – in part no doubt driven by a political impulse to pluralise and render multicultural a society that for too long spoke only in the thunderous conflicting monologisms of Loyalist and Nationalist orthodoxies – but also, from the other side of that once murderous divide, by such writers of 'Catholic' provenance as Seamus Heaney and Paul Muldoon, the latter giving MacNeice more space than any other poet in his *Faber Book of Contemporary Irish Poetry* (1986).

Peter McDonald, whose superb, definitive edition of MacNeice's *Collected Poems* was published by Faber and Faber on the centenary of his birth in 2007,[2] and who had previously co-edited a selection of MacNeice's plays and produced a critical study of his work, has his own take on all this. His

1997 book *Mistaken Identities*[3] took issue with a number of Northern poets, whether of Protestant provenance like Paulin and John Hewitt, or Catholic, like Heaney and John Montague, for acting as undercover agents of influence for a Nationalist agenda. McDonald's own motives were themselves a little conflicted, in that he sought to liberate MacNeice, and his other preferred writers (foremost of whom were Longley and Muldoon), from the chains of nationality and an oppressive 'identity politics' while, as his subtitle *Poetry and Northern Ireland* indicated, simultaneously ghettoising them in a poetic province to which he himself laid claim to privileged access 'as a Belfast-born Presbyterian', 'no more free than any other writer from the pressures of identity discourses', with 'his own origins [...] visible plainly enough in the book's style and in certain emphases of its polemic' (18). That polemic, while striving to avoid anything as compromising as mere sectarianism, was indubitably 'unionist' in its *parti pris*, but with a small 'u' and in a decidely postmodernist inflexion.

McDonald took exception, for example, to J.N. Browne's dismissal of MacNeice in 1951 as evincing 'little in either his work or his outlook to identify him as an Ulsterman' (19), while at the same time rebuffing more recent attempts to recruit Ulster's Protestant poets to an all-encompassing, ecumenical 'Irish' identity. On the contrary, McDonald insisted, MacNeice, like W.R. Rodgers, with whom MacNeice had sought to co-edit a finally abandoned anthology, *The Character of Ireland*, realised that 'ambitions for "identity" in a place like Northern Ireland are inevitably worn down by what they hope to transcend, the "acute and terrible attritions" of that "determined place"' (40). McDonald cited in substantiation MacNeice's verse 'Prologue' to *The Character of Ireland*, first republished in Jon Stallworthy's 1995 biography.[4] 'Prologue' is reprinted in the invaluable appendices to McDonald's edition of the *Collected Poems*, along with other uncollected verses published between 1932 and 1963, the texts of the previously unavailable first volume *Blind Fireworks* (1929), of his 1940 Cuala Press volume, *The Last Ditch*, and of the song cycle *The Revenant*, written for his wife Hedli Anderson, together with a selection of uncollected early poems and juvenilia, and his various prefaces and introductions.

Though MacNeice's 1941 study of Yeats had sought to resolve under the figure of paradox the problematics of Irishness, aphoristically summed up in his 'final antinomy', 'It is easy to be Irish; it is difficult to be Irish,'[5] McDonald was keen to emphasise in *Mistaken Identities* that 'Prologue' questions the very idea of a fixed national or ethnic identity:

'The Character of Ireland? Character?
A stage convention? A historical trap?
A geographical freak? Let us dump the rubbish

Stan Smith

Of race and talk to the point: what is a nation?

McDonald may be (partially) correct in his gloss that '[t]he recognition of "identity" for a country, or indeed for a self-identifying "race" within that country, as "a historical trap", makes good the kind of poetic intuition which MacNeice's "Prologue" explores' (38). But one should be sensitive, too, to the poem's faint echo of another exchange about nationality in Irish literature. 'What is your nation if I may ask?', demands the chauvinist Citizen in *Ulysses*. 'Ireland', the Irish Jew Leopold Bloom replies: 'I was born here. Ireland.' However, as a 'lover of women and Donegal', as Auden called MacNeice in his moving elegy for him in 1964, 'The Cave of Making',[6] he had learnt enough about the fickleness of the heart's affections never to pin too absolute a faith on the prospect that, this time, the commitment would be total, the relation enduring.

It was the pioneering study by Terence Brown in 1975, *Louis MacNeice: Sceptical Vision*,[7] that made the essential case for a more ambivalent Anglo-Irishness at the core of MacNeice's writing, something which accounted for his deep and abiding distrust of all systems of thought and feeling that laid claim to absolute and unquestioning allegiance. Himself a Dublin man of Presbyterian extraction, born in China to missionary parents, Brown took as epigraph to his study a maxim of Marcel Proust's that '[t]hrough art we can know another's view of the universe'; and it was this ability to recognise the authenticity of another's view-point and, in consequence, the fallibility or at least relativity of one's own, which for Brown was crucial to MacNeice's sense of self, as of cultural identity.

Brown quoted to good effect the words of the Southern-born Ascendancy Nationalist Stephen Gwynn, who, in ironic recollection of Molière's M. Jourdain's discovery that all his life he had been speaking prose without knowing it, reported in 1926 that, 'brought up to think myself Irish, without question or qualification', he had been shocked to discover that 'the new nationalism prefers to describe me and the like of [me] as Anglo-Irish', so that 'all my life I have been spiritually hyphenated without knowing it'.[8] For Brown, MacNeice's real territory – something, I'd argue, that makes his fellow-feeling with the left-wing poets of the 1930s, forever on the frontier, between two worlds, more than an accident of historical convergence – lies in that hyphen interposed between the absolutist demands on loyalty of English and Irish claimants. An equally hyphenated, in this case Anglo-Australian, poet, Peter Porter has reported, in a private communication, his contretemps at some conference or other with the Northern poet Matthew Sweeney, a Donegal man himself, on this very matter of 'patriality', in which Sweeney insisted on MacNeice's incontrovertible Irishness without any sense that this was at all problematic. Somewhat improbably, however, it is a writer of working-class Catholic provenance such as Ciaran Carson who best matches MacNeice's position. Brought up in a Belfast household where Gaelic was spoken, not on ideological principle but as the normal language of everyday, though unshared by any of the neighbours, in collections such as *HMS Belfast* and *The Twelfth of Never* Carson makes much of the idea that every positive 'identity' carries with it its own moral and conceptual shadow, evoking those antipodes of the spirit where dissidence blossoms and difference instates itself.

MacNeice's father, a Church of Ireland rector, later a bishop, in the small Co. Antrim town of Carrickfergus, a district now swallowed up in Belfast's environs, used to recall nostalgically the Connemara where he had grown up. In a minority of one amidst his Unionist flock, he sympathised with the Nationalist cause but refused to visit the newly-created Irish Free State because, according to his son, he couldn't bring himself to 'mix with people who might be murderers without you knowing it'.[9] Louis himself only visited what he called, in inverted commas, the 'South' in his seventeenth year. Since the 'South' in this case was Donegal, actually to the northwest of the Six Counties, its northernmost point further north than anywhere in the Ulster statelet's 'Black North', MacNeice's scare quotes round the concept indicate his own wry sense of the absurdity of confusing political topography with the geographies of the soul (a word at which he might have raised a sceptical eyebrow).

Auden's valedictory poem speculates that MacNeice would have taken a scholar's interest in the fact that, four miles to the east of the village in lower Austria where he penned it, 'at a wood palisade, Carolingian / Bavaria stopped, beyond it / unknowable nomads'. Not just a scholar's, one might add, but an Anglo-Irishman's interest also, that 'palisade' recalling various Pales, literal and metaphorical, which have divided the landscape and the peoples of Ireland. But Auden was thinking also of the Iron Curtain, by that time somewhat further east, which until recently had run through the middle of that pacified, neutralised country where he himself had sought final refuge from the noisy divisions of history. Frontiers of one kind or another, Auden's elegy implies, are the very stuff of existence, and always have been, and they run and always have run through the core of the self, testifying to the ultimately factitious nature of this transient creature of circumstance. For MacNeice, an ineluctably Protestant atheist born amidst contending absolutisms where, as the poem 'Belfast' records, '[t]he sun goes down with a banging of Orange drums', educated to be a professional Englishman at Marlborough and Oxford University (after which, *Autumn Journal* confesses, 'You can never really again / Believe anything that anyone says and that of course is an asset / In a world like ours'), the strings were always false. Deprived by death of his mother when he was only five, he knew that reality would always betray you, as you would most likely betray it. It's scarcely surprising then, that the grown man found himself consorting, whether consciously or not, with spies and double agents, as John Banville grasped in merging him fictively as the protagonist of *The Untouchable*[10] with his lifelong friend and mentor, the Queen's Own Soviet Spy, Sir Anthony Blunt, with whom he first visited Spain in 1936 just before the Civil War erupted. As our man in Athens with the British Council during the next decade's Greek Civil War, he was suspected in some quarters of being a (British) spy himself. MacNeice's generation, after all, was much taken with E.M. Forster's glib phrase-making in *Two Cheers for Democracy*, that '[i]f I had to choose between betraying my country and betraying my friend, I hope I should have the guts to betray my country'. If 'World is crazier and more of it than we think', as MacNeice wrote in the poem 'Snow', it is also 'more spiteful and gay than one supposes'. There is more than window-glass between more things than the dissolving, dissolute snow and the hyperbolically life-affirming roses.

Reviewing MacNeice's radio verse drama *They Met on Good Friday* in *The Observer* on 8 December 1959, in an article headed 'Language on the Boil', Dylan Thomas's biographer Paul Ferris objected to the Third Programme's revival of 'the old literary habit of unnecessary subtitles', which described the play as 'a sceptical historical romance'. But the description was probably MacNeice's own. As 'the only poet of stature still in the fold of the BBC', Ferris wrote, MacNeice's programmes 'usually sound as if he designed them as private entertainments; they don't, like most features, appear to have been conceived at a committee of seventeen, all drinking canteen tea'. If 'the result is sometimes a bit backboneless, a bit frothy', when he 'attaches himself to a sturdy theme, preferably an historical one, the result can be dazzling'. 'Attaching himself to an historical theme': that casual formula in a way catches the essence of the man, with his suspicion that he too, perhaps, was merely a figure in 'a sceptical historical romance'.

The author of those early volumes, *Poems* (1935), *Letters from Iceland* (1937), *The Earth Compels* (1938) and, particularly, *Autumn Journal* (1939) is the quintessential MacNeice – the man who could write, in his unfinished autobiographical memoir, *The Strings Are False*, of returning from a Barcelona in December 1938 poised to accept final defeat at the hands of Franco's fascists, that 'I began to hate the English […] who had passed by on the other side. Passed by under an umbrella. And then, very logically, I found myself hating myself' (196). This is the MacNeice who could also write, in 1942, in his (poetic) 'Epitaph for Liberal Poets', of 'us who walked in our sleep and died on our Quest', who were – the paradox is pointed – 'Conditioned to think freely', and now had to confront 'the tight-lipped technocratic Conquistadores' who 'shall supersede us and cannot need us', facing up to the prospect that 'our way of life goes west / And some shall say *So What* and some *What Matter*', with the only consolation that 'The Individual has died before, Catullus / Went down young, gave place to those who were born old.'

By the time of his death, MacNeice had come to terms with that melancholy recognition. I didn't, in 1963, go back for the rest of the lectures, chilled by their tiredness, their world-weariness. His heart didn't seem to be in them. Knowing the biographical reasons in retrospect, it's easy to account for his dispirited performance; but the fact that I went to that lecture in the first instance, almost uniquely in my undergraduate career, when so many other writers were available performing on the Cambridge scene, says something about his distinctive appeal. Both he and his 1930s contemporaries had ceased to be fashionable by the early 1960s, a superseded generation, as 'Epitaph for Liberal Poets' had foreseen, only significant to the middle-aged dons who organised such things as the Clark Lectures. But MacNeice remained different, and an object still of intellectual curiosity. I'd found his poems, along with those of Auden and the others, on the shelves of my grammar school library, in first editions from the 1930s and 1940s, which one would never find in a school library now, if such things even still exist in the state-run sector of secondary education. And I'd found him much more interesting than the other MacSpaundays, largely, I think, because he didn't assume large political and public postures, but spoke with a restrained, sleekit, melancholy personal voice, in a handful of lyrics that stuck in the memory. The voice, that is, of a man whom Oxford, according to *Autumn Journal*, had taught to ask: 'In a world like ours, / Why bother to water a garden / That is planted with paper flowers?' – but who could nevertheless write, at the end of the same poem, of the stubborn hopeless resistance of the people of Barcelona and urge his 'various and conflicting / Selves I have so long endured', not to 'hanker / For a perfection which can never come', but 'If you have honour to spare, employ it on the living'. The voice, too, of that consummate lyric, 'The Sunlight on the Garden', with its reworking of a perennial Classical topos, *tempus edax rerum*, but inflected with the specific urgency of 1930s apocalypse, predicting in the rueful tones of the rentier intellectual, simultaneously anxious and gleeful at the expected righting of ancient wrongs, that 'Our freedom as free lances / Advances towards its end.' MacNeice's private melancholy, that is, quietly resonated with undertones of a larger, historic and public crisis and, importantly, a sense of personal responsibility. The same mixed feelings underlie his remark in the essay 'Poetry Today' that 'the "freedom" of the free lance' was 'a gross misrepresentation [...] The best English poets have been those most successfully determined by their context.'[11] MacNeice was precisely a political poet because, like Auden at his best, he didn't write overtly about politics, but about the very structure of the self as a 'dated' being, its complicitous and inequitable dealings with the world of others compromised by the processes of its always historical formation. He may have written in the Note prefaced to *Autumn Journal* that he was 'not attempting to offer what so many people now demand from poets – a final verdict or a balanced judgment. It is the nature of this poem to be neither final nor balanced.' But, observing that 'I have been asked to commit myself about poetry', he had also reported in the *New Verse* double issue on 'Commitments' in Autumn 1938 that 'I have committed myself already so much *in* poetry that this seems almost superfluous', adding however that, while a poem 'cannot live by morals alone', nevertheless, 'The poet at the moment will tend to be moralist rather than aesthete.'[12]

'It is convenient to imagine that poets die at the right time. MacNeice did not', wrote Cyril Connolly in his 1967 review[13] of the posthumous *Collected Poems* edited by MacNeice's old friend and former Head of Department at Birmingham University, the Classical scholar, E.R. Dodds, himself a Northern Irish Presbyterian, born in Co. Down but growing up in Dublin from the age of ten. Connolly spoke of that collection as 'a rudderless ship; the pilot is gone; nothing can be added or subtracted. It is a memorial'. In a sense, though, MacNeice's death, premature for the mortal creature, was timely in terms of its cultural moment. That seems to be the tenor of the superficially sprightly poem 'Budgie', which provided the title for his last, virtually posthumous collection, *The Burning Perch* (1963). Casting himself self-deprecatingly as that semi-comic pet so popular in post-war Britain, the solitary budgerigar (in US parlance, parakeet) making ecstatic love to its own image in a little mirror rimmed in baby-pink plastic, 'Its voice a small I Am', the poet 'stands at his post on the burning perch', like the boy on the burning deck in the comic rhyme. Beyond the bird's cage there is a vast universe, galaxy on galaxy, 'But for all this small blue bundle could bother / Its beak, there is only itself and the universe', as 'I twitter Am'. An earlier poem in the same volume, 'Pet Shop', spelt out MacNeice's abiding sense of a shameful, venal complicity. Whether 'Cold blood or warm, crawling or fluttering', the poet is simply another pet, though 'most of the customers want something comfy'; and 'all are here to be bought'. The purchaser's words actually express the self-contempt of the hireling poet: 'Purr then or chirp, you are here for our pleasure, / Here at the mercy of our whim and purse.'

Connolly wished that the posthumously published 'Thalassa', the final poem both in Dodd's *Collected* and in the main body of McDonald's, had been known in time for the memorial service, where Auden gave the oration. In a sense, though Connolly doesn't spell this out, it is a defiant antidote to the self-laceration of 'Budgie' and 'Pet Shop'. It is addressed presumably to his fellow poets from the 1930s, those 'ignoble comrades, / Whose record shall be noble yet', invited, like the ageing fellow-travellers of Tennyson's and Dante's

Ulysses, to 'Put out to sea' for one final voyage. The poem's insistently repeated 'comrades', a word compromised now by the sarcastic undertones of post-war disillusion, catches the ambivalent period flavour. As the title suggests, it is not the hopes of a brave new world the other side of catastrophe that links these comrades now, but the shared nostalgia for old familiar things of a defeated remnant, the cry, in Xenophon's *Anabasis*, of routed Greek mercenaries who, having struggled home through Middle-Eastern deserts, finally greet the sea again. Connolly quotes the poem's middle stanza, with its mid-life-crisis ruminations on what must have seemed at the time for MacNeice a failed, a 'ruined' life. It doesn't pull any punches about the backslidings and venalities such a life involved for these 'feckless men', 'broken' and 'heartsick' comrades:

> You know the worst: your wills are fickle,
> Your values blurred, your hearts impure
> And your past life a ruined church –
> But let your poison be your cure.

The poem's closing crescendo, proclaiming that 'By a high star our course is set, / Our end is Life. Put out to sea', speaks however with an almost camp defiance. It may be that his poison (and all his contemporaries knew what that was, by then) was not his cure, but it offered a degree of Dutch courage. The defiance is double-edged. MacNeice wants still to believe that the now blurred values of his youth, lived under the sign of 'the god Bogus', may still be seen as 'noble yet'. But the friend of Anthony Blunt knows too that in that 'ruined church', motives were always 'impure' and wills 'fickle.'

Auden's elegy for MacNeice knew precisely where the fickleness and the impurity lay. Exact contemporaries (their centenaries both fell in 2007), both of them

> watched with mixed feelings
> the sack of Silence, the churches empty, the cavalry
> go, the Cosmic Model
> become German, and any faith if we had it, in immanent
> virtue died. More than ever
> life-out-there is goodly, miraculous, lovable,
> but we shan't, not since Stalin and Hitler,
> trust ourselves ever again: we know that, subjectively,
> all is possible.

Writing in his cave-like study, with his desk deliberately 'averted' from the window that might distract with daydreams and 'plausible videnda', Auden nevertheless registered that for MacNeice the poet's vocation was always to consider the 'life-out-there' even as he acknowledged his own abstraction from it, on the inside of the window against which, in the poem 'Snow', the snow swirls and melts. That indoor poet 'with whom I / once collaborated, once at a weird Symposium / exchanged winks as a juggins / went on about Alienation', knew, like Auden, the real alienation the poet experiences in his cave of making, withdrawn alike from the sack of silence, from ruined choirs where late the sweet birds sang, and from the receding cavalry, in a cosmos which is itself only a passing human construct, a modelled space, simply a bigger cave haunted by flickering Platonic shadows.

Cyril Connolly's final assessment of 'MacNeice's complete oeuvre' is tinged with more than a little self-regard, from this self-styled victim of the enemies of promise, but it catches one essential quality of MacNeice's best work:

> Talent, not genius, but talent unfailingly set to work and well-husbanded: a dogged determination to make the most of it; great metrical facility, varied images, vivid imagination but much difficulty in sustaining poems, many of which are uneven. Besetting sin: journalism. [...] His real preoccupation was with everyday life in bohemian London ('a smell of French bread in Charlotte Street') and holidays in Scotland or Ireland.

'We cannot cage the minute / Within its nets of gold', MacNeice had written in 'The Sunlight on the Garden'. But if any poet could, it was Louis MacNeice. The great virtue of Faber and Faber's handsomely produced complete edition is that, in restoring the poems to the volumes and the sequence in which they first appeared, it enables us to recover in all its circumstantial specificity MacNeice's politics of the everyday, in a world which is 'suddener than we fancy it', to share as if for the first time the 'smell of French bread in Charlotte Street'.

Notes

1   Louis MacNeice, *Varieties of Parable* (Cambridge: Cambridge University Press, 1965).
2   Louis MacNeice, *Collected Poems*, ed. Peter McDonald (London: Faber and Faber, 2007). Subsequent quotations from MacNeice's poetry are all from this volume.
3   Peter McDonald, *Mistaken Identities: Poetry and Northern Ireland* (Oxford: Clarendon Press, 1997).
4   Jon Stallworthy, *Louis MacNeice* (London: Faber and Faber, 1995).
5   Louis MacNeice, *The Poetry of W.B. Yeats* (London: Faber and Faber, 1941), 46.
6   W.H. Auden, *About the House* (London: Faber and Faber, 1966), 18–21.
7   Terence Brown, *Louis MacNeice: Sceptical Vision* (Dublin: Gill and Macmillan, 1975).

8 Stephen Gwynn, *Experiences of a Literary Man* (London: Butterworth, 1926), 11; cited in Brown, *Louis MacNeice*, 10.
9 Louis MacNeice, *The Strings are False* (London: Faber and Faber, 1965), 226.
10 John Banville, *The Untouchable* (London: Picador, 1997).
11 Louis MacNeice, 'Poetry Today', in Geoffrey Grigson (ed.), *The Arts To-day* (London: The Bodley Head, 1935), 30–31.
12 Louis MacNeice, 'A Statement', *New Verse* 31–2 (Autumn 1938), 7.
13 Cyril Connolly, 'Louis MacNeice', repr. in *The Evening Colonnade* (San Diego: Harcourt Brace Jovanovich, 1985), 323–6.

Keywords

Scouse

Scouse, an important term in the discourse of contemporary British culture, has a long and complex history; it originates in a contraction of 'lobscouse', an early modern English nautical term for a basic dish consisting of meat, vegetables and ship's biscuit. This substandard standard fare was first recorded in a satire on the English navy (1708): 'He has sent the Fellow a thousand times to the Devil, that first invented Lobscouse.' Yet although the term was evidently coined pre-eighteenth century, its roots are obscure. One possibility is that 'lobscouse' was a corruption of 'lob's course', as in Smollett (1751): 'a mess of that savoury composition known by the name of lob's-course'. This would suggest the sense of 'a meal served to a lob' (a sixteenth-century coinage meaning 'clumsy fellow, country bumpkin, clown or lout'). Given this, it seems plausible that the dish may have originated in England and spread through maritime trade (in which of course Liverpool played a central role in the eighteenth and nineteenth centuries). Evidence to support this hypothesis lies in the appearance of a series of related terms for this type of stew across the northern European languages (modern Norwegian 'lapskaus', Swedish 'lapskojs', Danish 'skipperlabskovs', Dutch 'lapskous' and German 'labskaus'), and the fact that 'lobscouse' was used in American English from the early-to-mid nineteenth century. The transition to the shortened form **scouse** appears to have been made in Liverpool by the last decades of the eighteenth century, chiefly in references to institutional food. Eden's *The State of the Poor: or, an History of the Labouring Classes in England, From the Conquest to the Present Period* (1797), for example, makes reference to the expenditure on food in the Liverpool poorhouse: 'Beef, 101 lbs. for scouse'; '14 Measures potatoes for scouse' (420 lbs); and 'Onions for ditto' (28 lbs).

Yet if this accounts for the history of scouse the dish, the development of the transferred senses of the term is more complicated and difficult to trace. The fifth edition of Eric Partridge's *Dictionary of Slang and Unconventional English* (1961) records 'Scouseland', meaning Liverpool, as 'nautical and (Liverpool) dockers" usage of the late nineteenth and early twentieth century (though there is no evidence in support of the claim). But the crucial shift, which associates people, place and cultural (culinary) tradition, appears to have taken place around the First World War in Forces' slang. In fact the evidence suggests that the use of **scouse**, and the derivative 'scouser', was a negative, or at least playfully disrespectful way of referring to the inhabitants of Liverpool by people from elsewhere. This pejorative sense is confirmed by the first reports of the use of **scouse** within the city, which note that it referred to denizens of the Scotland Road area (one of the poorest, and most Irish, districts). Indeed, while it remained as the name used in army and naval slang for Liverpudlian members of the Forces, **scouse** failed to displace 'Dicky Sam', the most widely used nickname for a Liverpudlian which dated from the early nineteenth century, until the 1920s–30s (at which point it began to contend with 'wacker' – the alternative form until the 1970s).

Strikingly, the use of **scouse** to refer to the language of Liverpool (usually the accent, though it can also mean the local dialect), is relatively recent; the first recorded use is in a headline in the *Liverpool Echo* – 'Scouse Lingo – How it all Began' (1950). Though there is evidence of a sustained interest in the local language from the early twentieth century, the overt link between people, place and a form of speech only appeared and became consolidated through the activities of a small group of local historians, folklorists, entertainers and journalists in the 1950s. In many ways this was an 'invention of tradition' which, as so often, took the form of a combination of historical fact, myth, nostalgia, pride, ambivalence and pragmatic storytelling. And it produced a powerful if reductive narrative of the history of the city, one which belies Liverpool's intricate multicultural past, through the history of its language (in essence: **scouse** = Lancashire dialect + Irish-English). Yet the most significant element that distinguishes the appearance of **scouse** is the fact that it was promulgated in influential early modes of popular culture and indeed became integral to them as a way of representing aspects of Northern working-class life. From the early and important BBC TV documentary on Northern working-class city life, *Morning in the Streets* (1958), to the earliest forms of TV drama, *No Trams to Lime Street* (1959) and *Z-Cars* (from 1962), through the impact of *The Beatles* and, later, *The Liver Birds*, *A Family at War*, *The Wackers*, *Boys from the Blackstuff*, *Bread*, *Merseybeat* and, for twenty-one years, *Brookside*, **scouse** was enregistered as the language of Liverpool. This was always an open and ambivalent process and **scouse** was and is both a familiar and flexible ideological marker. It has been used at specific moments to represent the lovable, cheeky, witty rogue ('the scouse git' of *Till Death Do Us Part*, 1965); the malingering and socially damaging trade union militant (frequently figured in the broadcast news of the late 1970s); the whining, self-pitying victim (Hillsborough, 1989); the confident, assertive and irreverent maker of fashion and culture (the European Capital of Culture, 2008). Thus although it retains its former senses of a type of stew and a person from Liverpool, **scouse** is perhaps best understood as a prime and indicative contemporary example of a mode of cultural representation that is peculiarly British: that curious, powerful and often damaging concatenation of language, class, geography, identity and political significance.

Tony Crowley
School of English, University of Leeds

Stuart Hall (1932-2014): A Personal Tribute

The obituaries posted across the press and radio with the news of Stuart Hall's death on 10 February this year suggested that he has been known chiefly as a political theorist, above all for his analysis of Thatcherism as a form of 'authoritarian populism'. This appeared, in what now seems another era, in *Marxism Today* and in *The Politics of Thatcherism* (1983). The left, he argued, had no answer to the way Thatcherism tuned into and exploited popular attitudes so as to govern under a new right-wing consensus. He was to extend this analysis to Tony Blair's New Labour which he saw as colluding with the Thatcherite programme after John Major. With others, including Martin Jacques, he framed the alternative of 'New Times' and subsequently co-authored a response to neoliberalism, known as 'The Kilburn Manifesto', with the editorial group associated with the journal *Soundings*. This argues that the financial crisis of 2008-9 has reinforced the power of the financial and class elites and calls for a coalition of oppositional groups, new and traditional, to rethink strategies for defending the principles of an egalitarian, participatory democracy.

Stuart Hall was indeed, then, a significant political thinker, public intellectual and activist. He was also a teacher, at the Open University and before that at the University of Birmingham, where he joined Richard Hoggart as a Research Fellow at the Centre for Contemporary Cultural Studies which Hoggart had founded in 1964. He had previously abandoned his study at Oxford of Henry James and had, with others, founded *Universities and Left Review* which was to become *New Left Review*.

I met Stuart when I joined the first group of research students at the Centre in 1968, then housed in a hut which was set in a telling position below the English Department housed in the main Arts Building. Cultural Studies had not at that time gained sufficient respectability for the Centre to be placed in the Arts Building or permitted to award PhD degrees. My preparation, such as it was, had been Roland Barthes's *Writing Degree Zero*, Stuart Hughes's *Consciousness and Society* and an enthusiasm for Black Mountain College and the poetry of Ed Dorn. Stuart and Richard Hoggart were my supervisors on what soon seemed a bizarre MA thesis of 50,000 words on 'Stylistics and Cultural Studies', which included a case study of Basil Bunting. Along the way, I discovered Chomsky's transformational grammar and Stuart said, yes, go ahead with that. Around me were students, research fellows and associates working on rock music, advertising, the press, everyday life, football and gay film. I joined a subgroup studying the Western and attended research seminars on readings in the definition of culture, the Frankfurt School and on Structuralism and Semiotics. The very first joint seminar, though, as I remember it, was on

Stuart Hall (1932–2014): A Personal Tribute

Blake's 'Tyger', chaired by Richard Hoggart with Stuart in attendance. Later the same day they led a discussion of the representation of women in advertising. Hoggart was then Director and his *The Uses of Literacy* and a pamphlet on 'The Literary Imagination and the Study of Society' (1967) gave impetus to the foundation of the Centre. He had not wanted to omit literature, and nor did I. When he left after a year for UNESCO and Stuart became Acting Director, the Centre's work shifted to the study of the mass media and continental theory, along with the continuing question of the methodology of Cultural Studies. I wrote my first ever 'paper', a structuralist analysis of the 'B' Western, and was the first student at the Centre to complete a postgraduate degree. Like other Centre students I had also started teaching classes in popular culture in FE colleges. This wasn't 'Cultural Studies', which didn't exist outside the Centre, but 'Liberal' or 'Complementary Studies'; not unlike the teaching Stuart had been doing at Chelsea College before his appointment to Birmingham.

My two years at the Centre had comprised two days of seminars, speakers and group project work a week, the last being at the time a quite distinctive innovation. The scheme of work was orchestrated by Stuart, who was also careful to bring students together intellectually and socially. My time there ended with a conference where E.P. Thompson, Leslie Fiedler and Peter Wollen were speakers. The whole experience was challenging, formative and unforgettable. I left Birmingham for London in 1971 and used Stuart and Paddy Whannel's *The Popular Arts* and Stuart's *Teaching Film* in my own teaching. The Centre publications also had begun to appear as at first stencilled A4 pamphlets, then the journal *Working Papers in Cultural Studies*, then a book series and individual studies. The Cultural Studies agenda accordingly moved in the 1970s and 1980s, and then beyond, through theories of ideology, language, feminism, post-Marxism, postmodernism and race and ethnicity, changing its course and character, sometimes radically, under the impact of new thinking. There always remained, too, the question of what purchase the study of culture could have on real life events. But, if anything, Cultural Studies grew stronger, and it was in the period under Thatcher that Stuart and the Centre gained a more public, indeed an international reputation.

I met him and we chatted half a dozen times after I left Birmingham. I wish it had been more. He had a personal grace and great charm and was always generous and interested and on the button. On most of these occasions he was an invited speaker at an academic or public event. Richard Hoggart's access to cultural meaning had been by way of what he called 'reading for tone'. In Stuart's case one had only to listen. An early characteristic move had been to 'map the field' and this was what he did: beginning gently, laying out the coordinates, critiquing and synthesising positions in a delivery laced with humour and intent which then rose to a rich and decisive analysis that showed

Stuart Hall (1932–2014): A Personal Tribute

a way forward. It was exhilarating and magnetic. This is what I and many, many more will remember. Recently I saw the documentary film of Stuart's life and ideas by John Akomfrah titled *The Stuart Hall Project*. I wrote a note to Stuart to say how moved I was by the film, personally, intellectually and politically. I'm pleased I did. Because this is what I would always have said. He was and remains, for me and countless others, an inspiration. We have yet to catch up with him.

Peter Brooker
University of Nottingham

Reviews

Matthew Beaumont, *The Spectre of Utopia: Utopian and Science Fictions at the Fin de Siècle. Ralahine Utopian Studies 12.* Oxford: Peter Lang, 2012, xii + 307 pp. £40 pb. ISBN 978-3-0343-0725-3

Like the curate's egg, Matthew Beaumont's *The Spectre of Utopia* is good – indeed, very good – in parts. But, again like the curate's egg, it sometimes adds up to rather less than the sum of those parts.

The book's 'Introduction' opens with an absolute howler of a mistake: 'Yevgeny Zamyatin's *We*, banned in the Soviet Union in 1921, appeared in England in 1924' (1). No, it didn't. Gregory Zilboorg's English-language translation of Zamyatin's *Mi* did indeed appear in 1924, but in New York and without either a British publisher or a British distributor. Which explains why both George Orwell and Aldous Huxley knew Zamyatin's novel through Cauvet-Duhamel's 1929 French translation *Nous autres*. Beaumont's 'Introduction' closes with an equivalent howler: 'The chapter looks at the beginnings of utopian thought in More's *Utopia*' (25). Thomas More certainly coined the name 'Utopia' in 1516 for his 'nova insula', but he knew full well that there was a long tradition of what we now call utopian thought reaching back at least to Plato. Hence, the explicit reference to Plato in the book's epigraphic hexastichon.

Between howlers, we are given a brief guide to Jacques Derrida's *Specters of Marx* (4–11, 14–17), whence Beaumont derives his title, and to the 'structure' (17) and chapter plan of his own book (17–25). Derrida is, of course, an acquired taste and one, I confess, I haven't managed to acquire. It is with some relief, then, that I can report that he rates only two or three mentions in the remainder of the book and seems to function not so much as an integral theoretical resource, as a source of external academic legitimation. The real problem comes with the chapter plan, which suggests what the book eventually confirms, that it has no overall coherent structure; or rather, that it has two which don't quite add up.

The first five chapters are, in effect, a short (125 pages) monograph, mounting an original and ultimately persuasive defence of Edward Bellamy's *Looking Backward 2000–1887* against the long tradition of British left-literary condescension inaugurated by William Morris's famously hostile review in the June 1889 issue of *Commonweal*. The most interesting of these from a strictly cultural materialist point of view is almost certainly the fifth, on William Reeves's 'Bellamy Library', which published the first complete British edition of Bellamy's novel in three different formats. Beaumont carefully demonstrates how the 'material form' of the cheapest format, the sixpence edition, 'made the text accessible to the foot soldiers of any future movement of reform' (141). These sixpenny editions were aimed, he demonstrates, at 'an interpretive community of working-class and lower-middle-class autodidacts' (142). As such, they attempted to radically humanise the reading experience, Beaumont concludes, by transforming the reader into 'the active participant in a collective act of production, the practical task of social reform' (149).

Almost equally interesting, however, are Chapter 2 on Bellamy's politics of consumption, Chapter 3 on the psychology of utopian time-travelling and Chapter 4 on Bellamy's proto-modernist sense of space. In the first, Beaumont takes as his springboard the way Bellamy's Julian West encounters shopping as his first sociable experience of twenty-first-century Boston. This is a 'consumerist utopia' (67), Beaumont concludes, its model the recently established department store (57–63), but one in which consumption is 'coolly ascetic, almost entirely machinic' (69). As such, it represents a 'dream of democratic consumption', which marks 'the point of convergence' between late-nineteenth century capitalist and socialist utopias (71–2). The novel is thus not 'without desire', as Raymond Williams once argued, but is rather an 'anticipatory insight' into the desiring economies of the more fully formed consumerist cultures of late capitalism.

Chapter 3 confronts head on Morris's famous dismissal of 'the slight envelope of romance' in *Looking Backward*, which has become something of a received wisdom on the British Left. To the contrary, Beaumont insists that the novel is 'possessed of considerable psychological depth' and that Bellamy's 'finest achievement' is 'his portrait of the protagonist's psychology' (76). Julian, he argues, is traumatised as a result of his time-travelling, so that his identity is in a sense doubled and his personality 'terminally troubled by existential doubt and psychic uncertainty' (82). Moreover, Beaumont continues, this psychological depth is directly informed by contemporary research on what was then diagnosed as 'psychogenic fugue'. Utopian fiction 'becomes more sophisticated at this time', he concludes, 'because it is shaped by contemporaneous developments in psychology' (95).

Beaumont's fourth chapter carefully locates the 'socially empty' grand spaces of Bellamy's utopia in relation to both earlier dystopias of depopulation and subsequent modernist images of the city. Such spaces are a source of anxiety and inspiration for Bellamy's Julian, prompting a kind of agoraphobia only overcome through resocialisation by means of shopping. The modernist 'city of the absent', Beaumont argues, 'is simultaneously a dream of being freed from the constraints of capitalist modernity and a nightmare of being cut loose from its consolations' (120). Beaumont's readings of Bellamy are so consistently provocative – running directly contrary, as they do, not only to

Morris, but also to both E.P. Thompson and Raymond Williams – that one is left asking for more.

This is not, however, what one gets. The remaining five chapters are a collection of essays on loosely related topics: Margaret Shurmer Sibthorp's liberal feminist newspaper *Shafts*; late-nineteenth century spiritualism; Oscar Wilde's *The Soul of Man Under Socialism*; H.G. Wells's *The Time Machine*; and the role of estrangement in science fiction, from Wells to Ian Watson by way of Arkady and Boris Strugatsky. Each of these is interesting in its own right – although I am least persuaded by the last – but, the chapter on Wells aside, none seem to add much to the initial treatment of Bellamy. And the obviously relevant text, which clearly connects *Looking Backward* to *The Time Machine*, Morris's *News from Nowhere*, though referred to throughout, is nonetheless refused a chapter to itself.

Beaumont's treatment of *The Time Machine* deploys Freud's concept of *das Unheimliche* (the Uncanny) and Bloch's of *das Noch-Nicht-Bewusste* (the Not-Yet-Conscious) in order to demonstrate what is surely already well-known, that the nineteenth-century bourgeoisie and proletariat evolve into Wells's Eloi and Morlocks. Whilst 'Bellamy resolves the problem of class struggle by abolishing it', Beaumont observes, 'Wells finds a more sophisticated, but far less optimistic, solution' (232) in Morlock cannibalism. The despair that pervades the novel's last pages is thus an expression of Wells's lower-middle-class ambivalence towards the working class. So the novel 'points in horror to the presence in late-Victorian society of a force that both elicits sympathy and threatens the ruin of civilization' (251). It isn't clear to me that Freud and Bloch contribute very much to this understanding of the text, but the reading itself is powerful nonetheless.

Here, too, Beaumont introduces the idea of 'anamorphosis', which will provide the organising theme for his closing chapter on science fiction. The term itself derives from painting, where it refers to the use of perspectival distortion to produce eccentric spectator positions: the most famous example, which Beaumont cites, is Holbein's 'The Ambassadors' (252–61). Beaumont's central argument here is that 'the defamiliarizing devices characteristic of science fiction are equivalent to anamorphosis' (261). The notion that science fiction works by way of *Verfremdungseffekte* (estrangement effects), in the Brechtian sense of the term, is by no means original. It is in fact one of the central theses in Darko Suvin's groundbreaking 1979 *Metamorphoses of Science Fiction*. And, as Beaumont notes, Suvin does at one point casually refer to these estrangement effects as anamorphic.

But Beaumont insists that Suvin 'discards' anamorphosis 'without developing its metaphorical potential' (266). As with *das Unheimliche* and *das Noch-Nicht-Bewusste*, I'm not entirely convinced. For there is nothing necessarily pictorial about the estrangement effects in Wells's *When the Sleeper Awakes* and *The War of the Worlds*, nor in the Strugatsky brothers' *Piknik na obochine* nor in Watson's short story 'Slow Birds'. And, stripped of its specifically pictorial aspects, anamorphosis surely becomes more or less synonymous with *Verfremdungseffekt*. That said, the book's treatment of Bellamy commands both attention and respect and secures its place both in utopian studies and in science fiction studies.

Andrew Milner
Monash University

Tony Crowley, *Scouse: A Social and Cultural History.* Liverpool: Liverpool University Press, 2012. xvi + 190 pp. £16.99 pb. ISBN 978-1-846-31840-5.

When did the distinctive form of English known as 'Scouse' first appear? This is the deceptively simple question that Tony Crowley's study sets out to address, but almost immediately another, much more complex set of questions imposes itself: what is Scouse? Why did such a distinctive linguistic and cultural construct appear in Liverpool? How does a 'non-prestige' form of speech come to acquire a whole range of cultural associations, such that it becomes synonymous with a complex, internally diverse city? To put it another way, how, as Crowley asks, 'does a 'bastard brogue' become a city-speech?' (22).

There is, as Crowley outlines, a received account of the history of Liverpool's distinctive English, according to which the characteristic dialect and intonation were produced by the convergence of waves of immigration during Liverpool's transformation from small coastal town to global port city (xiv). In this version, the major factor in the development of an identifiable form of Liverpool English was mass Irish immigration in the 1840s, plus large-scale nineteenth-century migration from Wales (compounded, in some versions, by the effects of industrial pollution); before about 1830, the story goes, Liverpool people spoke the same as the rest of Lancashire. This story, repeated even by professional linguists, is revealed to be untenable by extensive research showing that a distinctive form of speech was associated with the city well before the turn of the nineteenth century, the most intriguing piece of evidence being an obscure comedy of 1768, *The Sailor's Farewell*, by Thomas Boulton (32).

With the official story duly discarded, *Scouse* becomes less a linguistic history of a certain variant, dialect or accent (even deciding which of these applies to Scouse is shown to be impossible) and instead an account of how the concept has been constructed, disseminated and received. The official account, in which Liverpool only developed a distinctive linguistic form after the 1830s, is revealed to rest on a misreading of a single, humorous anecdote, given in a single text published in 1830, Robert Syers's *The History of Everton* (17). The most striking claim arising from this is that Scouse, as it is usually understood, is a mid-twentieth-century construction, invented by a group of local cultural figures (especially the mercurial Frank Shaw) who concertedly formed a 'Scouse industry' (63) during the difficult period of the 1950s and 1960s in which the city 'boomed culturally and yet stagnated economically and politically' (64). Intriguingly, this recasts the origins of Scouse not in Liverpool's centrality to the expansion of trade, but as a cultural effect of Britain's contraction as a global economic power. The proponents of the 'Scouse industry' tapped into, but also actively fostered, the cultural nostalgia that appeared in the decades immediately after the war, prompted in part by the dislocating effects of redevelopment and housing clearances, and which manifested itself in popular interest in the etymologies of local place names, words and phrases, discussions of which ran in the columns and letters pages of local newspapers for decades (42–3). The 'naturalized tradition' of Scouse (111), then, originates in this moment, and in the need for a sense of place in a time of transition, but also in the active interventions of a handful of people.

The counter-intuitive force of this, at least for a non-specialist, is considerable, bringing into view the surprisingly central role that an individual can play in processes of linguistic and cultural formation that might be more conventionally thought of as, by definition, social and to some extent collective. Moreover, Frank Shaw and his investment in Scouse appear to be deeply paradoxical. A skilled manipulator of the media, he nonetheless set out to present the standardising and homogenising effects of mid-century popular culture as threatening the authenticity of Scouse. Shaw's myth-making in relation of Liverpool language is also ambiguous; although seeming to celebrate its authenticity as resistance of linguistic standardisation, he also berated 'that catarrhal, adenoidal singsong' (70), and proposed to cleanse the 'worst locutions' in the name of 'good Scouse' (72). The greatest success of this paradoxical 'industry' was the *Lern Yerself Scouse* book series, intended to codify a certain version of the city's language culture for visitors during the 1966 World Cup, but which enjoyed enduring popularity both in and beyond the city. Central to the argument is the claim that these representations were the means by which Scouse was 'staged, sung and celebrated, and, literally turned into an object of knowledge' (77). Scouse, it turns out, is not properly a linguistic category at all, but is rather a complex 'mode of cultural value and social distinction' (94), which requires quite different analysis than it has previously received, and which exposes the inadequacy of the methods and disciplinary frameworks that have been invoked to study it. The implications of this clearly go well beyond the language of Liverpool, extending into searching questions of how the interrelations of language, history, culture and location can be examined.

A final, partly autobiographical chapter reveals the author's own investment in the relationship between language and place, describing a life lived progressively further away from his birthplace in the Dingle, first as a result of post-war rehousing and later as a result of the mobility of scholarship education and academic life. Crowley is acutely sensitive both to the power of Scouse to support a sense of being from a particular place, and its potential to conspire in linguistic and cultural stereotyping, which are, he notes, some of the last forms of prejudice to remain 'socially respectable' (xiv). Scouse, Crowley concludes, can become a stultifying abstraction that denies the complexity of the city's history, which is one of 'conservatism, conformity and orthodoxy' as much as much as it is of radicalism and creativity (136), as well as repressing its internal diversity and fragmentation. The refusal to simplify these issues means that the questions the book initially raises about the origins of Liverpool English go unanswered (and are, perhaps, unanswerable), but instead *Scouse* offers a compelling account of how a city's identity is formed through its language, drawing on a rich range of sources and generating a wealth of unexpected insights.

Elinor Taylor
University of Salford

Katharine Cockin (ed.), *The Literary North*. Basingstoke: Palgrave MacMillan, 2012. xiv + 269 pp. £53 hb. ISBN 978-0-230-36740-1.

The film director Ken Loach has often spoken of his past struggles to get stories set in the north of England into cinemas and onto television screens. When he attempted a film adaptation of David Storey's novel *Flight into Camden* (1961) in the late 1960s he was told by film producer Joseph Janni: 'The North is finished in films.' It was an area of the country – in this instance Yorkshire – seen by Janni as 'a trend that had gone out of fashion'. 'It's still there, Jo', Loach replied (quoted in Anthony Hayward, *Which Side Are You On? Ken Loach and His Films* (London: Bloomsbury, 2004), 86). Such dismissive rhetoric about the north, which Loach continues to challenge, implies that it is a geographical area which not only warrants minimal representation but also one which is knowable as a coherent and reified space: it can be depicted, understood, and then the creative gaze can move on elsewhere. *The Literary North*, an essay collection edited by Katharine Cockin, explores such simplified portrayals, contesting the clichés and mythologies built upon a homogeneous idea of a traditional north of England. With a focus on literary texts from the mid-nineteenth up to the twenty-first century, the book includes new approaches to the work of Elizabeth Gaskell, Arnold Bennett, W.H. Auden and Alan Sillitoe. While these chapters feature well-worn texts, albeit within some radical reappraisals, the collection also offers refreshing readings of children's literature, local newspapers, the poetry of Tony Harrison, the plays of Ewan MacColl and contemporary responses to the Moss Side area of Manchester. Such a diverse mixture allows for a challenge to the dominant idea of the north as a fixed entity; as Cockin explains in the introduction, it 'is rather still forming, or becoming' (3), a dynamic and diverse place which defies generalisation.

The Literary North explores the idea of the region as a constructed other, as a place defined by both placing it in binary opposition to London and by offering a portrayal of it for a metropolitan audience and reader. This notion of the north being written and explained for the benefit of England's capital forms the basis of Josephine Guy's opening chapter on Gaskell. *Mary Barton* (1848) and *North and South* (1854–55) are described as attempts by the novelist to position Manchester as a slum, inferior and incomparable to the sophistication and national importance of London. This was at a time when Manchester was beginning to challenge, momentarily at least, the political, cultural and economic power of the metropolis (31). By 'reducing Manchester to the singularity of the "chimneyed city"' (31) however, overlooking the complexity of the city's industries and the investment in buildings, parks and civic projects (as well as its emerging radical, intellectual, and artistic cultures), Gaskell reaffirms London as the country's power base and Manchester becomes the archetypal northern mill town. Moving onto the period 1880 to 1914 (the essays are presented chronologically), Jan Hewitt looks at attempts to construct a unified northern industrial identity through the fictional stories published in the evening newspapers of Middlesbrough and the northeast. The success of such a construction is destabilised by the 'diverse and problematic groupings' (43) of a new urban working class and by differences arising from local variations in topography and industry. Landscape also plays a significant role in two successive chapters which address works by Staffordshire writer Arnold Bennett. Ann Heilmann compares Bennett to the Irish naturalist George Moore, whose 1885 novel *A Mummer's Wife* depicts Hanley as a place which, surrounded by the 'imprisoning walls' (60) of the Staffordshire hills, is complicit in the destruction of its central character Kate Ede. While Moore's heroine represents the suffocating presence of Hanley, Bennett's Anna Tellwright in *Anna of the Five Towns* (1902) is able to accept and overcome 'the insidious long-term effects' (61) of her northern industrial environment. The absence of 'potential … individual and communal political change' (70), replaced by an emphasis in Bennett on 'spiritual grandeur' (70), is noted by Heilmann and this in particular would warrant further study. Ruth Robbins's chapter, instead, takes issue with Virginia Woolf's notorious attack on Bennett's dogged realism and the '"detailism" of (his) descriptions of provincial life' (76). Robbins argues that the intention in a work such as *Clayhanger* (1910) is to show individualised characters: Bennett is 'demanding that his readers see them not as "sweepings" but as people' (79).

Landscape with Chimneys, a 1951 play by Ewan MacColl, brings the collection into the post-war period. Although this chapter compares MacColl's work to Walter Greenwood's *Love on the Dole* (1933), there is little engagement in the collection more widely with the 1920s or 1930s. The northwest, or more specifically Wigan and Salford, is often the reference point for the poverty and unemployment of this interwar period. Part of *The Literary North*'s stated aim is to get beyond such a repetitive and restricted focus which often renders the northern landscape as one enormous '1930s theme park' (7). For that reason alone, the contributions to this collection should be applauded. Claire Warden's essay on MacColl does suffer, however, from a collapsing of *Landscape with Chimneys* with the more well-known Salford texts *Love on the Dole*, Shelagh Delaney's *A Taste of Honey* (1958) and Friedrich Engels's *The Condition of the Working Class in England* (1845). The emphasis falls on the similarities between these fictional and non-fictional works when an extended teasing out of the differences would have been even more stimulating. Nonetheless, it is a refreshing engagement with MacColl as a playwright and illuminates the political, personal and class tensions of an ambitious play that invokes Salford as both 'revolutionary, familiar and vibrant' and 'oppressive, hierarchical and desolate' (104): themes and reflections emanating from his working-class upbringing in Lower Broughton, which MacColl returned to throughout his career. An artist's childhood memories are also reflected upon in Tony Sharpe's appraisal of W.H. Auden. The poet's distant relationship and personal identification with the north offers an alternative reading of a landscape which offers both generic and particular meaning (113). Auden's 'sacred landscape' (112) was formed out of a childhood fascination which re-imagined a birthplace he had dreamed about but only first visited as a 12-year-old (113). These 'northern imaginings', suggests Sharpe, offer a 'potent and unusually stable point of reference for a career' marked by 'abrupt self-disownings' (110–11).

Representations of northern working-class youth are the focus of Nick Bentley's essay, with the habitual placing of Richard Hoggart's *The Uses of Literacy* alongside readings of *Saturday Night and Sunday Morning* (1958) and *Billy Liar* (1959). The latter novel by Keith Waterhouse depicts its eponymous character's struggle with and negotiation of the shifting social and cultural trends taking place in 1950s Britain. Whilst Hoggart, Bentley argues, assumes that the shiny barbarism of American consumerism will be universally and passively embraced by an emergent youth culture (dissipating traditional working-class culture in the process) (126), Waterhouse portrays the complexity of positions taken by characters such as Billy Liar, along with the growing anxieties about identity and the search for value in emergent but also dominant and residual cultural traditions (132). In Alan Sillitoe's novel, Arthur Seaton's narrative is imbued with a perspective which is 'northern', 'universal' and 'existential', according to Bentley (140). He has empathy for the struggles of his parents' generation while also recognising the enhancement, rather than the devaluation, of their lives in the post-war years (141). Both novels are presented as influenced by, but in different ways resistant to, the cultural analysis offered by Hoggart's seminal text. The inspiration behind the poetry of Philip Larkin, Douglas Dunn and Peter Didsbury is the focus of Sean O'Brien's compelling chapter. Through a deep engagement with the mysterious surprise that is Hull – the 'most isolated large city in England' (145) – a dense and contrasting city of anonymity, humour, 'serenity and horror' (153) emerges from the very different poetic perspectives of the three writers in question. The poetry of Dunn's 'near-contemporary' (149) Tony Harrison is analysed by Jo Gill, who considers the Leeds poet's work as engaging with the social changes experienced within a deindustrialised north. Of particular note in Gill's essay is the description of Harrison's use of poetic verse and traditional meter. She argues that he 'rattles the bars' of the hegemonic form (iambic parameter), disrupting 'our notions of proper and improper use of language' (162). More problematic is the positioning of Harrison's poetry as a lament for the country's old grammar school system (169–70).

As with many of the writers featured in Cockin's collection, Harrison closely identifies with the landscape of his home county while, according to Gill, the poems in *Continuous* (1981) mourn 'the self he might have been' (161), and elegise a 'nostalgic construction of something which may never have existed' (167). Themes of escape, loss and displacement permeate the work of many of these northern writers, and what emerges in three successive chapters on children's literature is a sense of individual identities built upon complex and shifting notions of belonging. The pitfalls of nostalgia appear to loom large in the work of Robert Westall, which Nolan Dalrymple describes as 'celebratory of the region's past' in comparison with an 'apprehension at the region's present condition' (187). His novels, centred upon the northeast of his formative years, are figured, however, as challenges to and debunking of the stereotype of the 'region as a grim, industrialized slumland' (184). Robert Lee, to whom the collection is dedicated following his death in 2010, suggests 'that there is a valuable, little-mined seam of children's books, waiting to tell us something of what it means to belong (or not to belong) in the north-east of England' (188). A nuanced understanding of local social and political difference is located within the novels of David Almond, Catherine Cookson,

Reviews

Frederick Grice and Westall (he describes Westall, incidentally, as acutely aware of the delusions of nostalgia). And Lee concludes that 'the scale and complexity of the spectrum of belonging that operates in the North-East' (203) is explored by such writers. Tess Cosslett draws attention to how studies of the childhood pastoral often place emphasis on an exclusively southern setting, overlooking the influence or involvement of the north within such literary models. The northern landscape, in texts such as *The Secret Garden* (1911), *Swallows and Amazons* (1930) and *Earthfasts* (1966), allows for an exploration of 'something beyond the safe, enclosed world of the pastoral idyll' (218), according to Cosslett. Rather, it 'provides a geography that leads the characters towards adulthood' (219).

The strengths of *The Literary North* are exemplified by Lynn Pearce's illuminating article on contemporary fiction written about and from Moss Side. Her research emanates from the AHRC-funded Moving Manchester project which looked at the 'mapping of Manchester as a migrant city' (231) from 1960 onwards. Joe Pemberton's *Forever and Ever Amen* (2000), *Moss Side Massive* (1994) by Karline Smith and Peter Kalu's *Lick Shot* (1993) are approached as texts which manipulate and utilise the tropes of both realist and genre fiction – predominantly crime fiction – in order to 'deliver a sharp, political comment' on social inequality 'specific to Britain's northern cities' (236). The focus on collective experience and structural oppression rather than the individualistic approaches taken by some of the writers in this collection is both refreshing and imperative. Whereas Auden laments the passing of his relationship with a landscape and region which has changed largely due to his own personal choices, the writers Pearce features portray the 'destabilizing, if not overtly traumatic, consequences' (221) of so-called slum clearances and the repeated demolition and regeneration of areas such as Moss Side and Hulme. If, as Cockin asserts, the north has been 'trapped by its relationship to realism, and the long shadow cast by Orwell's (rail)road trip' (251), then Pearce's exploration of a contemporary northern fiction, which pushes the conventions of genre, allows new perspectives and progressive approaches to emerge around questions of what (and where) the north is, how our image of it is constructed and how our understanding of it can shape the pressing social, economic and political issues of the twenty-first century.

Phil O'Brien
University of Manchester

Philip Bounds, *British Communism and the Politics of Literature 1928–1939*. Pontypool: Merlin Press, 2012. vi + 320 pp. £18.95 pb. ISBN 978-0-85036-594-8

Benjamin Kohlmann (ed.), *Edward Upward and Left-Wing Literary Culture in Britain*. Farnham: Ashgate, 2013. xxii + 206 pp. £60 hb. ISBN 978-1-4094-5060-3

'Much of the "Marxist" writing of the thirties was in fact the old Romantic protest that there was no place in contemporary society for the artist and the intellectual, with the new subsidiary clause that the workers were about to end the old system and establish Socialism, which would then provide such a place', Raymond Williams wrote in his chapter on 'Marxism and Culture' in *Culture and Society* (1961, 263). This is a key reference point for Philip Bounds's invaluable study of the relations between Communist Party affiliation and literary practice in the 1930s. Substantial chapters on Comintern cultural policy before World War II, and its effects on the British party, offer shrewd analyses of the 1920s 'Class against Class' phase ('The critic as left sectarian'), and of the rightward turn in the 1930s to the class collaborative strategies of the Popular Front (drolly epitomised here as 'revolutionary traditionalism') and to the doctrine of 'Socialist Realism' pronounced by Zhdanov at the 1934 Congress of Soviet Writers. At the centre of the study are subtle and persuasive readings of the CPGB's three leading literary luminaries, Alick West, Ralph Fox and Christopher Caudwell, all of whom are here shown to enter into complex relations with Party orthodoxy at national and international levels throughout their careers. West remained fiercely opposed to what he saw as the bourgeois deviation of the Popular Front strategy; the gravitational pull of English cultural conservatism drew Fox into what Bounds calls 'unconscious dissidence' (135); while Caudwell's autodidactic eclecticism often wandered into heterodoxy.

Bounds's 'guiding assumption' is that the revisionist account of Party history, based on extensive archival research by such political historians as Andrew Thorpe, Matthew Worley, Kevin Morgan and Mike Squires, is 'crucial not merely to our understanding of the CPGB's *political* evolution' but also 'to our understanding of its intervention in the cultural sphere', demonstrating that 'the relationship between the CI [Communist International] and the British Party was never as rigidly hierarchical as orthodoxy insists', and that indeed, the British Party not only maintained a degree of relative autonomy but also at times 'could *exercise a reciprocal influence on the CI*' (3), often with 'remarkably unorthodox consequences' (234). A final wide-ranging chapter, recalling the *Daily Worker* series 'The Past is Ours', surveys the attempts of such Communist critics and historians as Edgell Rickword, A.L. Morton and Jack Lindsay to appropriate the English radical tradition to a kind of retroactive 'Popular Front', seeking precursors and prefigurements in a swathe of writers from Langland and Thomas More to Dickens and Morris; while a brief Conclusion tentatively suggests continuities between the Party's 1930s intelligentsia, many of whom continued to write into the post-war period, and the New Left *risorgimento* of the 1950s and 1960s, including 'the founding texts of Cultural Studies […] in which Williams laid out his proposals for cultural reform' (236). Citing George Steiner's unexpected tribute to the Soviet Union on its deathbed in 1990, which spoke of the '"compliment to man" implicit in communism's hunger for "intellectual-philosophic sustenance"' (239), Bounds closes with a challenging assertion (though his arithmetic may be a little wonky): 'Although thousands of people had their lives ruined by communism, thousands of others were redeemed by it. Once we have condemned them for perpetrating or defending Stalinist barbarism, we must still acknowledge that the constituent parties of the world communist movement were among the greatest *spiritual* institutions of the twentieth century – and perhaps of all time' (240). Some of the evidence for this bold claim can be found in this extensively researched and informative account of a decade which was not always low and dishonest, but often honourable, brave and tragically idealistic.

The 'making-over of the workers' cause into the intellectuals' cause', Raymond Williams went on to add in 'Marxism and Culture', 'was always likely to collapse: either as the intellectuals found a place in different ways, or as the workers' cause asserted its primacy and moved in directions not so immediately acceptable or favourable' (263–4). One notable exception is 'The Case of Edward Upward', as Valentine Cunningham dubs it in his contribution to Benjamin Kohlmann's new collection, the first really comprehensive survey of an author whose influence was ubiquitous on the 1930s literary Left. Williams is a frequent reference point for many of these essays, despite his dismissal, cited here (83), of Upward's trilogy *The Spiral Ascent* as exemplifying 'a sense in which a significant number of left writers of the thirties were saying: we must have a revolution so that we can write our poems' (*Politics and Letters*: 1979, 73). On the contrary, Upward remained loyal to and active within a Leninist version of Communism throughout a remarkably long life (1903–2009), walking out of the CPGB in 1948 not in revulsion at Stalin's crimes but rather in protest against the Party's post-war revisionist agenda and 'Labourist' collaboration with capitalism (89–90 and *passim*), a *cause célèbre* explored at length in *The Rotten Elements* (1969). Indeed, the more usual criticism, originated by his erstwhile acolyte Stephen Spender and elaborated by Samuel Hynes, was that Upward was an 'arid, unimaginative, and unreadable realist' whose political commitment destroyed his literary gift, a description convincingly contested (83 *et seq.*) in

Ben Clarke's cogent reconfiguration of Upward within a larger revaluation of 1930s literary and political contexts.

Dislodged by the shifting cultural formations of the post-war world, too intransigent to take the path of recantation trodden by his one-time admirers, Upward declined into the posture of a resentful, forgotten 'Job' (Kohlmann's analogy, 17), that *Unmentionable Man* he styled himself in the title of a late short story collection. His reaction to what he saw as a deliberate, politically motivated marginalisation of his achievement was diagnosed by Ian Hamilton in 1995 as the 'sour-smug note' of a 'straightforward case of back-number paranoia'. Joseph Elkanah Rosenberg, who cites this, argues instead that the 'over-determined' fantasies of Upward's late fictions are symptoms of a literary illness Walter Benjamin diagnosed as 'left-wing melancholy', in which 'loyalty to the politics of the past comes at the expenses of any real political action in the present' (175–6). Several essayists remark on the peculiar symbiosis of apocalyptic fantasy, evinced particularly in those early Mortmere stories, with the sullen accidie of thirty years teaching at the Alleyn's School, Dulwich, a post which, *In the Thirties* confessed, 'meant becoming educationally a reactionary' (1962, 126). Charlotte Charteris, considering his Cambridge years, finds a biographical source for the radical fantasising on the playing fields of Repton. Simon Grimble, interpreting the figure of the teacher in Upward's work, focuses on '[t]he tensions involved in this relationship between revolt and constraint [...] the regularity of the school bell and revolution' (70). But the same tension runs right down the middle of Upward's political allegiances, succinctly epitomised by Cunningham as a recurrent clash in his diegesis between the imperative authoritarian 'must' and the wishful subjunctive 'would' and 'should' (58–62). As *The Spiral Ascent* trilogy reveals at length, once the dream of imminent revolution faded, the ardent cadre discovered that political engagement required much the same dull diurnal plod as being head of English at a private school.

Helen Small takes head on the 'emphatically low-key [...] inconsequential [...] muted' quality of Upward's late stories, his 'perilous experiment with a style that mimics the banality of everyday life without offering an image of its political transformation' (145), calling on Henri Lefebvre, *inter alios*, to justify the alleged '"flatness" of Upward's writing, when not in explicitly political or dream-visionary mode', which 'has commonly been read as the persistent stylistic trace of his earlier flirtation with Soviet realism' (147). Though Small demurs, she concedes that '[t]he term is recurrent in Upward criticism' (147). It is indeed evident in several of the essays collected here, though a businesslike reading by Rod Mengham of the thematics of walking in the late fiction scrupulously avoids the word 'pedestrian'. Steven Matthews's incisive discussion of Upward's 'comic historiographies' takes on the debate about those moments, across the writing, which 'court unreadability' (106); while Nick Hubble's perspicacious chapter on 'Radical Eccentricity and Post-war Ordinariness' interprets the antithesis suggested by his title in the perspective afforded by Williams's account of the Bloomsbury Group in *Problems in Materialism and Culture* (1980). Reading *The Spiral Ascent* in tandem with the fascist Henry Williamson's 'postwar *Künstlerroman*', Mark Rawlinson throws considerable light on 'the tension between romanticism and flatness' (128) in the work of both authors, and memorably casts Upward's trilogy as a (deliberate and self-conscious) 'study in priggishness' (123). If, as Stuart Christie observes in a penetrating re-examination of the later stories, 'the absence of a public readership haunts Upward scholarship today', so that his 'achievement remains consistently ill-defined [...] reckoned primarily in relation to someone else's influence, someone else's writing, indeed as marginal or antithetical to someone else's movement' (133), this fine collection of essays, ably edited and introduced by Benjamin Kohlmann, will go a long way towards righting that injustice. For all his limitations, Upward remains a figure to be reckoned with.

Stan Smith
Nottingham Trent University

Notes on Contributors

Peter Brooker is Emeritus Professor in the Department of Culture, Film and Media at the University of Nottingham. Most recently, he was Director of the AHRC-funded Modernist Magazine Project (2005–2010) and lead editor of the resulting three-volume *Oxford Critical and Cultural History of Modernist Magazines* (2009, 2012 and 2013). He was Chair of the Raymond Williams Society from 2005–2011. He is currently attempting to write a short biofiction of Ford Madox Ford and learning to paint in egg tempera.

Rosalind Brunt is a Visiting Research Fellow in Media Studies at Sheffield Hallam University and Research Associate of the Media Discourse Group, de Montfort University, Leicester.

Tony Crowley was born in Liverpool and is the Chair of English Language at the University of Leeds. He is the author of *Scouse: A Social and Cultural History* (Liverpool University Press, 2012).

Michael Malay recently completed his PhD at the University of Bristol. His thesis, a study of representations of animals in modern and contemporary poetry, focused on the writings of Ted Hughes, Marianne Moore, Elizabeth Bishop and Les Murray. Later this year he will take up a post as a Teaching Fellow at the University of Bristol.

Sean McQueen is a PhD candidate in the School of Comparative Literature and Cultural Studies at Monash University, Australia. He has been published in *Science Fiction Film and Television*, *International Journal of Baudrillard Studies* and *Science Fiction Studies*.

Andrew Milner is Professor Emeritus of English and Comparative Literature at Monash University in Melbourne, Australia. He is the author or editor of twenty-one books and his work has been published in English in Australia, India, the UK and the USA and in translation into Chinese, German, Korean, Persian and Portuguese. His most recent publications include *Tenses of Imagination: Raymond Williams on Utopia, Dystopia and Science Fiction* (2010) and *Locating Science Fiction* (2012).

Deborah Mutch is Senior Lecturer at De Montfort University, Leicester. She published a major works collection of socialist fiction entitled *British Socialist Fiction, 1884–1914* in September 2013 and is currently working on a monograph tentatively entitled *Socialist Space: Space and Place in British Socialist Fiction, 1884–1914*.

Phil O'Brien is a PhD candidate at the University of Manchester. His research looks at representations of the working class and neoliberalism in twenty-first-century British fiction.

Tony Sharpe was formerly head of English and Creative Writing at Lancaster University, where he still teaches. He has written books about Vladimir Nabokov (1991), T.S. Eliot (1991), and W.H. Auden (2007), and is the author of *Wallace Stevens: A Literary Life* (Macmillan, 2000), as well as of chapters and articles principally concerned with modern poetry. He has most recently edited *W.H. Auden in Context* (Cambridge University Press, 2013). His essay '"The difficultest rigor": Writing about Wallace Stevens' appears in the current issue of *Twentieth-Century Literature* (Spring, 2014).

Stan Smith, a fellow and trustee of the English Association and Professor Emeritus in English at Nottingham Trent University, is the author of many books and articles on modern literature, including *Irish Poetry and the Construction of Modern Identity* (2005), *Poetry and Displacement* (2007) and *Patrick Kavanagh* (ed., 2009). A student under Raymond Williams in the 1960s, he contributed an Introduction to the 2011 Spokesman Books reprint of *The Country and the City*.

Liane Tanguay is Assistant Professor of English at the University of Houston, Victoria, US, and the author of *Hijacking History: American Culture and the War on Terror* (McGill-Queen's University Press, 2012). She holds a PhD in English from the University of Manchester and was recently an External Fellow with the York Centre for International and Security Studies in Toronto.

Elinor Taylor recently completed her PhD in English at the University of Salford. Her research concerns left-wing writing in Britain from 1934 to 1939. She has interests in working-class writing, historical novels and genre fiction.

Chris Witter (whose prize-winning essay appeared in *Key Words* 11) recently completed his doctorate at Lancaster University, with a thesis on the American short story in the 1960s. His research explores the concealed history and politics of literary experimentation in the context of the Cold War. He won the 2012 Raymond Williams Postgraduate Essay Prize, with research on the connections between Grace Paley's fiction and the Popular Front. He is currently teaching at Lancaster University and pursuing a number of research projects, including work on Kettle's Yard, Tillie Olsen and the year 1964.

Raymond Williams Foundation (RWF)

Jim McGuigan gave the Annual Lecture of the Raymond Williams Society on 'A Short Counter-Revolution – Raymond Williams Towards 2000 Revisited' at Wortley Hall in November 2013. The second edition of *Towards 2000* will be published in the autumn this year with that McGuigan title, edited and updated by Jim, who makes the case, as in his lecture, that the book is a 'contemporary classic' which illustrates the present in remarkable, decisive ways.

Crucially, the dystopian 'Plan X' which Williams engaged with in the early 1980s defines with extraordinary prescience the neoliberal 'precariat' position currently experienced daily by so many.

Despite neoliberalism and 'austerity', which have created a desolate landscape in Britain for Adult Education, RWF continues to provide, however modestly, 'resources for a journey of hope'.

Analysing and debating the contemporary crisis, using Williams's works and ideas to better inform the process, remain vital aims.

These are examples of recent achievements:

- Wortley Hall residential courses, each gaining 40-plus participants: November 2013 on *Scandinavian Politics and Culture*, with keynote lecture by Lesley Riddoch. The Annual Lecture of the RWS, as above, took place during this weekend ensuring a combined audience of over sixty for Jim's talk;
- May 2014 on *War – and Peace*, with Paul Rogers giving the keynote lecture on this wide-ranging theme. Contact with, and support from, Noam Chomsky for this event;
- residential seminars with between ten and fifteen participants at the RMT Education Centre, Doncaster, on *Politics and the State* and *Ted Hughes in 2013* with two more planned for 2014 on *Dylan Thomas* and *The North – Governance, Community and Culture*;
- grants, and support for events: a Salford University conference on 'Culture, Journals, and Working-Class Movements, 1820–1979' at the Working-Class Movement Library; Shallowford House Literature weekends continuing the Wedgwood Memorial College, Barlaston, linked tutorial weekend traditions; discussion seminars (also supported by Merseyside PiPs) on *Keywords* at Liverpool-Tate during the art exhibition based on *Keywords*;
- grants to support individuals on reading and research retreat study breaks;
- Philosophy in Pubs (PiPs); Discussion in Pubs (DiPs) and similar networks, with several RWF Trustees, notably Paul Doran – National PiPs

Raymond Williams Foundation (RWF)

Coordinator – extending the links between community philosophy groups and RWF residential courses on similar themes;
- *The Sylvia Pankhurst Library* at Wortley Hall now incorporating the former WMC, Barlaston library has been developed to the point where we now plan an on-line catalogue of the most significant books and pamphlets within the collection. Reading and research retreats will be encouraged and subsidized by RWF;
- planned for November 2014: a Wortley Hall residential weekend based on the Open University/openDemocracy project *Participation Now*.

Derek Tatton
www.raymondwilliamsfoundation.org.uk

Style Notes for Contributors

Presentation of Copy
Key Words is an internationally refereed academic journal. In the first instance typescripts for prospective publication should be submitted as an email attachment to the Contributions Editor Dr Catherine Clay, Nottingham Trent University, at catherine.clay@ntu.ac.uk. Articles should normally be no longer than 6,000 words; reviews should typically be between 1,500 and 2,000 words. Articles should be double spaced, with generous margins, and pages should be numbered consecutively. For matters of style not addressed below, please refer to *The Chicago Manual of Style*, 15th edn or http://www.chicagomanualofstyle.org/contents.html. Contributors who fail to observe these notes may be asked to revise their submission in accordance with them.

Provision of Text in Electronic Format
Key Words is prepared electronically. Consequently, contributors whose work is accepted for publication will be asked to supply a file copy of their work to the Contributions Editor.

References and Bibliographic Conventions
Notes should be kept to a minimum, with all discursive material appearing in the text. Citations in *Key Words* appear as endnotes at the conclusion of each contribution. Essays presented for prospective publication should adopt this style. Endnote markers should be given in arabic numerals and positioned after, not before, punctuation marks, e.g. '.¹' rather than '¹.'. With no bibliography, full details must be given in a note at the first mention of any work cited. Subsequent citations should be given in the text. If following straight on a reference to the same work, only the page number should be given within brackets. If cited again later in the article, the author's name should be given with the page number; and if several works by the same author are quoted within the essay, also a short form of the title or a cross-reference needs to be added. Headline-style capitalisation is used. In headline style, the first and last words of title and subtitle and all other major words are capitalised. Titles of books and journals should be formatted in italics (not underlined).

Please cite books in the following manner:

> On first citation: Raymond Williams and Michael Orrom, *Preface to Film* (London: Film Drama, 1954).

Style Notes for Contributors

On subsequent citations: Williams and Orrom, *Preface to Film*, 12.

Please cite journal articles in the following manner:

Patrick Parrinder, 'Politics, Letters and the National Curriculum', *Changing English* 2, no. 1 (1994): 29.

Chapters in books should be referenced in the following way:

Andrew McRae, 'The Peripatetic Muse: Internal Travel and the Cultural Production of Space in Pre-Revolutionary England', in *The Country and the City Revisited: England and the Politics of Culture, 1550–1850*, ed. Gerald MacLean, Donna Landry, and Joseph P. Ward (Cambridge: Cambridge University Press, 1999), 41–57.

For internet articles:

Raymond Williams Society Executive, 'About the Raymond Williams Society', Raymond Williams Society, http://www.raymondwilliams.co.uk/ (accessed 26 March 2012).

Please refer to newspaper articles in the following way:

John Mullan, 'Rebel in a Tweed Suit', *The Observer*, 28 May 2005, Features and Reviews section, 37.

A thesis should be referenced in the following manner:

E. Allen, 'The Dislocated Mind: The Fictions of Raymond Williams' (PhD diss., Liverpool John Moores University, 2007), 22–9.

Conference papers should be cited in the following style:

Dai Smith, 'Translating Raymond Williams' (paper presented at the Raymond Williams's Culture and Society@50 conference, Canolfan Dylan Thomas Centre, Swansea, 7 November 2008).

Quotations

For quotations use single quotation marks, and double quotation marks for quotations within quotations. Punctuation is used outside quotations. Ensure that all spellings, punctuation, abbreviations etc. within a quotation are rendered exactly as in the original, including errors, which should be signalled by the authorial interpolation '(*sic*)'.

Book Reviews
Book reviews should open with full bibliographic details of the text under review. These details should include (in the following order): in bold type, first name(s) and surname(s) of author(s), or first name(s) and surname(s) of editor(s) followed by a parenthetic '(ed.)' or '(eds)'; in italics, the full title of the volume followed by a period and a hard return; then, in regular type, the place of publication, publisher and date of publication; the page extent of the volume, including front papers numbered in Roman numerals; the price (where available) of the supplied copy and an indication of 'pb.' or 'hb.'; and the ISBN of the supplied copy.

For example:

> **Dai Smith,** *Raymond Williams: A Warrior's Tale*. Cardigan: Parthian Books, 2008. xviii + 514 pp. £24.99 hb. ISBN 978-1-905762-56-9.